# The Billion Dollar Heist: How Hackers Nearly Stole from Bangladesh Bank

David G. Stone

Published by ELC Publishing, 2025.

THE BILLION DOLLAR HEIST: HOW HACKERS NEARLY STOLE FROM BANGLADESH BANK

**First edition. October 9, 2025.**



ISBN: 979-8232950316

Written by David G. Stone.

# Table of Contents

# Introduction: February 4, 2016 - 8:45 PM (Dhaka Time)

The clock struck 8:45 PM in Dhaka, and the world was about to witness one of the most audacious cybercrimes in banking history. While most Bangladeshi citizens were settling into their evening routines—sharing meals with family, watching television, or preparing for the next workday—something sinister was unfolding in the digital shadows. The Bangladesh Bank, the nation's central banking institution and financial guardian, was under siege. Not by armed robbers or political insurgents, but by an invisible enemy that moved through computer networks with the precision of a surgeon and the ruthlessness of a seasoned criminal mastermind.

## The Moment Bangladesh Bank's Systems Were Compromised

In the hushed corridors of Bangladesh Bank's headquarters on Motijheel Road, the building stood quiet, nearly deserted as evening descended upon the capital. The institution, which served as the monetary authority for a nation of over 160 million people, had entrusted its security to systems that were supposed to be impenetrable. Yet at this precise moment, malicious software was weaving its way through the bank's computer infrastructure like a digital parasite, silently burrowing deeper into the network's core.

The compromise had actually begun weeks earlier, but this Thursday evening marked the culmination of meticulous planning and patient execution. Cybercriminals had successfully infiltrated the bank's network through sophisticated spear-phishing campaigns—carefully crafted emails that appeared legitimate but contained deadly payloads. Once inside, they had moved laterally through the system, mapping the network architecture, identifying critical access points, and positioning themselves for the ultimate strike. The attackers had studied the bank's operational rhythms, understanding when security would be most lax, when transactions would be least scrutinized, and when their activities would blend into the background noise of normal banking operations.

What made this intrusion particularly devastating was its focus: the SWIFT system. The Society for Worldwide Interbank Financial Telecommunication represented the backbone of global banking, the trusted messaging network that facilitated trillions of dollars in international transfers daily. Bangladesh Bank's connection to this system was their gateway to the Federal Reserve Bank of New York, where Bangladesh maintained its foreign currency reserves. The attackers had successfully installed malware that would allow them to forge SWIFT messages, making fraudulent transfer requests appear completely legitimate. They had effectively created a skeleton key to one of the world's most secure financial vaults.

## Setting the Scene: A Thursday Evening in Dhaka

Dhaka in early February carries a particular atmosphere—the winter chill has begun to fade, replaced by the gentle warmth that precedes the scorching summer months. The streets of Motijheel, the financial district where Bangladesh Bank towered over neighboring buildings, were beginning to empty as businesses closed for the evening. Street vendors were packing their wares, office workers streamed toward bus stops and rickshaw stands, and the cacophony of horns and conversation that characterized daytime Dhaka was gradually diminishing into the evening calm.

Inside the bank's offices, a skeleton crew remained, their presence minimal on this Thursday evening. Thursday holds special significance in Bangladesh—it marks the final workday before the weekend, as Friday and Saturday serve as the official days of rest in this predominantly Muslim nation. This timing was no accident. The attackers had chosen their moment with calculated precision, understanding that the approaching weekend would create crucial delays in detection and response. By the time Monday morning arrived and the full staff returned, the money would have already begun its journey through a complex web of international accounts, each transfer designed to obscure the trail and complicate recovery efforts.

The physical environment of the bank building itself told a story of an institution caught between two worlds. Modern computer terminals sat alongside aging file cabinets. Sophisticated security cameras monitored hallways, yet the building's network infrastructure contained vulnerabilities that more advanced institutions had long since addressed. This juxtaposition—cutting-edge aspirations implemented through occasionally outdated systems—would prove to be a critical factor in the unfolding disaster. The bank had access to SWIFT's global network, connecting it to the world's financial elite, yet its internal security protocols had not evolved at the same pace as the threats it faced.

Outside the windows of the bank's trading floor, Dhaka's skyline stretched into the gathering darkness, punctuated by the lights of other financial institutions, multinational corporations, and government buildings. The city hummed with the energy of a nation on the rise, an economy growing steadily, ambitious and forward-looking. None of the millions of people going about their evening activities could have imagined that at this very moment, their nation's financial sovereignty was being challenged by adversaries they would never see, operating from locations they might never definitively identify.

## The Invisible Digital Invasion Begins

Digital intrusions possess a unique horror—they are completely invisible, utterly silent, and devastatingly effective. Unlike traditional bank robberies with their ski masks and weapons, their shouted demands and physical violence, cybercrimes unfold in the abstract realm of ones and zeros, leaving no footprints in the physical world and requiring no face-to-face confrontation. The attackers orchestrating this heist could have been anywhere on Earth—in a government-sponsored facility in Pyongyang, in a sophisticated criminal operation in Eastern Europe, or in an anonymous apartment complex in Southeast Asia. The digital nature of their crime rendered geography almost irrelevant.

The malware they had planted was a marvel of malicious engineering. It didn't just allow them to send fraudulent SWIFT messages; it also concealed its own activities from the bank's monitoring systems. When legitimate banking personnel checked their screens, everything appeared normal. The software manipulated the very tools designed to detect anomalies, creating a false reality where unauthorized transactions simply didn't exist in the bank's records. It was as if the thieves had not only broken into the vault but had also gained control of the security cameras, editing the footage in real-time to show empty, undisturbed rooms while they systematically stripped the contents.

The technical sophistication displayed was remarkable and deeply troubling. These weren't amateur hackers experimenting with stolen credit card numbers or teenage pranksters defacing websites. The individuals behind this operation possessed intimate knowledge of banking protocols, SWIFT messaging formats, international wire transfer procedures, and the specific vulnerabilities in Bangladesh Bank's security architecture. They understood not just how to breach the system, but how to exploit it in ways that would maximize their take while minimizing early detection. This level of expertise suggested either extensive insider knowledge or significant resources devoted to reconnaissance and planning—possibly both.

As the evening progressed, the malware lay in wait, its code poised to execute commands that had been carefully programmed weeks in advance. The attackers were playing a complex game of timing, waiting for the precise moment when New York's banking day would begin—the narrow window when they could submit transfer requests to the Federal Reserve that would be processed before anyone in Dhaka realized what was happening. They had weaponized the Earth's rotation itself, exploiting time zone differences to create gaps in oversight and response capabilities.

## What Was at Stake: $951 Million in Attempted Theft

The numbers involved in this cyber heist transcended ordinary comprehension. Nine hundred fifty-one million dollars—nearly one billion dollars—represented the total amount the attackers attempted to steal from Bangladesh Bank's account at the Federal Reserve Bank of New York. To put this figure in perspective, it exceeded the annual gross domestic product of several small nations. For Bangladesh, a developing country still struggling with poverty, infrastructure challenges, and economic inequality, this sum represented a catastrophic potential loss that could have destabilized the national economy and set back developmental progress by years.

This wasn't money sitting idle in an account; these were Bangladesh's foreign currency reserves, the financial buffer that nations maintain to manage their exchange rates, pay for international obligations, and provide economic stability during crises. These reserves represented decades of accumulated earnings from exports, remittances sent home by Bangladeshi workers abroad, and foreign investments in the country's growing economy. They were the financial foundation upon which monetary policy was built, the reserves that gave international creditors confidence in the nation's ability to meet its obligations. To lose nearly a billion dollars in a single night would have been economically devastating and politically explosive.

The attackers had crafted thirty-five separate fraudulent SWIFT transfer requests, each carefully designed to avoid triggering automated fraud detection systems. Most transfers were for amounts between twenty and thirty-five million dollars—substantial sums, but not so enormous as to immediately raise red flags. The destinations were equally strategic: accounts in the Philippines and Sri Lanka, jurisdictions known for their vibrant financial sectors but also, unfortunately, for certain regulatory gaps that could be exploited by sophisticated money launderers. The Philippine transfers were directed to accounts at Rizal Commercial Banking Corporation (RCBC), while the Sri Lankan requests targeted institutions in Colombo.

What makes the $951 million figure even more staggering is that it represented only the amount requested, not necessarily the maximum the attackers could have attempted. The actual balance in Bangladesh Bank's Federal Reserve account was sufficient to cover these transfers, but the thieves had shown some restraint—perhaps to avoid immediately depleting the account in ways that would trigger automatic safeguards, or perhaps because they had calculated that this amount represented the maximum they could successfully launder through their pre-established network of destination accounts. Either way, the ambition was breathtaking and the potential damage almost incomprehensible.

Had the entire scheme succeeded, Bangladesh would have faced not just immediate financial catastrophe but long-term reputational damage. International confidence in the nation's financial management would have cratered. The value of the Bangladeshi taka would likely have plummeted. Foreign investors would have fled, and the country's credit rating would have suffered severe downgrades. Beyond the immediate loss of capital, the secondary effects could have cost billions more in lost economic growth, increased borrowing costs, and diminished international standing. The attackers weren't just stealing money; they were attempting to strike at the very heart of a nation's economic sovereignty and future prospects.

## Preview of the Global Implications

This attack on Bangladesh Bank represented far more than a single nation's financial crisis—it exposed fundamental vulnerabilities in the global banking infrastructure that everyone had assumed was secure. The SWIFT network, used by more than 11,000 financial institutions in over 200 countries and territories, had been considered virtually impregnable. Banks worldwide relied on it to transfer trillions of dollars daily, confident that the system's security protocols and message authentication mechanisms provided ironclad protection against fraud. The successful compromise of Bangladesh Bank's SWIFT connection shattered that confidence and sent shockwaves through the international financial community.

If it could happen to Bangladesh, it could happen anywhere. That was the terrifying realization that dawned on banking security professionals worldwide as details of the breach emerged. The attack methodology didn't rely on any specific weakness unique to Bangladesh Bank, though the institution certainly had security gaps that more advanced banks had addressed. Instead, the attackers had identified vulnerabilities in the broader SWIFT ecosystem—in the human factors that surrounded it, in the assumption that endpoint security at individual banks could be trusted, and in the protocols for verifying transaction authenticity. These vulnerabilities potentially existed at thousands of institutions worldwide, from major international banks to smaller regional players, from central banks to commercial lenders.

The geopolitical dimensions added another layer of complexity and concern. Strong evidence would eventually point toward North Korea's involvement in the attack, specifically a hacking group known as Lazarus, which had connections to the North Korean government. This suggested that nation-states were actively targeting the international banking system as an asymmetric warfare tactic—a way for isolated, sanctioned regimes to generate revenue and project power without conventional military engagement. If true, this represented a new frontier in international conflict, where cyberattacks on financial infrastructure could serve as weapons of economic warfare, potentially more devastating than traditional military strikes and far more difficult to defend against or deter.

The attack also highlighted the uncomfortable reality of global financial inequality and digital infrastructure disparities. Developing nations, often operating with limited cybersecurity budgets and less sophisticated technical expertise, had become soft targets for highly skilled attackers. While institutions in New York, London, and Tokyo were investing heavily in cutting-edge security systems and employing teams of cybersecurity experts, banks in Dhaka, Manila, and other developing financial centers struggled to keep pace. This created a two-tiered global banking system where some institutions served as weak links that could potentially be exploited to attack the entire network. The security of global finance was only as strong as its most vulnerable participant—a sobering thought that demanded international cooperation and resource sharing.

Furthermore, the incident previewed the coming wave of cybercrime that would characterize the late 2010s and early 2020s. The Bangladesh Bank heist wasn't an isolated incident but rather a harbinger of increasingly sophisticated and audacious cyberattacks targeting critical infrastructure, government systems, and financial institutions. In the years that followed, the world would witness ransomware attacks crippling hospitals, pipeline operators, and municipal governments; state-sponsored hacking groups breaching defense contractors and government agencies; and cryptocurrency exchanges losing hundreds of millions to sophisticated thieves. The techniques pioneered or perfected in the Bangladesh Bank attack—patient reconnaissance, supply chain compromise, exploitation of trust relationships, and strategic timing—would become standard elements in the cybercriminal playbook.

## Why This Story Matters Today

Nearly a decade after that fateful February evening, the Bangladesh Bank heist remains profoundly relevant, offering lessons that extend far beyond the financial sector. In our increasingly interconnected digital world, where everything from power grids to healthcare systems relies on networked computer infrastructure, the vulnerabilities exposed by this attack serve as a cautionary tale about the risks we face collectively. Every time we transfer money electronically, make an online purchase, or trust a digital system to protect sensitive information, we are implicitly relying on security measures that determined adversaries continue to probe and exploit.

The story matters because the fundamental tensions it revealed remain unresolved. How do we balance the efficiency and connectivity that digital systems provide with the security requirements those systems demand? How do developing nations and smaller institutions acquire the resources and expertise necessary to defend against sophisticated state-sponsored attackers? How do we create international norms and enforcement mechanisms for cybercrimes that transcend borders and jurisdictions? These questions have become only more urgent as our dependence on digital infrastructure has deepened and the sophistication of cyber threats has evolved.

For professionals working in cybersecurity, banking, or technology, the Bangladesh Bank heist serves as an essential case study in how complex attacks unfold and how seemingly small security gaps can cascade into catastrophic breaches. The incident demonstrates the critical importance of defense-in-depth strategies, where multiple layers of security compensate for individual weaknesses. It highlights how human factors—from spear-phishing susceptibility to communication failures—often determine success or failure in cybersecurity. It shows why security cannot be viewed as a one-time implementation but must instead be understood as an ongoing process of assessment, improvement, and adaptation to evolving threats.

For ordinary citizens, this story matters because it affects the systems we trust daily. When we check our bank balance on a mobile app, deposit a paycheck, or transfer funds to pay bills, we are participating in the same global financial infrastructure that was compromised in Dhaka. The security of our personal finances depends on the same protocols, the same networks, and faces the same categories of threats that Bangladesh Bank confronted. Understanding how these systems can be compromised helps us become more informed consumers of financial services, more vigilant about our own digital security practices, and more engaged in demanding accountability from the institutions that hold our assets.

The Bangladesh Bank heist also matters as a human story—a narrative of oversight and response, of heroes and victims, of technical detective work and international cooperation. In the hours and days following that Thursday evening, individuals within Bangladesh Bank, the Federal Reserve, SWIFT headquarters, and law enforcement agencies around the world would be forced to confront a crisis unlike any they had experienced before. Their decisions, actions, and occasional failures would determine not just how much money was ultimately stolen, but how the global financial system would respond to this new category of threat. Their story reveals much about institutional resilience, crisis management, and the human dimension of technological challenges.

Finally, this story matters because it isn't finished. While some of the stolen funds were eventually recovered and security improvements were implemented throughout the banking system, the perpetrators were never conclusively brought to justice. The techniques they pioneered continue to be refined and deployed in new attacks. The geopolitical tensions that may have motivated the attack remain unresolved and have in some respects intensified. The digital arms race between attackers and defenders continues to escalate, with each side developing new capabilities and strategies. Understanding what happened on February 4, 2016, provides essential context for understanding the cyber threats we face today and will continue to confront in the future.

## Conclusion

As evening settled over Dhaka on that February Thursday, a line was being crossed that would reverberate through the global financial system for years to come. The invisible digital invasion of Bangladesh Bank represented more than just an ambitious theft—it was a watershed moment that exposed how vulnerable our interconnected financial infrastructure had become to sophisticated cyber adversaries. The attempt to steal nearly a billion dollars through fraudulent SWIFT messages challenged fundamental assumptions about banking security and demonstrated that no institution, regardless of its connections to the world's most trusted financial networks, could consider itself immune to attack.

The story that began at 8:45 PM Dhaka time would unfold over the coming hours and days into a complex international crisis involving central banks, law enforcement agencies, cybersecurity experts, and government officials across multiple continents. It would expose security gaps, reveal the devastating effectiveness of patient, well-resourced attackers, and ultimately force a global reckoning with the realities of financial cybersecurity in the twenty-first century. What was at stake that evening extended far beyond Bangladesh's foreign reserves—it was the integrity and trustworthiness of the systems that undergird global commerce and international finance.

Understanding this story, with all its technical complexity and geopolitical implications, provides essential insights into the world we now inhabit—a world where the greatest threats often come not from conventional weapons or traditional criminals, but from adversaries who wage war in the digital realm, striking from the shadows with devastating effect. As we delve deeper into the details of how the attack unfolded, how it was discovered, and how the world responded, we gain not just historical knowledge but practical wisdom about the challenges and imperatives of securing our digital future. The events of February 4, 2016, forever changed how we think about banking security, international cybercrime, and the hidden vulnerabilities in the systems we trust most—lessons that remain critical as we navigate an increasingly digital and interconnected world.

# Part One: The Setup

## Chapter 1: The Target

The selection of a target in the world of sophisticated cybercrime is never random. It requires meticulous research, strategic calculation, and a cold assessment of opportunity versus risk. For the architects of what would become one of history's most audacious bank heists, Bangladesh Bank presented an irresistible combination of factors: substantial assets, critical vulnerabilities, and systemic weaknesses that could be exploited by patient adversaries. This chapter explores how and why Bangladesh's central banking institution became the focal point of an attack that would expose fundamental flaws in global financial security and forever change how institutions approach cybersecurity. Understanding the target means understanding not just an institution, but an entire ecosystem of financial relationships, technological infrastructure, and human factors that converged to create a perfect storm of vulnerability.

### Bangladesh Bank's Role in the Nation's Economy

Bangladesh Bank stands as far more than merely another financial institution in South Asia—it functions as the very foundation upon which the nation's economic structure rests. Established on December 16, 1971, the same year Bangladesh achieved independence from Pakistan, the central bank was created to serve as the monetary authority for a newly sovereign nation. From its headquarters on Motijheel Road in Dhaka's bustling financial district, Bangladesh Bank exercises powers and responsibilities that touch every aspect of the country's economic life, from the money in citizens' pockets to the nation's standing in international financial markets.

The bank's primary mandate encompasses several critical functions that make it indispensable to Bangladesh's economic stability and growth. First and foremost, it serves as the issuer of the national currency, the Bangladeshi taka, controlling the money supply and managing inflation through monetary policy decisions. This responsibility alone places immense power in the institution's hands—the ability to influence interest rates, credit availability, and ultimately the pace of economic growth. When Bangladesh Bank adjusts its policy rates or reserve requirements, the effects ripple through the entire banking sector, affecting everything from mortgage rates for families to borrowing costs for businesses seeking to expand operations.

Beyond currency management, Bangladesh Bank serves as the banker to the government itself, managing the state's accounts, facilitating tax collection processes, and coordinating the nation's borrowing and debt repayment activities. When the government of Bangladesh needs to fund infrastructure projects, pay civil servants' salaries, or meet international obligations, those transactions flow through Bangladesh Bank's systems. This intimate relationship with government finance means that any compromise of the bank's operations could potentially disrupt not just commercial banking but the fundamental operations of the state itself.

The institution also functions as the supervisor and regulator of Bangladesh's entire banking and financial sector. Commercial banks, investment firms, insurance companies, and other financial institutions operate under licenses granted and monitored by Bangladesh Bank. The central bank sets capital requirements, conducts inspections, enforces compliance with banking regulations, and has the authority to intervene when institutions face insolvency or engage in unsound practices. This regulatory role makes

Bangladesh Bank the guardian not just of monetary stability but of confidence in the entire financial system—a confidence that can evaporate in moments if the guardian itself appears vulnerable.

Perhaps most relevant to the events of February 2016, Bangladesh Bank manages the nation's foreign currency reserves. These reserves, accumulated through export earnings, foreign investment, and international borrowing, represent Bangladesh's financial insurance policy—the buffer that allows the country to manage exchange rate fluctuations, pay for essential imports, and demonstrate to international creditors that it can meet its obligations. In early 2016, these reserves totaled approximately $28 billion, a substantial sum for a developing nation and a testament to Bangladesh's economic progress over the preceding decades. A significant portion of these reserves was held in an account at the Federal Reserve Bank of New York, the institution that would become unwittingly entangled in the unfolding cyber heist.

The economic context in which Bangladesh Bank operated in 2016 was one of cautious optimism mixed with persistent challenges. Bangladesh had achieved impressive economic growth rates, averaging around six percent annually, driven by a robust ready-made garment industry that made the country one of the world's leading textile exporters. Remittances from millions of Bangladeshi workers overseas provided another crucial source of foreign currency and domestic purchasing power. Yet poverty remained widespread, infrastructure was inadequate, and the nation still ranked among the lower-middle-income countries by World Bank classifications. In this environment, Bangladesh Bank's role as steward of economic stability and growth was more critical than ever.

The institution employed thousands of staff members, from senior policy advisors with international training to clerical workers processing routine transactions. Like many large bureaucracies, it blended modern technological capabilities with entrenched procedural traditions, cutting-edge aspirations with resource constraints that forced difficult prioritization decisions. This mixture of old and new, of advancement and limitation, would prove significant when sophisticated attackers began probing for vulnerabilities. The bank had modernized many of its operations, connecting to international financial networks and implementing digital systems, but this modernization had occurred unevenly, creating gaps that more uniformly advanced institutions had managed to avoid.

Understanding Bangladesh Bank's role in the national economy helps clarify what was truly at stake when attackers compromised its systems. This wasn't just about stealing money from one institution among many—it was an assault on the economic nervous system of a nation of over 160 million people. The psychological and economic fallout from a successful theft of nearly a billion dollars from the central bank would have extended far beyond the immediate financial loss, potentially triggering currency crises, bank runs, capital flight, and a catastrophic loss of international confidence in Bangladesh's financial management. The attackers weren't just targeting a bank; they were targeting a nation's economic sovereignty and its people's aspirations for prosperity and development.

## The SWIFT Network: Banking's Nervous System

To understand how the Bangladesh Bank heist was possible, one must first comprehend the Society for Worldwide Interbank Financial Telecommunication—universally known by its acronym, SWIFT. This cooperative organization, founded in 1973 and headquartered in Belgium, has evolved into something far more significant than its creators likely envisioned: it has become the central nervous system of global banking, the communication infrastructure that enables the movement of money across borders and between institutions. Without SWIFT, international trade as we know it would grind to a halt, foreign currency markets would collapse, and the integrated global economy would fragment into isolated national systems.

SWIFT does not actually move money—this crucial distinction often confuses those unfamiliar with international banking mechanics. Instead, SWIFT provides the secure messaging system that allows financial institutions to communicate payment instructions to one another. When a bank in Tokyo needs to transfer funds to a bank in London, it sends a SWIFT message containing standardized information about the sender, recipient, amount, and purpose of the transfer. The receiving bank, upon validating this message's authenticity, then credits the recipient's account and handles the actual movement of funds through correspondent banking relationships or central bank settlement systems. SWIFT messages are essentially highly structured, authenticated digital letters of instruction that banks trust implicitly because of the network's robust security protocols.

The security architecture that made SWIFT trusted by thousands of banks worldwide rested on several foundational principles. First, each member institution received unique credentials and encryption keys that allowed them to send messages that could be authenticated by recipients. These credentials were supposed to be carefully guarded, with access restricted to authorized personnel and systems isolated from general internet connectivity. Second, SWIFT messages followed standardized formats with strict requirements for syntax and content, making them difficult to forge without intimate knowledge of banking operations and protocols. Third, the network itself was designed to be resilient and redundant, with multiple data centers and backup systems ensuring continuous operation even during technical failures or disasters.

By 2016, SWIFT connected more than 11,000 financial institutions in over 200 countries and territories, facilitating millions of messages daily representing trillions of dollars in transfers, securities transactions, and trade finance operations. The network had become so integral to global commerce that being disconnected from SWIFT represented one of the most severe financial sanctions that could be imposed on a nation or institution—effectively cutting it off from the international banking system and severely limiting its ability to engage in cross-border commerce. Iran experienced this isolation in 2012 when SWIFT compliance with international sanctions resulted in Iranian banks being cut off from the network, devastating the country's economy and demonstrating just how dependent modern nations had become on this Belgian cooperative's infrastructure.

For Bangladesh Bank, SWIFT connectivity was essential to managing the nation's foreign currency reserves and facilitating international transactions. The bank's SWIFT terminal allowed it to communicate directly with the Federal Reserve Bank of New York, where a substantial portion of Bangladesh's dollar reserves were held. When Bangladesh needed to make payments in dollars—perhaps to pay for oil imports, service international debt, or support the taka's exchange rate—officials at Bangladesh Bank would generate SWIFT messages instructing the Federal Reserve to transfer specific amounts to designated recipient accounts. These instructions, once authenticated, would be executed automatically, with the Federal Reserve treating them as legitimate orders from its correspondent institution.

This system worked on a foundation of trust—trust that the SWIFT credentials belonged exclusively to authorized personnel at Bangladesh Bank, trust that the messages originated from the institution they claimed to represent, and trust that internal controls at each member institution were sufficient to prevent unauthorized access to SWIFT terminals. This trust had been generally well-placed throughout SWIFT's history; while occasional frauds and errors occurred, the system's overall integrity had remained intact. Major security breaches were virtually unknown, and the assumption that SWIFT-connected institutions could be trusted to manage their endpoint security adequately had become ingrained in global banking culture.

However, this trust model contained a critical vulnerability that the Bangladesh Bank attackers would exploit with devastating effectiveness: SWIFT's security ended at the network level. The cooperative provided a secure communication channel between institutions, but it could not control what happened within each member's internal systems. If attackers could compromise a bank's computers and gain access to its SWIFT credentials, they could send fraudulent messages that would appear completely legitimate to recipients. The authentication protocols would verify that the message came from the correct institution using valid credentials, but they couldn't determine whether the person initiating the message was authorized to do so or whether the transaction was legitimate. This was the digital equivalent of stealing someone's house key—once you have it, you can enter and act as though you belong there, and the lock can't tell the difference between the rightful owner and an imposter.

The SWIFT network's architecture also created timing vulnerabilities that sophisticated attackers could exploit. Messages sent through SWIFT were typically processed during business hours, with international transfers requiring coordination across time zones. This created predictable windows when messages would be received and acted upon, and other periods when responses might be delayed by weekends, holidays, or the simple fact that it was the middle of the night in one location while business hours in another. Attackers who understood these rhythms could time their fraudulent messages to maximize the delay between sending instructions and detection of fraud, creating opportunities to move stolen funds through multiple accounts before anyone realized something was wrong.

For all its sophistication, SWIFT had been designed in an era when the primary security threats came from technical failures, communication errors, and relatively unsophisticated fraud attempts. The network's security model assumed that member institutions would maintain robust internal controls, that access to SWIFT terminals would be carefully restricted, and that the primary risk was message interception or alteration rather than endpoint compromise. By 2016, these assumptions were increasingly out of step with the reality of cyber threats—nation-state actors with enormous resources, criminal organizations with sophisticated technical capabilities, and attack methodologies that focused on exploiting the human and organizational weaknesses that no amount of network-level security could address.

The Bangladesh Bank heist would force SWIFT to confront these uncomfortable realities and recognize that its trust-based security model required fundamental revision. The network remained secure, but that security was meaningless if member institutions' connections to it could be compromised. The attack would spark a major overhaul of SWIFT's security framework, including new mandatory security controls, enhanced information sharing about threats, and more aggressive auditing of member institutions' cybersecurity practices. But in February 2016, those reforms lay in the future, and the system operated on assumptions that were about to be catastrophically invalidated.

## Security Vulnerabilities in Developing

## Nations

The cybersecurity divide between developed and developing nations had become one of the most consequential disparities in the modern world by 2016, yet it received far less attention than more visible gaps in infrastructure, education, or healthcare. While major financial institutions in New York, London, Tokyo, and Frankfurt were investing tens of millions of dollars annually in cybersecurity—employing dedicated security teams, implementing cutting-edge defensive technologies, and conducting regular penetration testing to identify vulnerabilities—many of their counterparts in developing economies struggled to allocate even basic resources to digital security. This disparity created a dangerous situation where the global financial system's overall security was undermined by weak links that sophisticated attackers could identify and exploit.

Bangladesh Bank's security posture in early 2016 exemplified many of the challenges that developing nation institutions faced. The bank operated with limited cybersecurity budgets that had to compete with numerous other pressing needs—from upgrading aging physical infrastructure to training staff on new banking regulations to managing the day-to-day operations of monetary policy. When forced to prioritize spending, cybersecurity often lost out to more immediately visible needs. After all, the benefits of preventing an attack that might never come were abstract and difficult to quantify, while the benefits of a new branch office or improved customer service systems were tangible and immediate.

The institution's technical infrastructure reflected these budget constraints and competing priorities. While Bangladesh Bank had successfully connected to SWIFT and implemented various modern banking systems, the underlying network infrastructure contained significant vulnerabilities. The bank's computers were not adequately isolated from internet connectivity, creating potential pathways for external attackers to penetrate internal networks. Firewall configurations were insufficient, allowing more traffic between network segments than security best practices would recommend. Software patching was inconsistent, leaving systems vulnerable to exploits that had been publicly known and addressed by vendors months or even years earlier. These weren't necessarily the result of incompetence or negligence—they reflected the reality of managing complex technical systems with limited resources and expertise.

Human factors compounded these technical vulnerabilities. Bangladesh Bank, like many institutions in developing economies, struggled to attract and retain top cybersecurity talent. The most skilled professionals could command significantly higher salaries in the private sector or in developed nations, creating a brain drain that left critical positions filled by less experienced personnel or remained vacant altogether. The bank's IT staff certainly included dedicated and competent professionals, but they were often stretched thin, managing too many responsibilities with insufficient support, making it difficult to maintain the constant vigilance that effective cybersecurity demands.

Training and awareness programs, essential for building a security culture within organizations, were inadequate or inconsistent. Many employees had not received comprehensive education about cybersecurity risks, making them vulnerable to social engineering attacks like the spear-phishing campaigns that would be used to initially compromise Bangladesh Bank's networks. The concept of "security awareness" was often treated as a perfunctory exercise—perhaps an annual presentation or a circulated memo—rather than an ongoing cultural commitment. Employees might understand that they shouldn't share passwords, but they might not recognize a sophisticated phishing email crafted to appear as though it came from a trusted colleague or legitimate institution.

The regulatory environment in Bangladesh, while improving, had not kept pace with the evolving cyber threat landscape. Banking regulators imposed various security requirements on institutions, but these requirements often focused on traditional risks—fraud prevention, physical security, business continuity planning—rather than the sophisticated cyber threats that had emerged in the 2010s. Audits and inspections might verify that a bank had implemented basic security controls without deeply assessing whether those controls were effective against modern attack methodologies. This created a false sense of security, where institutions could technically comply with regulations while remaining fundamentally vulnerable to sophisticated attackers.

International cooperation and information sharing on cybersecurity threats were limited, leaving institutions in developing nations potentially unaware of attack campaigns that had successfully compromised similar organizations elsewhere. While banks in developed nations participated in information-sharing arrangements—both formal organizations and informal networks where security professionals exchanged threat intelligence—many developing nation institutions lacked access to these channels. They might not learn about new attack techniques, emerging threat actors, or specific vulnerabilities until after they had been successfully exploited, putting them perpetually behind the curve in defensive preparations.

The procurement processes for security technology in government and quasi-government institutions often involved bureaucratic complexity that hindered rapid response to emerging threats. Even when security professionals at Bangladesh Bank identified needs for specific security tools or systems, the process of budgeting, approving, tendering, and implementing solutions could take months or years. By the time new security controls were finally implemented, the threat landscape might have evolved significantly, and what had once been cutting-edge protection might now be merely adequate or even insufficient. This lag between threat identification and defensive implementation created windows of vulnerability that attackers with good intelligence could identify and exploit.

Cultural factors also played a role in cybersecurity vulnerabilities. In some institutional cultures, raising concerns about security problems might be perceived as criticism of leadership or as creating unnecessary alarm, discouraging staff from reporting suspicious activities or advocating for security improvements. Hierarchical organizational structures could create situations where information about potential threats didn't flow freely to decision-makers who had the authority to respond. The "save face" dynamics common in many Asian cultures might make individuals reluctant to admit they had been fooled by a phishing email or had made a security mistake, delaying incident response and allowing compromises to deepen before being detected.

These vulnerabilities were not unique to Bangladesh—they represented systemic issues affecting financial institutions throughout the developing world. Banks in the Philippines, Sri Lanka, Vietnam, Kenya, and numerous other countries faced similar challenges: limited resources, talent shortages, inadequate awareness, and regulatory frameworks struggling to keep pace with evolving threats. This created what security researchers sometimes called "cyber risk geography"—a global map where some regions were significantly more vulnerable to successful attacks than others, not because of any inherent deficiency in their people or intentions, but because of structural factors related to economic development, resource availability, and the maturity of their cybersecurity ecosystems.

The international banking system's interconnected nature meant that these localized vulnerabilities had global implications. A successful attack on a bank in Dhaka could compromise transactions involving institutions in New York, London, and Tokyo. Stolen funds could be laundered through banks in Manila, Singapore, and Hong Kong. The security of the entire system was only as strong as its weakest participant—a sobering reality that the Bangladesh Bank heist would dramatically illustrate. The attack would serve as a wake-up call that cybersecurity in developing nations was not just their problem but a shared challenge requiring international cooperation, resource sharing, and a recognition that global financial security demanded investment in improving defenses everywhere, not just in the developed world's financial capitals.

## The Federal Reserve Bank of New York Connection

The Federal Reserve Bank of New York occupies a unique and powerful position in global finance, serving not only as one of the twelve regional banks in the United States Federal Reserve System but also as the primary interface between U.S. monetary policy and international financial markets. Located at 33 Liberty Street in Lower Manhattan, the imposing fortress-like structure houses one of the world's largest gold repositories, manages open market operations for the entire Federal Reserve System, and maintains correspondent banking relationships with central banks and international financial institutions around the world. For Bangladesh Bank, the relationship with the New York Fed was essential to managing the nation's dollar reserves and facilitating international transactions.

Correspondent banking relationships between central banks represent a fundamental architecture of the international monetary system. Most countries maintain substantial foreign currency reserves, particularly U.S. dollars given the greenback's role as the global reserve currency and the currency in which many international commodities and transactions are denominated. However, actually holding physical dollars in vaults in Dhaka or anywhere else would be impractical and would prevent those reserves from earning any return. Instead, central banks like Bangladesh Bank maintain accounts at the Federal Reserve Bank of New York, where their dollar reserves are held electronically and can be easily deployed for various purposes—from supporting exchange rate interventions to paying for imports to servicing international debt.

Bangladesh Bank's account at the New York Fed contained approximately $951 million in early February 2016—a substantial sum representing years of accumulated reserves. This wasn't idle money sitting unused; it was actively managed capital that served multiple strategic purposes. When Bangladesh needed to stabilize the taka's exchange rate by purchasing domestic currency and selling dollars, these reserves at the New York Fed could be drawn upon. When the government needed to make payments in dollars to international creditors or for essential imports, the reserves facilitated those transactions. The account represented financial security, flexibility, and sovereignty—the ability to meet international obligations without having to borrow or accept unfavorable terms from international lenders.

The operational mechanics of this correspondent relationship were built around the SWIFT messaging system. When Bangladesh Bank needed to transfer dollars from its Federal Reserve account, authorized officials in Dhaka would generate SWIFT messages with specific formatting and information—the amount to be transferred, the recipient bank details, the purpose of the transfer, and various codes and references that allowed both institutions to track and reconcile transactions. These messages would be transmitted securely through the SWIFT network to the New York Fed's payment processing systems. Upon receiving and authenticating the messages, the Federal Reserve would execute the transfers, debiting Bangladesh Bank's account and crediting the specified recipient accounts at other financial institutions.

This system operated on established protocols and trust relationships that had been functioning smoothly for years. The Federal Reserve maintained strict procedures for validating SWIFT messages, verifying that they contained proper authentication codes, originated from recognized terminals at correspondent institutions, and followed required formatting standards. However, these validation processes were primarily technical rather than contextual—the system verified that a message was properly authenticated and formatted, not whether the underlying transaction made economic sense or fit normal patterns for the correspondent institution. This distinction would prove crucial during the attack.

The New York Fed's relationship with Bangladesh Bank involved regular communications and coordination on various matters beyond just processing payment instructions. The institutions exchanged information about reserve balances, discussed technical aspects of payment processing, and maintained channels for resolving discrepancies or addressing questions. However, this was primarily a transaction-processing relationship rather than a close operational partnership. The Federal Reserve provided services to hundreds of correspondent institutions worldwide, making it impossible to maintain intimate knowledge of each one's internal operations, typical transaction patterns, or current priorities. This limited institutional familiarity would later become relevant when unusual transfer requests arrived from Bangladesh Bank's compromised systems.

The security protocols surrounding Bangladesh Bank's interaction with the Federal Reserve reflected established practices that had generally proven reliable throughout decades of correspondent banking. Bangladesh Bank maintained dedicated SWIFT terminals for communicating with the New York Fed, operated by trained personnel who understood the procedures for generating payment instructions. Access to these terminals was supposedly restricted, with authentication required before messages could be sent. The Federal Reserve, for its part, maintained systems designed to detect obvious anomalies—transfers to sanctioned entities, amounts that exceeded account balances, or messages with technical errors that suggested fraudulent activity.

However, this security architecture assumed that Bangladesh Bank's internal systems and controls were secure—that if a SWIFT message arrived with proper authentication from Bangladesh Bank's credentials, it genuinely represented an authorized transaction. The Federal Reserve couldn't monitor what was happening inside Bangladesh Bank's networks, couldn't know whether the person generating a message was authorized to do so, and couldn't independently verify that senior officials at Bangladesh Bank had actually approved each transaction. The correspondent banking model relied on each institution maintaining adequate internal controls, with the correspondent (the Federal Reserve) trusting that its clients' security and authorization processes were functioning properly.

This trust-based model worked effectively when security threats primarily came from external attempts to intercept or alter messages in transit, or from relatively unsophisticated frauds involving forged documents or impersonation. But it was poorly adapted to insider threats or to sophisticated attackers who had successfully compromised a correspondent institution's internal systems. Once attackers gained access to Bangladesh Bank's legitimate SWIFT credentials and terminals, they could generate messages that appeared completely authentic to the Federal Reserve—they bore the correct authentication codes, originated from recognized systems, and followed all technical requirements. The New York Fed's validation processes had no way to determine that these messages, while technically valid, were actually fraudulent instructions from unauthorized parties.

The time zone difference between New York and Dhaka would become a critical factor in the attack's execution. When it was Thursday evening in Dhaka, it was Thursday morning in New York—the beginning of a business day at the Federal Reserve when payment processing systems were actively staffed and transfers were being executed routinely. The attackers understood this rhythm and timed their fraudulent SWIFT messages to arrive during New York business hours when they would be processed automatically as part of the normal flow of transactions. By the time Friday morning arrived in Dhaka and bank officials might notice irregularities, it would be Thursday night in New York, with the Federal Reserve's offices closing for the day and the weekend approaching. This timing gap created crucial hours or even days during which stolen funds could be moved through multiple accounts before anyone in Dhaka could contact the New York Fed to halt the transfers.

The Federal Reserve Bank of New York's role in this story extends beyond being the custodian of stolen funds—it represents a critical junction point in the global financial system where trust, technology, and established procedures intersected with emerging cyber threats. The institution would find itself caught in an uncomfortable position when the fraud was discovered: technically blameless in following established procedures and executing what appeared to be legitimate instructions, yet undeniably central to a massive theft that exploited the very systems designed to facilitate secure international banking. The incident would force the Federal Reserve and other correspondent banks to reassess their validation procedures, invest in more sophisticated anomaly detection, and develop better coordination mechanisms with correspondent institutions to quickly identify and respond to potential frauds.

## Why Bangladesh Became the Target

The selection of Bangladesh Bank as the target for this sophisticated cyber heist was neither random nor opportunistic—it represented a calculated decision based on thorough reconnaissance and strategic assessment of various factors that made this particular institution an attractive target for attackers willing to invest significant time and resources into planning and executing a complex operation. Understanding why Bangladesh was chosen requires examining the unique combination of accessibility, vulnerability, potential reward, and systemic factors that distinguished this target from thousands of other financial institutions worldwide that might have been compromised.

The most obvious factor was the substantial sum held in Bangladesh Bank's Federal Reserve account. Nine hundred fifty-one million dollars represented an extraordinary potential payoff that could justify months of preparation and considerable resource investment in developing customized malware, conducting reconnaissance, and planning the laundering operation. While there were certainly wealthier institutions with larger reserve holdings, few presented the same combination of substantial assets and exploitable vulnerabilities that Bangladesh Bank offered. For attackers conducting a cost-benefit analysis of potential targets, Bangladesh Bank likely ranked extremely high in terms of potential return relative to the difficulty of compromise.

The security vulnerabilities discussed earlier in this chapter made Bangladesh Bank more accessible to compromise than many peer institutions. Sophisticated attackers conducting preliminary reconnaissance—perhaps through passive monitoring of internet-connected systems, analysis of the bank's technical job postings that revealed details about their infrastructure, or even initial probing attacks to test defenses—would have identified characteristics that marked Bangladesh Bank as a relatively soft target. The institution's cybersecurity posture was simply not on par with major international banks, creating opportunities that more hardened targets would not have presented.

Bangladesh's geopolitical position and international relationships may have influenced target selection in ways that extend beyond purely financial motivations. If, as evidence suggests, the attack was conducted by North Korean state-sponsored hackers, Bangladesh represented a target from a nation with no particular security alliance with North Korea's primary adversaries. Attacking a bank in the United States, South Korea, Japan, or other nations with which North Korea had direct geopolitical conflicts might have provoked more aggressive responses—both in terms of cyber counterattacks and potential escalation of conventional tensions. Bangladesh, as a relatively neutral developing nation, presented less risk of severe retaliation, making the attack more politically palatable even if it was discovered and attribution was established.

The structure of Bangladesh's foreign reserve management created technical opportunities that the attackers could exploit. Unlike some nations that distribute their reserves across multiple correspondent institutions or maintain more complex approval processes for large transfers, Bangladesh Bank's concentration of dollar reserves in a single Federal Reserve account and its established patterns of periodic transfers created an operational environment that attackers could study and manipulate. The bank had legitimate reasons to transfer substantial sums from its Federal Reserve account, meaning that large transfer requests wouldn't necessarily appear anomalous if they occurred during normal business hours and followed proper formatting.

The regulatory and oversight environment in Bangladesh, while functional, lacked some of the redundant security checks and balances that existed in more developed financial systems. In some countries, transfers above certain thresholds required multiple authorization signatures, independent verification by separate departments, or advance notification to regulatory authorities. Bangladesh Bank's procedures, while following established norms, may have been less cumbersome than those at other institutions, allowing the attackers to exploit systems where a single compromise could enable complete control over the transfer process without requiring additional authorizations or approvals.

The laundering infrastructure that would be needed to convert stolen funds into usable assets also influenced target selection. The attackers had clearly prepared destination accounts in the Philippines and Sri Lanka—jurisdictions where they believed regulatory gaps, casino operations, and other factors would facilitate rapid movement and conversion of stolen funds before authorities could freeze accounts or reverse transactions. The practical reality of money laundering meant that the source of funds had to be compatible with the destination accounts and laundering mechanisms that had been prepared. Bangladesh, as a developing nation without the intense scrutiny that might accompany transfers from major Western central banks, presented fewer immediate red flags when large transfers suddenly appeared in Philippine and Sri Lankan accounts.

Intelligence gathering opportunities may have given the attackers particularly good information about Bangladesh Bank's vulnerabilities. If insider information was available—whether from disgruntled employees, recruited informants, or simply from the natural challenges of maintaining operational security in a large bureaucratic institution—the attackers might have known specific details about security gaps, operational procedures, or technical infrastructure that made Bangladesh Bank especially attractive. Even without active insider cooperation, institutions in developing nations might have less sophisticated information security practices, making it easier for attackers to gather intelligence through social engineering, observation of employees' digital activities, or analysis of information inadvertently exposed through social media and other public channels.

The timing of the attack in early 2016 coincided with a period when Bangladesh Bank was not under particular scrutiny from international financial oversight bodies. The bank had not recently been involved in major scandals or regulatory problems that would have attracted heightened attention from correspondent institutions or international monitors. This relative anonymity meant that unusual transactions might not trigger the same level of scrutiny that would have been applied to institutions with troubled histories or those currently under close oversight for other reasons. The bank operated in the vast middle ground of international financial institutions—important enough to manage substantial assets but not prominent enough to receive constant attention from the international financial community.

Cultural and linguistic factors may have also played a role in target selection. Conducting sophisticated social engineering attacks requires understanding the target organization's language, cultural norms, and communication styles well enough to craft convincing phishing emails and other deceptions. Bangladesh's use of English as a business language, combined with communication styles that might be more formal and less suspicious of unexpected requests from apparent authority figures, could have made social engineering campaigns more likely to succeed than in countries where language barriers or cultural tendencies toward skepticism might have undermined phishing attempts.

The attackers' technical capabilities and resources also influenced which targets they could realistically compromise. Bangladesh Bank, while challenging to hack, was within the capabilities of a sophisticated state-sponsored or well-resourced criminal group. More hardened targets—major U.S. or European banks with mature cybersecurity programs, dedicated security operations centers, and advanced threat detection capabilities—might have been beyond the attackers' abilities or might have required resources they were unwilling or unable to commit. Bangladesh Bank represented a target that was both valuable enough to justify the effort and vulnerable enough to be realistically compromised by the capabilities the attackers possessed.

Finally, the element of novelty worked in favor of selecting Bangladesh Bank as a target. While cybersecurity communities were increasingly aware of threats to financial institutions, and major banks had begun investing heavily in defenses, the specific attack vector of compromising a SWIFT endpoint at a central bank had not been prominently featured in threat intelligence or widely anticipated by defenders. The attackers were pioneering a new approach, and Bangladesh Bank's characteristics made it an ideal test case for proving this methodology. If successful, the attack would not only yield a substantial financial reward but would also demonstrate a new capability that could potentially be replicated against other similar targets, multiplying the strategic value of the operation.

Understanding why Bangladesh became the target reveals how sophisticated attackers make strategic decisions, balancing opportunity, risk, reward, and practical considerations about their capabilities and objectives. Bangladesh Bank wasn't chosen because it was inherently flawed or because Bangladeshis were somehow less capable than their counterparts elsewhere. Rather, it was selected because structural factors related to economic development, security resource allocation, geopolitical positioning, and the specific configuration of its foreign reserve management created a unique convergence of vulnerability and opportunity. The attack on Bangladesh Bank could have happened to numerous other institutions facing similar challenges and operating under comparable constraints. That it happened in Dhaka rather than elsewhere was the result of cold strategic calculation by adversaries who understood not just how to breach computer systems but how to analyze the global financial landscape and identify the weak points where sophisticated attacks would be most likely to succeed.

## Conclusion

The convergence of factors that made Bangladesh Bank an attractive target for sophisticated cybercriminals reveals much about the vulnerabilities inherent in our globalized financial system. This wasn't simply a story of a single institution's security failures, but rather a systematic exploitation of the gaps that exist when developing nations' legitimate aspirations for participation in international finance encounter the harsh realities of sophisticated cyber threats. Bangladesh Bank's role as the guardian of the nation's economic stability, its connection to the SWIFT network and the Federal Reserve Bank of New York, and the security challenges common to institutions in developing economies created a perfect storm of vulnerability that patient, skilled attackers recognized and methodically exploited.

The institution's importance to Bangladesh's economy meant that enormous value concentrated in systems that, despite best efforts, could not match the security sophistication of institutions in wealthier nations. The SWIFT network, for all its technical excellence, was only as secure as its weakest endpoint—and Bangladesh Bank's endpoint presented exploitable vulnerabilities. The trust-based correspondent banking relationship with the Federal

Reserve created opportunities for attackers who understood that technical authentication of messages was not the same as verification of authorization and legitimacy. The systemic disadvantages faced by developing nation institutions—limited resources, talent shortages, regulatory gaps, and inadequate access to threat intelligence—created an environment where sophisticated adversaries enjoyed significant advantages.

The selection of Bangladesh as the target demonstrates the calculating nature of modern cybercrime and cyber warfare. The attackers assessed not just technical vulnerabilities but geopolitical factors, economic considerations, operational practicalities, and the likelihood of detection and response. They chose their target with the precision of surgeons, identifying an institution that offered substantial rewards while presenting manageable risks and exploitable weaknesses. This calculated approach to target selection represents a maturation of cyber threats from opportunistic attacks of convenience to strategic operations carefully planned and executed against selected victims.

As we move forward to examine how the attack unfolded, the preparation that preceded it, and the response that followed discovery, understanding the target—Bangladesh Bank itself, its role in the national and international financial systems, and the factors that made it vulnerable—provides essential context. This was not random misfortune or simple bad luck that brought catastrophe to Bangladesh's central bank. It was the predictable outcome when asymmetric warfare meets systemic inequality, when patient adversaries with substantial resources target institutions operating with constraints and vulnerabilities that more privileged counterparts have managed to address. The story of Bangladesh Bank's targeting is ultimately a story about the uneven distribution of security capabilities in our interconnected world and the consequences when that inequality is exploited by those who understand that the global financial system's security is only as strong as its weakest participant.

# Chapter 2: The Hunters

In the shadowy realm of state-sponsored cyber warfare, few actors have demonstrated the audacity, technical sophistication, and ruthless determination of the group that would come to orchestrate the Bangladesh Bank heist. These digital mercenaries operated at the intersection of criminal enterprise and geopolitical strategy, wielding code as a weapon and exploiting the vulnerabilities of interconnected systems with a precision that betrayed years of experience and substantial institutional support. Understanding who these attackers were, how they evolved their capabilities, and the methodical approach they took in planning and executing their assault on Bangladesh Bank reveals a chilling portrait of modern cyber warfare—where invisible adversaries can strike targets thousands of miles away, stealing hundreds of millions of dollars without ever setting foot in the targeted nation. This chapter explores the hunters who stalked Bangladesh Bank through cyberspace, tracing their origins, examining their capabilities, and reconstructing the patient reconnaissance that preceded one of history's most ambitious bank heists.

## Who Were the Lazarus Group?

The name "Lazarus Group" carries an almost biblical resonance—a reference to the figure raised from death, suggesting something that refuses to stay buried, that resurrects itself despite attempts to eliminate it. This moniker, assigned by cybersecurity researchers tracking the collective's activities, aptly captures the persistent, evolving nature of what would become one of the world's most notorious cyber threat actors. The Lazarus Group emerged into public consciousness gradually, their activities initially disconnected incidents that only retrospective analysis revealed to be components of a larger, coordinated campaign orchestrated by a sophisticated organization with substantial resources and clear strategic objectives.

The collective's origins trace back to North Korea's recognition, sometime in the late 1990s and early 2000s, that cyber capabilities could serve as an asymmetric warfare tool—a way for an economically isolated, technologically limited nation to project power and generate revenue despite its disadvantages in conventional military and economic competition. North Korea, officially the Democratic People's Republic of Korea (DPRK), found itself increasingly isolated following the Cold War's end, facing international sanctions, economic stagnation, and the challenge of maintaining regime stability while its population suffered through periodic famines and severe deprivation. In this context, cyber operations offered attractive advantages: they required relatively modest investment compared to conventional military capabilities, they could be conducted deniably through proxies and false flags, and they could potentially generate revenue to support the regime while simultaneously advancing strategic objectives.

The Lazarus Group, while not a formal organization with business cards and headquarters, functioned as an operational umbrella encompassing various teams, units, and campaigns all operating under the direction and support of North Korean state institutions. Cybersecurity researchers identified consistent patterns in malware code, attack methodologies, infrastructure usage, and targeting priorities that indicated these apparently separate incidents were actually connected efforts by related groups sharing resources, intelligence, and direction. The collective included specialists in various domains—malware developers who crafted sophisticated code, social engineers who designed convincing phishing campaigns, reconnaissance specialists who mapped target networks, and money laundering experts who understood how to convert stolen digital assets into usable funds.

Attributing cyber attacks to specific actors is notoriously difficult, involving analysis of technical indicators, operational patterns, geopolitical context, and sometimes human intelligence that remains classified. In the case of Lazarus Group, the attribution to North Korea rests on multiple converging lines of evidence. The malware used in their operations contained Korean language artifacts, compilation timestamps consistent with working hours in the Pyongyang time zone, and code similarities to malware previously linked to North Korean operations. The targets selected aligned with North Korean strategic interests and adversaries. The attack infrastructure occasionally revealed connections to IP addresses and hosting providers previously associated with North Korean operations. Perhaps most tellingly, defectors from North Korea's cyber warfare programs provided firsthand accounts of the training, organization, and operations of units that matched the activities attributed to Lazarus Group.

The organizational structure supporting Lazarus Group's operations was sophisticated and compartmentalized. North Korea's cyber warfare capabilities were primarily organized under two main institutions: the Reconnaissance General Bureau (RGB), the country's primary foreign intelligence service, and the Ministry of State Security, focused on internal security and counterintelligence. Within the RGB, specialized units handled different aspects of cyber operations—from developing exploits to conducting attacks to laundering proceeds. Bureau 121, in particular, gained notoriety as the primary cyber warfare unit, reportedly staffed by hundreds of highly trained operatives who had demonstrated exceptional mathematical and technical aptitude from an early age.

The recruitment and training pipeline for North Korean cyber warriors represented a substantial long-term investment by the regime. Promising students were identified in their early teens, selected for specialized education that emphasized mathematics, computer science, and foreign languages—particularly English and Chinese, essential for operating in international cyberspace. These elite students attended specialized schools like Kim Il-sung University and Pyongyang University of Science and Technology, receiving education that, in technical domains at least, rivaled what they might receive in more developed nations. The most talented graduates were recruited into cyber warfare units, where they received additional specialized training in offensive hacking techniques, malware development, and operational security.

What distinguished Lazarus Group from many cybercriminal organizations was the fusion of criminal and strategic objectives. While some cyber operations focused purely on espionage—stealing military secrets, political intelligence, or technological innovations—others were clearly profit-motivated, designed to generate revenue for the sanctions-squeezed regime. The Bangladesh Bank heist represented the latter category, though even financially motivated operations served strategic purposes by demonstrating capabilities, testing defenses, and maintaining the technical skills of operatives who might later be deployed for more overtly political or military objectives.

The group's evolution over time revealed increasing sophistication and ambition. Early operations in the mid-2000s were relatively crude—website defacements, distributed denial-of-service attacks that temporarily disrupted websites, and basic espionage campaigns. By the early 2010s, Lazarus Group had developed considerably more advanced capabilities, including custom malware families, sophisticated social engineering techniques, and the ability to conduct complex, multi-stage operations that could persist inside victim networks for months while evading detection. The progression from nuisance-level attacks to operations capable of stealing hundreds of millions of dollars or causing substantial physical damage demonstrated both learning from experience and investment in capability development.

The psychology and motivation of individual Lazarus Group members remain somewhat opaque, given the closed nature of North Korean society and the difficulty of obtaining firsthand accounts from active operatives. However, available evidence suggests a mixture of nationalistic commitment, pragmatic careerism, and the simple reality of having few alternatives in a totalitarian state with limited opportunities. Those selected for cyber warfare units enjoyed privileges unavailable to ordinary North Koreans—better food, housing, and access to foreign goods. They traveled abroad to China, Southeast Asia, and sometimes further afield, operating from hotel rooms and rented apartments while conducting attacks against targets worldwide. These perks, combined with the prestige associated with serving the regime in a strategic capacity, created powerful incentives for loyalty and performance.

The group's targeting priorities revealed the breadth of North Korea's interests and adversaries. Financial institutions obviously represented lucrative targets for revenue generation. South Korean and American entities faced persistent campaigns serving both espionage and harassment functions. The entertainment industry became a target following North Korea's anger over unflattering portrayals in film and media. Cryptocurrency exchanges offered opportunities to steal digital assets that could be laundered more easily than traditional banking funds. This diverse targeting demonstrated flexibility and opportunism—Lazarus Group pursued whatever objectives served the regime's interests at any given moment, from strategic intelligence gathering to profit generation to simple retaliation against perceived insults.

By February 2016, when the Bangladesh Bank operation reached its climax, Lazarus Group had evolved into one of the world's most capable and aggressive cyber threat actors. They had successfully conducted major operations against high-profile targets, stolen hundreds of millions of dollars across multiple campaigns, and demonstrated technical capabilities that rivaled those of cyber units in far wealthier nations. They operated with a combination of patience and boldness—willing to invest months in reconnaissance and preparation, yet audacious enough to attempt heists of unprecedented scale and complexity. Understanding this adversary—their origins, capabilities, motivations, and operational patterns—is essential to comprehending how a central bank's defenses could be breached and nearly a billion dollars almost stolen in a single night.

## North Korean Cyber Warfare Capabilities

To understand the threat that Lazarus Group posed to Bangladesh Bank and numerous other targets worldwide, one must examine the broader context of North Korean cyber warfare capabilities—how a nation of approximately 25 million people, with an economy smaller than many individual U.S. states, with limited internet connectivity and facing international sanctions, nonetheless developed offensive cyber capabilities that security experts ranked among the world's most dangerous. This seeming paradox—advanced cyber warfare emerging from one of the world's most isolated and economically challenged nations—reveals important truths about the nature of cyber conflict and the asymmetric advantages it offers to determined adversaries.

North Korea's investment in cyber warfare reflected strategic calculations made at the highest levels of regime leadership. The country faced existential security challenges: hostile relations with South Korea and the United States, international isolation following its nuclear weapons program, an economy crippled by sanctions and mismanagement, and the constant need to maintain internal control over a population living in severe deprivation. Conventional military competition was financially unsustainable—North Korea could not match the technological sophistication or resources of potential adversaries. Nuclear weapons provided deterrence but were essentially unusable without risking total annihilation. Cyber warfare, by contrast, offered a tool that was relatively inexpensive to develop, could be deployed with plausible deniability, and could generate both strategic advantages and financial returns.

The economics of cyber warfare heavily favored North Korea's asymmetric approach. Developing sophisticated malware, training elite hackers, and conducting cyber operations cost millions of dollars—substantial sums for North Korea, certainly, but trivial compared to the billions required for advanced conventional military capabilities. A few hundred highly trained cyber operatives could potentially cause disruption, steal intelligence, and generate revenue far exceeding their cost. Moreover, unlike missiles or tanks, cyber capabilities could be used repeatedly without depleting inventories, and successful operations might even fund their own continuation through stolen assets. This cost-benefit analysis made cyber warfare particularly attractive to a resource-constrained regime seeking maximum strategic impact from limited investments.

North Korea's approach to developing cyber capabilities emphasized both technical excellence and operational security. The regime created a pipeline for identifying and developing talent from an early age, concentrating resources on the most promising students in a way that democratic societies, with their broader educational mandates and individual freedoms, could not easily replicate. Students selected for cyber warfare training received education and opportunities unavailable to ordinary North Koreans, creating powerful incentive structures that helped retain talent despite the temptations of defection. The system produced technically skilled operatives who combined programming proficiency with understanding of networking, operating systems, and security mechanisms.

The organizational structure supporting North Korea's cyber operations balanced centralized control with operational flexibility. Strategic direction came from the top levels of regime leadership, with Kim Jong-un himself reportedly taking personal interest in cyber warfare capabilities. The Reconnaissance General Bureau provided institutional infrastructure, resources, and coordination across various cyber units. Individual teams enjoyed considerable autonomy in executing their assigned missions, allowing for operational creativity and adaptation to specific target environments. This combination of top-down strategic direction and bottom-up operational flexibility created an effective model for conducting diverse cyber campaigns across multiple domains simultaneously.

North Korea's use of overseas operatives added another dimension to its cyber warfare capabilities. Rather than conducting all operations from within North Korea's limited internet infrastructure, the regime stationed cyber operatives in China, Southeast Asia, and occasionally other regions. These operatives worked from hotel rooms, rented apartments, and sometimes even legitimate businesses that served as fronts for their activities. Operating overseas provided several advantages: better internet connectivity and infrastructure, reduced risk of having operations traced back to North Korean IP addresses, easier access to international banking and cryptocurrency systems for laundering stolen funds, and opportunities to acquire hardware, software, and other resources difficult to obtain under sanctions. This geographic distribution made attribution more challenging and complicated efforts to disrupt operations through network monitoring or physical intervention.

The malware development capabilities demonstrated by Lazarus Group and associated North Korean units revealed sophisticated technical expertise. Their custom malware families incorporated advanced features: polymorphic code that changed with each infection to evade signature-based detection, modular architectures allowing components to be mixed and matched for different operations, sophisticated persistence mechanisms ensuring malware survived system reboots and basic cleaning attempts, and anti-analysis techniques that hindered reverse engineering by security researchers. The malware showed evidence of continuous development and improvement, with new versions incorporating fixes for detected vulnerabilities and additions of new capabilities based on operational experiences.

Social engineering capabilities represented another area of strength in North Korean cyber operations. Lazarus Group demonstrated sophisticated understanding of how to craft convincing phishing emails and messages that exploited human psychology and organizational dynamics. They researched targets carefully, identifying individuals with access to critical systems and understanding enough about organizational context to craft messages that appeared legitimate. They created fake personas on professional networking sites, building relationships with targets over time before deploying malicious content. They spoofed trusted communication channels, making their messages appear to come from colleagues, business partners, or legitimate institutions. This combination of technical malware capabilities and social engineering sophistication made their attacks particularly difficult to defend against.

North Korea's willingness to cross lines that constrained other actors gave its cyber operations a particularly threatening character. While most nations conducting cyber espionage drew distinctions between intelligence gathering and destructive attacks, between military and civilian targets, between theft and destruction, North Korean operations showed fewer such restraints. They were willing to destroy data and cripple business operations, as demonstrated in the Sony Pictures attack. They targeted civilian financial institutions for theft, as the Bangladesh Bank heist illustrated. They appeared willing to take risks and attempt operations that other actors might have deemed too provocative or likely to trigger escalatory responses. This aggressive posture reflected both the regime's desperation for resources and its calculation that international responses would be limited by attribution difficulties and other nations' reluctance to escalate conflicts over cyber incidents.

The financial motivation behind many North Korean cyber operations created a somewhat unusual profile compared to other state-sponsored actors. While countries like China, Russia, and the United States primarily used cyber capabilities for espionage and strategic advantage, North Korea allocated substantial resources to operations with purely financial objectives. Bank heists, cryptocurrency exchange thefts, and ransomware campaigns all served to generate revenue for the sanctions-squeezed regime. Estimates of North Korean cyber theft revenues varied widely but generally suggested hundreds of millions of dollars stolen annually—substantial sums that could fund the regime's priorities, from weapons development to luxury goods for the elite, without requiring approval from legislative bodies or leaving paper trails that might be monitored by intelligence agencies.

The defensive challenges posed by North Korean cyber operations stemmed partly from the regime's isolation and the difficulty of imposing consequences. Unlike adversaries that might be deterred by threats of economic sanctions, North Korea was already heavily sanctioned and largely isolated from international commerce. Unlike nations that valued their international reputations and relationships, North Korea operated with limited concern for diplomatic consequences. Criminal prosecution of North Korean cyber operatives was nearly impossible given the lack of extradition relationships and the regime's protection of its operatives. Even when individuals were identified and indicted by foreign authorities, they remained safely beyond reach, continuing operations with minimal consequences. This relative immunity from retaliation created an environment where North Korean cyber units could operate more aggressively than counterparts in other nations who faced greater risks of meaningful consequences for their actions.

The evolution of North Korean cyber capabilities between the early 2000s and the mid-2010s demonstrated rapid learning and improvement. Early operations were often crude and easily detected, but the groups learned from their mistakes and from observing other cyber actors. They adopted techniques and tools developed by cybercriminal communities, modified and improved them, and integrated them into their operational playbooks. They studied defensive countermeasures and adapted their tactics to evade detection and response. By 2016, they had evolved into a mature cyber adversary capable of conducting complex, multi-stage operations against hardened targets—a remarkable achievement for a nation with such limited resources and international connections.

The psychological and cultural factors that shaped North Korean cyber operations created distinctive operational patterns. The regime's intense nationalism and cult of personality surrounding its leadership instilled a sense of mission and righteousness in operatives who viewed their attacks as serving the supreme leader and defending the homeland against hostile forces. The totalitarian control over information meant that operatives might genuinely believe the regime's propaganda about external threats and the justness of their cause. The cultural emphasis on loyalty, discipline, and collective purpose over individualism created operational security advantages—operatives were less likely to defect or leak information about operations than might be expected in less controlled environments. These cultural and psychological factors combined with technical capabilities to create adversaries who were not just skilled but highly motivated and mission-focused.

Understanding North Korean cyber warfare capabilities as they stood in early 2016 provides essential context for comprehending how the Bangladesh Bank heist was possible. This wasn't a case of lucky amateurs stumbling into success or opportunistic criminals exploiting an obvious vulnerability. Rather, it represented a sophisticated adversary with years of experience, substantial institutional support, advanced technical capabilities, and the boldness to attempt operations of unprecedented ambition deploying resources developed through substantial investment and refined through hard-won experience against numerous previous targets. The hunters stalking Bangladesh Bank were, in short, among the world's most dangerous cyber adversaries—patient, capable, and determined.

## Previous Attacks and Patterns

The Bangladesh Bank heist did not emerge fully formed as an isolated incident—it represented the culmination of years of evolution, learning, and increasingly ambitious operations by Lazarus Group and associated North Korean cyber units. Examining their previous attacks reveals patterns in targeting, methodology, and objectives that both foreshadowed the Bangladesh operation and provided the experiential foundation that made such an audacious heist possible. These earlier campaigns served as a testing ground where techniques were refined, vulnerabilities in defensive approaches were identified, and the group's confidence in their ability to execute complex operations without suffering meaningful consequences grew with each successful attack.

One of the earliest high-profile operations attributed to Lazarus Group was the 2009 "Operation Troy" campaign, a series of distributed denial-of-service (DDoS) attacks targeting websites in South Korea and the United States. While relatively unsophisticated by later standards—DDoS attacks simply overwhelm websites with traffic until they become unavailable rather than penetrating systems or stealing data—these operations demonstrated North Korea's willingness to conduct cyberattacks against perceived adversaries. The attacks targeted government agencies, financial institutions, and major commercial websites, causing temporary disruptions and sending a message about North Korea's cyber capabilities. The operations also provided training opportunities for cyber warfare units, allowing them to conduct offensive operations while observing how targets responded and what defensive measures proved effective.

The 2011 attack on South Korean banks and media organizations marked an escalation in destructiveness and sophistication. This operation, which occurred on March 20—a symbolically significant date in Korean history—deployed malware that destroyed data on infected computers, rendering them inoperable. The attack hit major banks including Shinhan Bank and Woori Bank, as well as television broadcasters KBS, MBC, and YTN, causing widespread disruption as tens of thousands of computers were disabled. The operation demonstrated several capabilities that would later appear in the Bangladesh Bank attack: the ability to conduct detailed reconnaissance to identify critical systems, the development of destructive malware designed to cause maximum impact, and the willingness to target financial institutions despite the risks of provoking strong responses.

The evolution of Lazarus Group's technical sophistication became particularly evident in the 2013 "Dark Seoul" attacks, another major assault on South Korean institutions. These attacks deployed malware called "WhiskeyAlfa" and "WhiskeyBravo" that featured advanced capabilities including the ability to steal data before destroying it, to spread through networks using various propagation techniques, and to execute at precisely scheduled times to maximize coordinated impact. The attacks targeted banks, broadcasters, and critical infrastructure, affecting over 48,000 computers and causing substantial economic disruption. The operation showed that Lazarus Group had moved beyond simple DDoS attacks to sophisticated network intrusions with capabilities for espionage, destruction, and disruption deployed strategically to achieve maximum effect.

Perhaps the operation that brought Lazarus Group into the global spotlight was the November 2014 attack on Sony Pictures Entertainment. This assault, which the U.S. government formally attributed to North Korea, represented a watershed moment in cyber conflict, demonstrating the potential for cyberattacks to cause substantial corporate damage, influence business decisions, and create international incidents. The attack was reportedly motivated by North Korean anger over the film "The Interview," a comedy depicting the assassination of Kim Jong-un. Lazarus Group operatives penetrated Sony's network, exfiltrated massive amounts of internal data including unreleased films, employee information, executive emails, and sensitive business documents, then deployed destructive malware that wiped systems across the company.

The Sony attack revealed several important characteristics of Lazarus Group's operational approach. First, it demonstrated their patience—the attackers had been inside Sony's network for months before deploying their destructive payload, using that time to map the network, identify valuable data, and position themselves for maximum impact. Second, it showed their willingness to weaponize stolen information, releasing embarrassing emails and private information to damage Sony's reputation and business relationships beyond just the technical destruction. Third, it illustrated their capacity for operations motivated by regime political interests rather than purely financial or strategic military objectives. The attack cost Sony tens of millions of dollars in remediation, lost business, and legal settlements, demonstrating that cyber operations could cause corporate-level damage comparable to major physical disasters.

The technical capabilities displayed in the Sony attack provided direct precursors to the Bangladesh Bank operation. The malware used included components designed to evade detection, persist in networks, and execute coordinated destructive actions across many systems simultaneously. The attackers demonstrated sophisticated understanding of corporate network architectures and the ability to move laterally through complex environments to reach high-value targets. The social engineering techniques used to gain initial access—spear-phishing emails carefully crafted to appear legitimate to targeted individuals—would be refined and redeployed in subsequent operations. The attack essentially served as proof-of-concept that Lazarus Group could successfully penetrate and compromise major corporate networks belonging to well-resourced targets in developed nations.

Following the Sony attack, Lazarus Group shifted focus increasingly toward financially motivated operations, likely reflecting North Korea's desperate need for revenue as international sanctions tightened. In 2015, several banks in various countries experienced cyberattacks that bore Lazarus Group's technical fingerprints. The Vietnam Tien Phong Bank, for instance, was targeted in a failed attempt to steal approximately one million dollars through fraudulent SWIFT transactions. While unsuccessful, this operation served as a direct precursor to the Bangladesh Bank heist, demonstrating that the group was specifically targeting the SWIFT system and developing capabilities for bank theft operations that exploited the trusted international banking network.

The patterns emerging across these various operations revealed a consistent operational methodology that would be fully deployed against Bangladesh Bank. Attacks typically began with reconnaissance phase, sometimes lasting months, during which the attackers gathered information about target networks, identified key personnel, and mapped the technical infrastructure they would need to compromise. This was followed by initial compromise, usually through spear-phishing or other social engineering techniques that exploited human vulnerabilities rather than requiring purely technical exploits. Once inside target networks, attackers moved laterally, escalating privileges and positioning themselves to access high-value systems while deploying malware designed to conceal their activities from security monitoring tools.

The malware families used across multiple Lazarus Group operations showed clear evidence of shared development and iterative improvement. Security researchers identified consistent code signatures, similar structural patterns, and common capabilities across malware samples from different operations. Variants of tools used in one attack would appear in subsequent operations with refinements and additional features. This pattern confirmed that these operations were products of a sustained program with continuity of personnel and institutional learning rather than disconnected incidents by unrelated actors. The group was clearly maintaining a malware arsenal that evolved through both internal development and incorporation of techniques observed in other actors' operations.

Target selection patterns revealed strategic thinking about risk versus reward and careful assessment of defensive capabilities. Early operations targeted South Korean entities—geographically close, politically significant, but also relatively well-defended given South

Korea's awareness of the North Korean cyber threat. As capabilities matured, targeting expanded to include entities in other nations where defensive postures might be less robust. Financial institutions in developing nations became increasingly attractive targets—they had valuable assets, connections to the international financial system, but often lacked the sophisticated cybersecurity programs of banks in more developed economies. This shift toward targets that offered better risk-reward profiles demonstrated the group's evolution from making political statements to conducting operations with clear practical objectives.

The persistence mechanisms employed across multiple operations showed particular sophistication. Lazarus Group malware didn't just infect systems and operate until detected—it was designed to survive reboots, persist through basic security scans, and maintain access even when some components were discovered and removed. The malware often included multiple redundant channels for command and control, ensuring attackers could maintain access even if primary communication paths were blocked. This persistence reflected both technical capability and strategic patience—the willingness to invest time in maintaining long-term access to compromised networks rather than conducting quick hit-and-run operations that might yield immediate results but sacrifice future opportunities.

The operational security practiced by Lazarus Group improved substantially over time as they learned from previous operations' exposure. Early attacks sometimes left obvious fingerprints that aided attribution and provided security researchers with intelligence about the group's tools and techniques. Later operations showed much more careful attention to avoiding detection and hindering forensic analysis. The group used proxy services and compromised systems to obscure the origin of attacks, deployed anti-forensic tools to wipe logs and cover their tracks, and carefully timed operations to maximize delays in detection and response. By 2016, they had evolved sophisticated operational security practices that made attacks harder to detect in progress and more difficult to attribute definitively after discovery.

The learning curve demonstrated across these operations was steep and continuous. Each attack, whether successful or thwarted, appeared to inform subsequent operations. When defensive measures proved effective, attackers adapted their techniques. When particular social engineering approaches succeeded, they were refined and reused. When malware was detected and analyzed, new versions appeared incorporating changes designed to evade the detection techniques that had exposed previous variants. This continuous learning and adaptation created a moving target for defenders—by the time security communities had developed countermeasures for one campaign, Lazarus Group had already evolved new approaches for the next.

The international dimension of Lazarus Group's operations expanded significantly over time. Early attacks primarily targeted South Korean entities with some U.S. targets as secondary objectives. By the mid-2010s, operations extended across Asia, into the Middle East, and occasionally into Europe and other regions. This geographic expansion reflected both growing ambition and practical considerations about where opportunities existed. It also complicated defensive efforts and international law enforcement responses—attacks originating from or transiting through multiple countries, targeting victims in other nations, and conducted by operatives in yet other locations created jurisdictional tangles that hampered coordinated responses.

By February 2016, when Lazarus Group turned its full attention to the Bangladesh Bank operation, the group had accumulated extensive experience attacking financial institutions, developing custom malware for specific targets, exploiting SWIFT systems, conducting sophisticated social engineering campaigns, and evading detection while maintaining persistent access to compromised networks. They had learned from past failures and successes, refined their tools and techniques, and developed the confidence to attempt an operation of unprecedented ambition—the theft of nearly a billion dollars from a central bank through the supposedly secure SWIFT network. The Bangladesh Bank heist represented not an aberration but the natural progression of a sophisticated adversary's capabilities matured through years of operations against increasingly ambitious targets.

## Reconnaissance and Planning Phases

The success of sophisticated cyber operations depends less on brilliant execution during the attack itself than on meticulous preparation in the months preceding the assault. For the Bangladesh Bank heist, Lazarus Group invested substantial time and resources in reconnaissance and planning—patiently gathering intelligence, mapping the target's network and procedures, identifying vulnerabilities, and preparing the customized tools and infrastructure necessary for a complex operation. This preparation phase, largely invisible to the target, determined whether the eventual attack would succeed or fail, whether the theft would go undetected long enough to launder the funds, and whether the attackers could escape attribution and consequences for their actions. Understanding how the hunters stalked their prey reveals much about the sophistication of modern cyber threats and the challenges defenders face in detecting and preventing attacks by patient, well-resourced adversaries.

The reconnaissance phase likely began months before the February 2016 attack, possibly as early as mid-to-late 2015 or even earlier. The initial stages involved passive intelligence gathering—collecting information about Bangladesh Bank that was publicly available or could be obtained without directly interacting with the bank's systems in ways that might trigger security alerts. The attackers would have studied the bank's organizational structure, identifying key personnel in IT departments, payment processing units, and executive leadership. They would have examined the bank's public communications, regulatory filings, procurement notices, and any other sources that might reveal information about technical infrastructure, security practices, or operational procedures.

Social media and professional networking platforms provided rich sources of intelligence that many organizations inadequately secure. Employees' LinkedIn profiles might reveal details about the technologies the bank used—when someone lists specific skills with particular software platforms or mentions projects involving certain systems, they inadvertently provide attackers with a map of the target's technical environment. Conference presentations, technical publications, and even job postings seeking personnel with specific skills all contributed to the intelligence picture. The attackers could piece together a remarkably detailed understanding of Bangladesh Bank's systems and operations without ever touching the bank's network simply by aggregating scattered pieces of publicly available information that individually seemed innocuous but collectively revealed significant detail.

The physical and organizational context surrounding Bangladesh Bank would have been studied carefully. The attackers needed to understand the bank's operational rhythms—when staff worked, when critical systems were most actively monitored, when security personnel might be less alert. They would have researched Bangladesh's banking holidays and working week structure, recognizing that Thursday evening preceded the weekend and that timing attacks to coincide with periods of reduced staffing could buy crucial time before discovery. They would have studied the bank's relationships with other institutions, identifying the Federal Reserve Bank of New York as the custodian of foreign currency reserves and understanding how transfers from that account were initiated and processed.

Technical reconnaissance likely progressed from passive to active stages as the attackers moved from gathering publicly available information to directly probing Bangladesh Bank's internet-facing systems. This active reconnaissance would have been conducted carefully to avoid triggering security alerts—perhaps using distributed scanning from multiple locations, limiting the frequency of probes, or focusing on systems that appeared less likely to be heavily monitored. The attackers would have identified the bank's internet-facing IP address ranges, mapped the services running on accessible systems, and looked for potential vulnerabilities that might provide initial access to internal networks. They would have studied the bank's email systems, looking for opportunities to conduct social engineering attacks against specific individuals.

The identification of specific personnel to target with social engineering campaigns required substantial research and psychological profiling. The attackers needed to identify individuals who had access to critical systems or whose credentials could provide a foothold in the network, but who might also be vulnerable to deception. They would have researched these individuals' professional backgrounds, interests, and social media activities, looking for information that could be exploited in crafting convincing phishing messages. They might have identified individuals who were relatively new to their positions and thus less experienced in recognizing sophisticated phishing attempts, or who had demonstrated trusting or helpful personalities in their online interactions that might make them more likely to respond to well-crafted deceptive messages.

The development of the attack infrastructure parallel to reconnaissance activities involved substantial effort. The attackers needed to establish command-and-control servers that could communicate with malware they would plant inside Bangladesh Bank's network, but these servers needed to be configured in ways that made them difficult to identify and take down once the attack was discovered. They likely used proxy chains, compromised legitimate servers in third countries, and bulletproof hosting services that were resistant to takedown requests. They created domain names that appeared legitimate, perhaps mimicking trusted entities or using patterns that would not appear suspicious if observed in network traffic logs. This infrastructure needed to be tested and ready well before the attack commenced, requiring parallel work-streams of technical preparation occurring alongside intelligence gathering.

The custom malware developed for the Bangladesh Bank operation represented a substantial software engineering effort. Based on subsequent analysis of the malware recovered from Bangladesh Bank's systems, security researchers determined that the attackers had created highly specialized tools designed specifically for this operation. The malware needed multiple capabilities: initial compromise and establishing persistence in the network, lateral movement through the internal network to reach SWIFT systems, keystroke logging and screen capture to steal credentials and learn operational procedures, manipulation of SWIFT software to send fraudulent transactions, and critically, concealment of evidence to prevent discovery until the theft was complete. Developing, testing, and debugging this customized malware suite while ensuring it would evade Bangladesh Bank's security controls required substantial time and technical expertise.

The planning of the theft itself involved careful consideration of how stolen funds would be moved and laundered. The attackers needed to establish destination accounts capable of receiving large transfers without immediately triggering fraud alerts, in jurisdictions where funds could be rapidly moved and converted before authorities could freeze accounts. The selection of the Philippines and Sri Lanka as destination countries appeared strategic—both had active financial sectors capable of processing large international transfers, both had some regulatory gaps that could be exploited, and both had mechanisms (particularly casinos in the Philippines) through which large amounts of cash could be laundered relatively quickly. Establishing these destination accounts and arrangements required coordination with money laundering networks—either existing criminal organizations or operatives specifically positioned for this purpose.

The testing phase for the attack likely involved operations against secondary targets that allowed the attackers to validate their approach without risking detection at their primary target. The 2015 attack on Vietnam's Tien Phong Bank, which attempted to steal funds through fraudulent SWIFT messages using similar methodologies to the later Bangladesh Bank attack, may have served this purpose. Although that operation failed to steal significant funds, it provided valuable operational experience that informed refinements to the approach. The attackers could test whether their malware successfully evaded detection, whether fraudulent SWIFT messages were processed by receiving institutions, and where the vulnerabilities in their operational plan existed. This empirical testing transformed theoretical attack plans into validated procedures with much higher probability of success.

The social engineering campaign that would provide initial access to Bangladesh Bank's network required careful orchestration. The attackers crafted spear-phishing emails that appeared highly legitimate—perhaps posing as job applications with attached resumes that actually contained malware, or official communications from trusted entities with links to compromised websites that would infect visitors' computers. These messages needed to be convincing enough to fool recipients who might have received general security awareness training about phishing threats. The attackers likely researched current events, upcoming bank initiatives, or professional contexts that would make their deceptive messages appear timely and relevant. They may have conducted preliminary social engineering—perhaps initiating benign correspondence with targets to establish trust before deploying malicious content in subsequent messages.

The timeline for the operation was carefully calculated based on multiple factors. The attackers needed to complete their reconnaissance and establish persistent access to Bangladesh Bank's network well before attempting the theft, allowing time to thoroughly map internal systems, identify the location of SWIFT terminals, and understand the operational procedures for initiating international transfers. They needed to time the actual theft to exploit time zone differences between Dhaka and New York, maximizing the delay before discovery. They selected a Thursday evening, knowing that the approaching weekend would further delay detection and response. This attention to timing details demonstrated sophisticated planning that considered not just technical factors but organizational rhythms, human behaviors, and the international nature of the financial system they were exploiting.

Risk assessment and contingency planning likely occupied significant attention during the preparation phase. The attackers needed to consider what could go wrong—partial detection that exposed their presence before the theft could be completed, technical failures that prevented fraudulent SWIFT messages from being transmitted, receiving institutions rejecting transfers as suspicious, or earlier-than-expected discovery triggering account freezes before funds could be laundered. They developed contingency approaches for various scenarios, building redundancy into their attack infrastructure and maintaining backup command-and-control channels in case primary methods were discovered. They prepared multiple destination accounts, presumably recognizing that some transfers might be blocked and planning to maximize theft from those that succeeded.

The legal and geopolitical context was almost certainly considered during planning. The attackers operated with knowledge that North Korea's isolation provided substantial protection from consequences—even if the operation was definitively attributed to North Korean actors, the lack of diplomatic relations, extradition treaties, or significant bilateral trade relationships limited potential retaliation. The choice of target in a developing nation with less sophisticated cyber forensics capabilities and more limited resources for international law enforcement cooperation likely reflected calculated assessment of where the operation was least likely to result in effective pursuit of the perpetrators. The planners understood they were operating in a largely consequence-free environment where successful operations would go essentially unpunished beyond possible diplomatic condemnations.

The compartmentalization of the operation across different teams and individuals served both operational security and practical organizational purposes. Different specialists likely handled different aspects—social engineering teams crafting phishing campaigns, malware developers creating custom tools, network penetration specialists conducting the actual intrusion, SWIFT specialists who understood banking protocols and could craft convincing fraudulent transactions, and money laundering coordinators who managed the destination accounts and conversion of stolen funds. This compartmentalization meant that no single individual necessarily understood the complete operation, reducing the risk that defection or capture of one operative would expose the entire campaign. It also allowed specialization, with each team focusing on their area of expertise rather than requiring individuals to master every aspect of a complex operation.

The intelligence gathering about Bangladesh Bank's specific SWIFT implementation was particularly critical and would have required detailed technical reconnaissance. The attackers needed to understand not just SWIFT protocols in general but the specific configuration and procedures used at Bangladesh Bank. They needed to know which software versions the bank used, how the SWIFT terminals were configured, what security controls were in place around SWIFT operations, and crucially, what the legitimate message formats and authorization procedures looked like. This level of detail likely required sustained access to the bank's network, observing legitimate SWIFT transactions over time to understand normal patterns that fraudulent messages would need to mimic.

The psychological preparation of operatives conducting the attack should not be underestimated. Executing an operation of this complexity under pressure, knowing that detection could occur at any moment and that improvisation might be necessary if circumstances changed, required individuals with particular temperaments and training. The operatives needed technical competence combined with operational discipline—the ability to follow procedures carefully, document their activities for coordination with other team members, and resist the temptation to deviate from plans in ways that might compromise the operation. The training and selection processes that produced such operatives represented significant institutional investment by North Korea's cyber warfare apparatus.

The documentation and standard operating procedures developed during the planning phase would have been extensive. Complex operations involving multiple teams working across time zones require careful documentation to ensure coordination and prevent miscommunication. The attackers likely developed detailed operational plans specifying the sequence of activities, the responsible parties for each task, the timing windows for different phases, and the contingency procedures if problems arose. They may have conducted rehearsals or simulations, walking through the operation to identify potential problems and refine procedures. This level of planning sophistication distinguished state-sponsored operations from opportunistic cybercrime, where planning might be minimal and operations more improvisational.

The final stages of preparation immediately preceding the attack involved positioning all the necessary components for rapid execution. The malware was finalized and ready for deployment. The command-and-control infrastructure was operational and tested. The fraudulent SWIFT messages were prepared with correct formatting, recipient account details, and amounts carefully calculated to maximize theft while avoiding immediate red flags. The money laundering teams were alerted and ready to rapidly move funds once they arrived in destination accounts. The timing was synchronized so that all elements would be ready to execute when the optimal moment arrived—that Thursday evening in Dhaka when the approaching weekend would buy crucial time for completing the theft before discovery.

Throughout this extended preparation period, the attackers maintained operational security discipline that prevented premature detection. They avoided activities that would trigger obvious alarms, limited their footprint within Bangladesh Bank's network, and carefully covered their tracks when conducting reconnaissance activities. They likely monitored security researchers' discussions and threat intelligence sharing to understand what indicators defenders were watching for, allowing them to adjust their techniques to evade known detection methods. This counter-intelligence awareness—understanding what defenders knew and adapting to avoid detection—represented sophisticated operational thinking that went beyond mere technical hacking skills.

The reconnaissance and planning phases ultimately determined the operation's outcome far more than the execution phase would. By the time the actual attack commenced in February 2016, months of preparation had created a situation where success was highly probable if the operation proceeded according to plan. The attackers understood their target intimately—its technical infrastructure, its procedures, its vulnerabilities, and its rhythms. They had prepared customized tools designed specifically to exploit the identified weaknesses. They had established the infrastructure necessary to move and launder stolen funds. They had timed the operation to maximize delays in detection and response. The careful preparation transformed what might have been an impossibly ambitious crime into a feasible operation with reasonable probability of success.

## Identifying the Weaknesses

The transformation of Bangladesh Bank from an institution among thousands of potential targets into the specific focus of Lazarus Group's ambitious heist depended on the attackers' ability to identify exploitable weaknesses that distinguished this bank from better-defended alternatives. The reconnaissance phase revealed multiple vulnerability categories—technical deficiencies in network security, procedural gaps in operational controls, human factors that could be exploited through social engineering, and systemic weaknesses in how the bank's SWIFT connection was secured and monitored. Understanding how the attackers identified and categorized these weaknesses provides insight into the analytical process that sophisticated cyber adversaries employ when selecting and preparing to attack specific targets.

The technical infrastructure weaknesses at Bangladesh Bank were numerous and, from the attackers' perspective, inviting. The bank's network architecture lacked the robust segmentation that security best practices recommended for protecting critical systems like SWIFT terminals. Rather than isolating SWIFT infrastructure on completely separate networks with stringent controls on any connections to other systems, Bangladesh Bank's configuration allowed network pathways between SWIFT terminals and more general-purpose systems. This meant that attackers who gained initial access to the broader network through conventional compromise methods could potentially reach SWIFT systems through lateral movement rather than needing to directly breach the more carefully protected payment processing infrastructure.

The firewall configurations protecting Bangladesh Bank's network contained gaps that the reconnaissance phase would have identified. Firewalls serve as gatekeepers, controlling what traffic can flow between different network segments and between internal networks and the internet. Properly configured firewalls implement the principle of least privilege—blocking everything by default and only allowing specific, necessary traffic based on explicit rules. Analysis of Bangladesh Bank's network after the attack revealed that firewall rules were less restrictive than they should have been, allowing more communication between network segments than was strictly necessary for legitimate business purposes. These overly permissive rules created pathways that attackers could exploit to move through the network once they had achieved initial compromise.

The patching and update practices at Bangladesh Bank presented another significant vulnerability that reconnaissance would have revealed. Software vendors regularly release security patches that fix vulnerabilities discovered in their products. Organizations that promptly apply these patches close security holes that attackers might otherwise exploit. However, Bangladesh Bank's patch management was inconsistent, with some systems running software versions that contained known vulnerabilities for which patches had been available for months. The attackers could identify these unpatched systems through their reconnaissance, then use publicly available exploit code to compromise them, gaining their initial foothold in the network through vulnerabilities that should have been closed through routine maintenance.

The endpoint security controls on individual computers at Bangladesh Bank were insufficient to detect and block the sophisticated malware that Lazarus Group had developed. The bank likely relied on antivirus software that used signature-based detection—comparing files against databases of known malicious software. While this approach works against common, widely-distributed malware, it is ineffective against custom malware developed specifically for a targeted attack. The attackers knew their malware would not appear in antivirus databases because it had never been used before, allowing it to evade these defenses. The absence of more advanced endpoint detection systems that might have identified suspicious behavior even when specific malware signatures were unknown left individual computers vulnerable to compromise.

The network monitoring and intrusion detection capabilities at Bangladesh Bank were limited in both scope and sophistication. The bank likely had some monitoring systems in place, but these were either not comprehensive enough to observe all critical network traffic or not sophisticated enough to identify the subtle indicators that would have revealed the attackers' presence. The attackers could observe during their reconnaissance what traffic patterns appeared normal and what activities triggered alerts, allowing them to operate within the gaps in monitoring coverage. They could move through the network using techniques that blended with legitimate activities, avoiding the behavioral patterns that might have triggered alerts from the bank's security systems.

The procedural weaknesses surrounding SWIFT operations presented exploitable opportunities that technical controls alone could not address. Bangladesh Bank's procedures for authorizing and reviewing international transfers apparently lacked sufficient segregation of duties and independent verification. In properly controlled environments, initiating a transfer, approving it, and reconciling it afterward should involve different individuals or departments, creating multiple checkpoints where fraudulent transactions might be detected. The attackers' reconnaissance revealed that Bangladesh Bank's procedures did not implement these controls as rigorously as they might have, creating opportunities to manipulate the process once they had compromised the relevant systems.

The physical security around SWIFT terminals and the facilities that housed them may have been adequate against traditional threats like theft or physical sabotage, but did not address the cyber threat the attackers posed. The bank likely focused physical security on preventing unauthorized physical access to sensitive areas, but the attackers had no need for physical presence—they accessed SWIFT systems remotely through the compromised network. The mental model that physical security of facilities equated to security of the systems within those facilities was outdated, but this outdated thinking persisted in many institutions that had not fully adapted to the realities of cyber threats.

The human vulnerabilities at Bangladesh Bank were perhaps the most critical weakness the attackers identified and exploited. Security awareness among bank staff was insufficient to reliably detect and resist sophisticated social engineering attacks. Employees had likely received basic training about not clicking suspicious links or opening unexpected attachments, but this training was inadequate preparation for dealing with carefully crafted spear-phishing campaigns that leveraged detailed research about the organization and the targeted individuals. The attackers identified specific employees who had access to systems they needed to compromise and who appeared potentially vulnerable to social engineering based on their digital footprints and professional profiles.

The organizational culture and communication patterns at Bangladesh Bank created additional exploitable vulnerabilities. In some organizations, junior staff might hesitate to question what appeared to be requests or instructions from senior management, even if those requests seemed unusual. This hierarchical deference could be exploited by attackers who successfully impersonated authority figures in social engineering attacks. The attackers studied how people communicated within the organization—the formality levels, the typical patterns of requests, and the circumstances under which unusual requests might be considered normal—allowing them to craft deceptive messages that fit the organizational culture and were therefore less likely to trigger suspicion.

The technical expertise available within Bangladesh Bank's IT department, while sufficient for routine operations, was insufficient for detecting and responding to sophisticated nation-state-level threats. The IT staff understood conventional security concerns and could handle typical technical problems, but they lacked specialized cybersecurity expertise in areas like advanced threat detection, forensic analysis, and incident response. The attackers recognized that the bank's internal capabilities for detecting sophisticated intrusions were limited, reducing the risk that their reconnaissance activities or persistent presence in the network would be discovered before they were ready to execute the theft.

The visibility gaps between Bangladesh Bank and the Federal Reserve Bank of New York represented a systemic weakness that the attackers carefully analyzed. The Federal Reserve processed payment instructions from Bangladesh Bank based on authenticated SWIFT messages, but had limited insight into Bangladesh Bank's internal approval processes, typical transaction patterns, or current operational context. The Federal Reserve couldn't know whether a large transfer request was genuinely authorized by senior Bangladesh Bank officials or whether it represented a fraudulent transaction initiated by attackers who had compromised the bank's systems. This information asymmetry—where the Federal Reserve trusted that properly authenticated messages represented legitimate transactions—created an exploitable gap that the attackers recognized and planned to exploit.

The timing patterns and operational rhythms at both institutions presented weaknesses that the attackers identified and incorporated into their planning. Bangladesh Bank followed a Thursday-Friday weekend schedule typical of Muslim-majority nations, different from the Saturday-Sunday weekend in the United States. The attackers recognized that initiating fraudulent transfers on Thursday evening Dhaka time would mean they were executed during New York business hours but would not be discovered in Dhaka until after the weekend when staff returned. This timing gap, created by the confluence of different working schedules and time zones, represented a weakness not in any specific security control but in the temporal coordination between the two institutions.

The backup and recovery procedures at Bangladesh Bank revealed vulnerabilities in the bank's ability to detect tampering and maintain reliable audit trails. The attackers identified that the bank's backup systems and logging infrastructure could potentially be compromised along with production systems, allowing them to manipulate or delete evidence of their activities. In properly secured environments, logs and backups are protected separately from the systems they monitor, ensuring that attackers cannot easily cover their tracks. The absence of such separation at Bangladesh Bank created opportunities to conceal evidence of the intrusion and the fraudulent transactions, buying additional time before discovery.

The regulatory oversight and audit processes to which Bangladesh Bank was subject apparently did not include sufficiently rigorous assessment of cybersecurity controls specific to SWIFT operations. Auditors may have verified that the bank had implemented various security measures without deeply testing whether those measures were effective against sophisticated attacks. The attackers recognized that regulatory compliance did not necessarily equate to genuine security, and that Bangladesh Bank might have passed audits while still remaining fundamentally vulnerable to the techniques they planned to employ.

The international coordination and information-sharing mechanisms available to Bangladesh Bank were limited, meaning the institution might not have timely access to threat intelligence about Lazarus Group's activities and techniques. While banks in some countries participated in information-sharing arrangements where members alerted each other about attack campaigns and emerging threats, Bangladesh Bank's participation in such networks was limited. The attackers knew that their previous operations might not have been studied by Bangladesh Bank's security personnel, meaning defenses might not be calibrated to detect the specific techniques and indicators associated with Lazarus Group operations.

The incident response capabilities at Bangladesh Bank were inadequate for quickly detecting and containing a sophisticated intrusion. Even if some indicators of compromise were observed, the bank lacked the expertise, procedures, and tools necessary to rapidly investigate and respond. The attackers recognized that delays in detection and response would work to their advantage—even if their presence in the network was eventually discovered, the time required for the bank to understand what had happened, how deep the compromise extended, and what actions were needed to remediate would provide crucial hours or days during which their operation could proceed.

The legal and jurisdictional complexities surrounding international cybercrime created another form of weakness that the attackers understood and incorporated into their planning. Even after the theft was discovered and attribution established, the practical challenges of pursuing criminal prosecution across international boundaries, particularly involving North Korea with its lack of extradition treaties and hostile relations with most of the international community, meant that meaningful consequences for the perpetrators were unlikely. This weakness in the international legal architecture surrounding cybercrime reduced the deterrent effect that might otherwise have prevented such audacious operations.

The comprehensive identification of these various weakness categories—technical, procedural, human, organizational, and systemic—demonstrated the sophistication of Lazarus Group's analytical capabilities. They didn't simply look for a single vulnerability to exploit; they identified how multiple weaknesses could be chained together into an attack path that would take them from initial compromise through to successful theft and laundering of funds. Each weakness they identified became a component in the overall attack plan, with specific techniques and tools developed to exploit particular vulnerabilities. The meticulous cataloging of weaknesses during reconnaissance transformed an ambitious theoretical operation into a practical plan with a clear path from beginning to end and reasonable probability of success.

## Conclusion

The hunters who stalked Bangladesh Bank through cyberspace were neither opportunistic amateurs nor isolated criminals operating in basements with stolen credit cards. They were sophisticated operatives of one of the world's most aggressive cyber warfare programs, backed by state resources, motivated by both ideological commitment and practical revenue needs, and equipped with technical capabilities refined through years of increasingly ambitious operations. Lazarus Group's evolution from conducting crude denial-of-service attacks to orchestrating near-billion-dollar bank heists represented one of the most remarkable capability progressions in cyber warfare history, demonstrating how determined adversaries with institutional support and learning opportunities can rapidly advance from nuisance to existential threat.

The group's connection to North Korea illuminated uncomfortable realities about cyber warfare in the modern era. A relatively poor, isolated nation could develop offensive capabilities that rivaled those of far wealthier countries by concentrating resources, identifying and developing elite talent, and recognizing that cyber operations offered asymmetric advantages unavailable through conventional competition. The financial motivations behind operations like the Bangladesh Bank heist revealed how cyber capabilities could serve dual purposes—generating revenue to support the regime while simultaneously maintaining and improving technical capabilities that might later be deployed for more overtly strategic or military objectives.

The previous attacks and patterns established by Lazarus Group provided essential context for understanding the Bangladesh Bank operation. The Sony Pictures attack demonstrated capabilities for penetrating major corporate networks and causing substantial damage. The attempted theft from Vietnam's Tien Phong Bank served as proof-of-concept for targeting SWIFT systems specifically. Each operation, whether fully successful or partially thwarted, contributed to an accumulated body of experience and refined techniques that informed subsequent campaigns. The Bangladesh Bank heist didn't emerge from nowhere—it represented the culmination of years of operational evolution and learning.

The reconnaissance and planning phases preceding the attack illustrated the patient, methodical approach that distinguished sophisticated cyber operations from opportunistic hacking. Months of intelligence gathering, target analysis, custom tool development, and infrastructure preparation transformed an audacious concept into an executable plan. The attackers studied not just technical systems but human behaviors, organizational rhythms, and systemic factors that might be exploited. They tested their approaches against secondary targets, refined their techniques based on observed results, and carefully timed their operation to maximize advantages and minimize risks of early detection.

The comprehensive identification of weaknesses at Bangladesh Bank—spanning technical infrastructure, procedural controls, human factors, and systemic gaps—demonstrated analytical sophistication that went far beyond simple hacking. The attackers understood that security was only as strong as its weakest link, and they identified multiple vulnerable links that could be exploited sequentially to achieve their objectives. They recognized how different weakness categories interacted and reinforced each other, creating attack paths that might not have been obvious when examining individual vulnerabilities in isolation.

As we transition from examining the hunters to exploring how the attack actually unfolded, understanding these adversaries—their capabilities, their methods, their patient preparation, and their analytical approach to identifying and exploiting weaknesses—provides essential context. The Bangladesh Bank heist was not random misfortune or simple bad luck. It was the predictable result when sophisticated, well-resourced adversaries identifying and exploiting a confluence of vulnerabilities that should have been addressed but were not. The hunters had identified their prey, studied its weaknesses, prepared their tools, and positioned themselves for the strike. The stage was set for one of history's most audacious cyber heists, an operation that would expose fundamental vulnerabilities in global financial infrastructure and forever change how institutions approached the security of international banking systems.

# Chapter 3: The Infiltration

The digital fortress that organizations spend millions constructing, reinforced with firewalls, intrusion detection systems, and elaborate security protocols, often falls not through brute force but through whispers—carefully crafted lies that exploit the one vulnerability no security patch can fix: human nature itself. The infiltration stage represents the pivotal moment when theoretical vulnerabilities transform into actual breaches, when reconnaissance crystallizes into access, and when patient attackers finally cross the threshold from outsider to insider. This chapter unveils the sophisticated methodologies that transform locked doors into open gateways, examining how modern threat actors orchestrate their initial compromise with the precision of master locksmiths and the cunning of confidence artists.

## How the Hackers Gained Access

The initial breach rarely announces itself with fanfare or flashing alerts. Instead, it slips through defenses like smoke through a keyhole, exploiting the microscopic gaps that exist in even the most fortified networks. Understanding how attackers gain that crucial first foothold requires examining the intricate dance between technical vulnerability and human fallibility, where success often hinges not on overwhelming security measures but on finding the single weak thread that unravels the entire tapestry.

Modern access methodologies have evolved far beyond the stereotypical image of hooded figures frantically typing in dark rooms. Today's sophisticated threat actors employ multi-vector approaches that combine technical prowess with psychological manipulation. They understand that networks are defended by technology but operated by people, and that the strongest encryption means nothing if someone willingly hands over their credentials. The contemporary infiltration begins long before any malicious code touches a target system, starting instead with the painstaking process of mapping the human terrain—identifying who has access to what, who responds to which psychological triggers, and where the organization's security awareness falters.

The pathway to initial compromise typically follows one of several well-worn routes, each selected based on the target's unique defensive posture and the attacker's capabilities. Some adversaries prefer the direct approach, exploiting known vulnerabilities in internet-facing applications or services that organizations have failed to patch. Others favor the indirect route, compromising third-party vendors or service providers who maintain trusted relationships with the ultimate target. Still others play the long game, compromising personal devices or home networks of employees who work remotely, then pivoting from these less-secured environments into the corporate infrastructure. The choice of entry vector reflects both opportunity and strategy, with sophisticated attackers often preparing multiple attack paths simultaneously, ready to pivot when one avenue closes.

What makes modern infiltration particularly insidious is the asymmetry of effort involved. Defenders must secure every possible entry point, maintaining perfect vigilance across thousands of potential vulnerabilities. Attackers need find only one weakness, one moment of inattention, one unpatched system or one trusting employee. This fundamental imbalance shapes every infiltration, rewarding patience and punishing complacency. The organizations that fall victim often discover, in painful retrospect, that their breach began not with sophisticated zero-day exploits but with something far more mundane: a missed software update, an overly permissive firewall rule, or a password that never should have been created in the first place.

The initial foothold, once established, becomes the beachhead for everything that follows. It might be as simple as valid credentials harvested through a successful phishing campaign, granting the attacker legitimate-looking access through the front door. It could be a backdoor implanted in a compromised software update, allowing remote control that bypasses traditional authentication. Or it might be access to a poorly secured remote desktop protocol port, left exposed to the internet and protected only by default credentials that took mere minutes to guess. Regardless of the specific mechanism, this initial access represents the critical failure point—the moment when theoretical risk becomes actual compromise, when external threat becomes internal presence.

## Phishing Attacks and Social Engineering

The art of phishing has matured from crude, typo-ridden emails promising fortunes from Nigerian princes into something far more dangerous: precision-crafted psychological weapons that exploit fundamental aspects of human cognition and organizational behavior. Modern phishing campaigns represent the perfect fusion of technical capability and psychological manipulation, leveraging detailed reconnaissance to create scenarios so convincing that even security-conscious individuals find themselves clicking links or entering credentials before their rational minds engage. This evolution has transformed phishing from a nuisance into the single most effective vector for initial compromise, responsible for an overwhelming majority of successful breaches across all sectors.

The anatomy of a sophisticated phishing attack begins long before any email arrives in an inbox. Attackers invest substantial effort in reconnaissance, harvesting information from social media profiles, corporate websites, professional networking platforms, and even data breaches affecting other organizations. They construct detailed profiles of their targets, understanding not just names and job titles but organizational relationships, current projects, communication styles, and the subtle cultural norms that make certain requests seem normal rather than suspicious. This intelligence gathering transforms generic phishing attempts into spear-phishing campaigns—highly targeted attacks aimed at specific individuals, crafted to exploit their unique circumstances, responsibilities, and psychological pressure points.

The messages themselves demonstrate remarkable sophistication in their construction. Rather than obvious requests for passwords or wire transfers, modern phishing emails embed themselves in the natural flow of business communications. An employee in accounting receives what appears to be a routine invoice requiring approval, complete with authentic-looking vendor branding and familiar formatting. An executive gets an urgent message seemingly from their CEO, referencing actual ongoing projects and using language that matches previous legitimate communications. An IT staff member sees what looks like an automated security alert, warning of suspicious activity and requiring immediate password verification through a link that leads to a flawlessly replicated login portal. The scenarios vary, but the underlying principle remains constant: make the fraudulent seem so normal, so expected, so time-sensitive that critical thinking surrenders to habitual response.

Technology amplifies these social engineering attacks in ways that previous generations of con artists could never have imagined. Email spoofing techniques make malicious messages appear to originate from trusted sources, with sender addresses that look legitimate at first glance. Sophisticated attackers compromise actual email accounts, sending phishing messages from genuinely legitimate addresses that have already established trust and bypassing many security filters in the process. They exploit features of modern communication platforms, using URL shorteners to disguise malicious links, embedding credentials-harvesting forms directly in emails, or leveraging cloud storage platforms to host malware that appears to come from trusted services. The technical sophistication serves the psychological manipulation, creating scenarios that pass both automated security checks and human skepticism.

Beyond email, social engineering extends into every communication channel an organization uses. Voice phishing, or vishing, involves attackers calling employees while impersonating IT support, vendors, or executives, using information gathered from reconnaissance to establish credibility before requesting sensitive information or convincing targets to take actions that compromise security. SMS phishing, or smishing, delivers malicious links through text messages that often bypass email security entirely. Social media platforms become venues for relationship-building attacks, where adversaries spend weeks or months cultivating trust with targets before finally making requests that leverage the established rapport. The multi-channel approach recognizes that different people respond to different communication styles, and that attacks arriving through unexpected vectors often face less scrutiny than those coming through channels where security awareness training has focused attention.

The psychological principles underlying successful social engineering remain remarkably consistent across all these variations. Attackers exploit authority, crafting scenarios where requests appear to come from legitimate figures whose directives employees feel compelled to follow. They leverage urgency, creating artificial time pressure that short-circuits careful consideration and triggers automatic responses. They tap into helpfulness, the natural human desire to assist others and solve problems, particularly when the person requesting help seems distressed or speaks the organization's cultural language. They use social proof, suggesting that others have already complied with similar requests or that the action being requested represents standard procedure. And they exploit the fundamental challenge of proving a negative—making it difficult for targets to verify that a request isn't legitimate without making phone calls or checks that seem paranoid or inefficient in the moment.

The evolution of phishing techniques continues to accelerate, incorporating emerging technologies in ways that make attacks even more convincing. Artificial intelligence now generates phishing content that lacks the grammatical errors and awkward phrasing that once served as red flags, producing text that flows naturally and matches organizational communication styles with eerie precision. Deepfake audio technology enables voice phishing attacks where attackers impersonate executives so convincingly that their own staff cannot distinguish the artificial from the authentic. Automated systems now run phishing campaigns that adapt in real-time based on recipient behavior, serving different content to different users and learning from failures to optimize future attempts. The arms race between attackers and defenders increasingly tilts in favor of those who understand that technology amplifies human psychology rather than replacing it.

## Malware Deployment Strategies

Once phishing or social engineering creates that initial opening—whether through stolen credentials, a clicked link, or a downloaded attachment—the next phase begins: deploying the malicious software that will provide persistent access and enable the attacker's ultimate objectives. Malware deployment represents a critical juncture where attackers must overcome not just perimeter defenses but also endpoint protection, network monitoring, and increasingly sophisticated behavioral analysis systems. The strategies employed reveal how threat actors think about stealth, persistence, and progression, balancing the need for robust access against the ever-present risk of detection that could terminate the entire operation before it achieves its goals.

The delivery mechanisms for malware have grown remarkably diverse, adapting to whatever weaknesses the reconnaissance and initial compromise phases reveal. When phishing succeeds in convincing a user to open a malicious attachment, that file might be a weaponized document—perhaps a Microsoft Word file, PDF, or Excel spreadsheet containing carefully crafted exploit code that takes advantage of vulnerabilities in the applications meant to open them. These documents often appear completely normal when viewed, displaying the invoice, report, or contract that the user expected, while simultaneously and invisibly executing code in the background that downloads and installs the attacker's tools. The dual functionality—providing the legitimate-seeming content that maintains the deception while simultaneously delivering the malicious payload—demonstrates the sophistication of modern malware packaging.

Alternative deployment vectors bypass traditional file-based delivery entirely. When attackers compromise credentials through phishing or other means, they might use legitimate remote access tools and administrative interfaces to deploy malware directly, their actions indistinguishable from routine administrative activity. They exploit trusted relationships between organizations, compromising software update mechanisms to distribute malware through channels that security systems have been specifically configured to trust. Supply chain attacks, where adversaries infiltrate software vendors and embed malicious code in legitimate applications before they ever reach end users, represent perhaps the most insidious deployment strategy—turning the very tools meant to enhance functionality into vectors for compromise. These approaches succeed precisely because they abuse trust rather than break through technical barriers, slipping past defenses designed to stop external threats but poorly equipped to validate internal or trusted sources.

The malware itself exhibits increasing sophistication in its design and capabilities. Rather than monolithic programs that perform all functions immediately, modern attack operations favor modular, staged deployments. The initial payload might be remarkably small and simple—sometimes called a dropper or loader—designed solely to establish a foothold and fetch additional components only when needed. This staged approach serves multiple purposes: it reduces the chances of detection by limiting the initially malicious code's footprint, it allows attackers to customize the operation based on what they discover after initial access, and it compartmentalizes the operation so that detection of one component doesn't necessarily compromise the entire toolkit. First-stage malware might do nothing more than establish a connection to a command-and-control server and wait for instructions, pulling down additional capabilities only after attackers verify that the initial deployment succeeded and assess what the compromised environment offers.

Evasion techniques represent another critical aspect of deployment strategy, as malware must survive scrutiny from antivirus software, endpoint detection and response systems, and increasingly sophisticated behavioral analysis tools. Attackers employ polymorphic code that changes its appearance with each deployment, making signature-based detection ineffective. They use encryption and obfuscation to hide malicious functionality, only decrypting or revealing true capabilities at the last possible moment before execution. Some malware incorporates environmental awareness, refusing to execute if it detects signs of virtual machines, sandboxes, or analysis tools commonly used by security researchers, remaining dormant until it confirms it has successfully infiltrated a genuine target environment. The most sophisticated variants employ techniques borrowed from legitimate software protection mechanisms, using anti-debugging tricks, code integrity checks, and execution guards that make reverse engineering extraordinarily difficult.

Persistence mechanisms ensure that malware survives system reboots, security scans, and routine maintenance that might otherwise dislodge the attacker's presence. These techniques range from straightforward registry modifications that cause malware to launch automatically at system startup to sophisticated hijacking of legitimate system processes and services. Attackers might replace or modify legitimate system files with malicious versions, install themselves as device drivers that load before security software initializes, or compromise the boot-loader itself to ensure their code runs before the operating system even fully loads. Advanced persistence sometimes eschews traditional file-based approaches entirely, with malware that exists only in memory, reconstructing itself from artifacts scattered across legitimate system locations or fetched from remote servers each time the system starts. The goal remains constant: ensure that the attacker's foothold survives detection attempts and maintains access regardless of routine security operations.

The deployment phase increasingly incorporates automation and artificial intelligence, enabling attacks that adapt to their environment without constant human intervention. Malware now includes decision-making logic that guides its own deployment, spreading through networks by evaluating the value of different systems, the security tools those systems run, and the likelihood of successful compromise. Some variants incorporate machine learning capabilities that help them identify and exploit local vulnerabilities, adapt their behavior to blend with normal network activity, and even modify their own code to evade specific security measures they encounter. This autonomous operation allows attacks to scale beyond what human operators could manage, simultaneously compromising multiple targets while requiring minimal ongoing attention from the threat actors who launched the campaign.

## Living Off the Land: Blending in with Normal Traffic

Perhaps the most challenging aspect of modern intrusions for defenders to detect and counter involves attackers who have largely abandoned custom malware in favor of legitimate system tools and normal network protocols. This approach, commonly known as "living off the land," transforms the victim's own administrative infrastructure into an attack platform, exploiting the reality that organizations maintain extensive capabilities for remote management, automation, and system administration—capabilities that, in the wrong hands, become potent instruments for data theft, lateral movement, and persistent access. By using tools that are meant to be on the network and traffic patterns that mirror legitimate activity, attackers achieve a form of operational camouflage that renders many traditional security measures nearly useless.

The philosophy underlying living-off-the-land attacks recognizes a fundamental challenge in cybersecurity: distinguishing malicious intent from legitimate use when the tools and techniques are identical. Every Windows system includes PowerShell, a powerful scripting environment that administrators use for automation and management but that attackers leverage for reconnaissance, credential theft, and malware execution. Every network supports remote desktop protocols and other remote access mechanisms that enable IT support and remote work but that also provide attackers with interfaces indistinguishable from authorized administration. Every organization maintains administrative shares, scheduled tasks, and management interfaces that exist for operational efficiency but serve equally well for malicious purposes when accessed by the wrong party. The attacker's genius lies not in creating new tools but in recognizing that the victim has already deployed everything necessary for a successful compromise.

Execution through native system utilities allows attackers to accomplish sophisticated objectives without introducing any obviously malicious files into the environment. Windows Management Instrumentation provides comprehensive capabilities for system querying and remote execution, allowing attackers to gather intelligence about the network, identify valuable targets, and execute commands on remote systems—all through interfaces that security software has been trained to regard as legitimate administrative activity. Command-line interpreters and scripting engines execute attacker commands that download additional tools, modify system configurations, or extract data, leaving behind only the same artifacts that routine administrative work would generate. Even the tools designed specifically for security and forensics—including network mapping utilities, password recovery tools, and system monitoring software—become weapons when employed by adversaries who understand that security operations teams often struggle to distinguish authorized security testing from malicious activity.

Credential theft exemplifies how living-off-the-land techniques exploit built-in functionality. Rather than deploying custom key-loggers or password stealers that antivirus might detect, sophisticated attackers use native Windows capabilities to dump credential material from memory where the operating system stores it for legitimate authentication purposes. Tools like Mimikatz, while well-known to security professionals, primarily leverage documented Windows features and protocols, accessing credential stores in ways that don't necessarily appear malicious to security software monitoring for file-based threats. Even more subtle approaches involve manipulating legitimate authentication mechanisms, creating golden tickets for Kerberos systems or forging authentication tokens that grant access without requiring actual passwords. These techniques succeed because they exploit fundamental aspects of how operating systems and networks function rather than bugs or vulnerabilities that can be patched away.

Network movement within compromised environments increasingly relies on protocols and services that organizations explicitly enable and require for normal operations. Attackers move laterally through networks using remote procedure calls, Windows Management Instrumentation, PowerShell remoting, and similar mechanisms that exist specifically to allow centralized management and remote access. They authenticate using stolen credentials through standard login interfaces rather than exploiting vulnerabilities, making their activity indistinguishable from a legitimate administrator connecting from an unusual location or at an odd time. File transfers occur through standard file-sharing protocols, web services, or even cloud storage platforms that the organization uses for legitimate purposes, with malicious data exfiltration hiding within the constant stream of normal business file movement. Every action mirrors something that happens thousands of times daily in the course of routine operations, rendering the malicious effectively invisible within the normal.

The command-and-control infrastructure supporting these operations demonstrates similar sophistication in blending with expected traffic patterns. Rather than communicating through unusual ports or protocols that network monitoring might flag, malware increasingly uses standard web traffic over ports 80 and 443, the same channels through which normal internet browsing occurs. Communications might tunnel through DNS queries, a protocol so fundamental to network operations that blocking unusual DNS patterns risks breaking critical functionality. Some operations leverage popular web services—social media platforms, cloud storage, code repositories, or collaboration tools—using these services' APIs to send and receive commands in ways that appear identical to legitimate application usage. By routing malicious traffic through the same channels and services that handle massive volumes of legitimate business communications, attackers achieve a needle-in-haystack dynamic where identifying the malicious requires sophisticated behavioral analysis rather than simple pattern matching.

Defenders face a profound challenge: the same capabilities that enable efficient IT operations also enable sophisticated attacks. Disabling PowerShell breaks countless legitimate scripts and administrative workflows. Blocking remote desktop access prevents flexible work arrangements and emergency system administration. Restricting administrative tools makes routine support and maintenance exponentially more difficult. The solution cannot be simply removing capabilities but instead requires organizations to implement monitoring and controls sophisticated enough to distinguish malicious use from legitimate activity based on context, behavior, and user intent—a far more complex undertaking than simply blocking known-bad files or network connections. Some organizations adopt application whitelisting, privilege management, and least-privilege architectures that limit even legitimate administrative tools to only those who specifically need them for documented purposes. Others invest heavily in behavioral analytics and user and entity behavior analytics that build baselines of normal activity and flag deviations, attempting to catch the subtle anomalies that might indicate compromised credentials or malicious use of legitimate tools.

# The Waiting Game

Once initial access has been achieved and persistent footholds established, sophisticated attackers often adopt a posture that seems counterintuitive to those imagining hackers racing against time to steal data before detection: they wait. This patient phase of operations, sometimes extending for weeks or months, represents perhaps the most challenging aspect of intrusions for defenders to counter because it involves adversaries who have already penetrated defenses and established presence, yet who generate minimal observable activity while they carefully expand access, study the environment, and position themselves for ultimate objectives. The waiting game transforms infiltration from a kinetic assault into a methodical siege, where time favors the patient attacker who understands that rushing increases detection risk while patience enables truly comprehensive compromise.

The strategic logic behind this patience reflects hard lessons learned from earlier, less sophisticated attacks. Rushing to accomplish objectives immediately after initial compromise increases the likelihood of detection dramatically. Security operations centers monitor for anomalous behavior, and sudden spikes in network activity, unusual system access patterns, or unexpected data movements often trigger investigations that can terminate an intrusion before it fully develops. Early-stage malware might remain dormant for days or weeks after deployment, allowing security scans and incident response procedures to run their course and potentially declare the environment clean before any obviously malicious activity begins. Attackers understand that defenders eventually experience alert fatigue, that initial heightened vigilance following suspicious activity tends to relax over time, and that patient adversaries outlast the immediate response to whatever detection hint led security teams to briefly intensify monitoring.

During this dormant or low-activity period, sophisticated threat actors engage in careful environmental mapping that makes their eventual operational phase far more effective. They conduct slow, methodical reconnaissance of the network infrastructure, identifying critical systems, data repositories, backup servers, and security infrastructure. They map organizational hierarchies and user privileges, understanding who has access to what and which accounts provide the most valuable capabilities for lateral movement and ultimate objectives. They study security monitoring and response capabilities, deliberately triggering minor alerts to observe how quickly and effectively the security team responds, learning the organization's defensive rhythms and blind spots. This reconnaissance occurs gradually, generating activity levels low enough to blend into normal operational noise, avoiding the concentrated scanning or probing that might alert defenders to the presence of an intruder.

The waiting game also allows attackers to establish redundancy that makes their presence extraordinarily difficult to eliminate even after partial detection. Rather than relying on a single access method or persistence mechanism, patient adversaries slowly deploy multiple backdoors across different systems using different techniques. They compromise multiple accounts across various privilege levels, ensuring that losing access to one doesn't terminate their presence entirely. They establish command-and-control channels through different protocols and infrastructure, creating fallback communication methods that survive disruption of primary channels. This redundancy takes time to implement properly but pays dividends throughout the remainder of the operation, enabling attackers to survive even substantial remediation efforts. Organizations that discover one aspect of an intrusion and focus remediation efforts there may believe they have expelled the attackers, not realizing that multiple other footholds remain intact, waiting for attention to relax before becoming active again.

Operational security during this phase requires exceptional discipline from threat actors. Communications with compromised systems occur infrequently and at irregular intervals to avoid establishing patterns that behavioral monitoring might detect. Commands execute during periods of high network activity when individual actions blend into overall traffic volume. Data staging occurs gradually, with attackers slowly copying files to intermediate locations rather than executing sudden, massive transfers that might trigger data loss prevention systems. The pace of activity carefully balances the need to accomplish objectives against the imperative of remaining undetected, with sophisticated actors showing remarkable patience in advancing their goals incrementally rather than rushing toward completion. This measured approach reflects professionalism and discipline often associated with state-sponsored actors and sophisticated criminal organizations rather than opportunistic attackers seeking quick scores.

The psychological dimension of this waiting game affects both attackers and defenders in profound ways. For security teams, the greatest challenge involves sustaining vigilance against adversaries who might be present but inactive, maintaining expensive detection capabilities and analyst attention for threats that manifest only intermittently and subtly. Alert fatigue sets in as analysts process thousands of false positives, making it progressively harder to identify the legitimate indicators of compromise hidden among them. Budget pressures and competing priorities tempt organizations to scale back security operations that haven't detected active intrusions recently, creating windows of reduced vigilance that patient attackers exploit. Meanwhile, the attackers themselves must maintain operational discipline over extended periods, resisting the temptation to accelerate operations or take shortcuts that might compromise the investment they have made in establishing and maintaining access.

This patient approach reaches its ultimate expression in advanced persistent threat operations, where nation-state actors or sophisticated criminal organizations maintain long-term presence in target networks, sometimes for years, slowly exfiltrating information of strategic value or positioning themselves for future objectives that may not even be defined at the time of initial compromise. These operations view access not as a means to an immediate end but as a strategic asset to be preserved and leveraged over time. The infiltration becomes not a one-time event but an ongoing relationship between attacker and victim, with the former having achieved such comprehensive understanding and control of the latter's environment that they operate almost as shadow administrators, present throughout the infrastructure yet invisible to those responsible for its security.

## Conclusion

The infiltration phase represents the culmination of reconnaissance, planning, and opportunity—the moment when theoretical vulnerabilities become actual compromise and external threats establish internal presence. As this chapter has revealed, modern infiltration rarely follows the dramatic scenarios popular culture portrays. Instead, it unfolds through carefully orchestrated combinations of technical exploitation and psychological manipulation, where success depends less on overwhelming defensive capabilities than on identifying and exploiting the inevitable gaps that exist in even sophisticated security architectures. The most sobering reality is that infiltration techniques continue to evolve faster than defensive measures can adapt, with attackers constantly discovering new methods to exploit the fundamental tensions between security, usability, and operational efficiency.

Understanding how adversaries gain initial access, deploy malware, exploit legitimate tools, and patiently expand their presence provides essential context for the comprehensive security programs organizations must implement. Defense requires moving beyond perimeter-focused thinking to embrace approaches that assume breach and focus on rapid detection and response. It demands security awareness programs sophisticated enough to counter increasingly convincing social engineering attacks. It necessitates architectural decisions that limit the value of any single compromised account or system. Most fundamentally, it requires organizations to recognize that infiltration is not an endpoint but a beginning—the first chapter in an adversarial relationship that will test every aspect of defensive capabilities.

As we transition to examining what attackers do after establishing initial access, remember that infiltration creates the conditions for everything that follows. The quality of that initial compromise—how many systems are controlled, which accounts are compromised, and how thoroughly the attacker understands the environment—directly determines what becomes possible in subsequent phases. Organizations that detect infiltration early, before attackers establish comprehensive presence and situational understanding, dramatically improve their chances of containing damage and expelling adversaries. Those who fail to recognize the signs of compromise face attackers who have had time to position themselves for maximum impact, transforming initial infiltration into comprehensive control that may take months or years to fully remediate. The stakes of understanding and countering infiltration techniques could not be higher, as this phase determines whether a security incident remains a contained intrusion or evolves into a catastrophic breach.

# Part Two: The Attack

## Chapter 4: The Perfect Storm

The moment of truth in any sophisticated cyberattack arrives not with fanfare but with calculated precision, when reconnaissance transforms into action, when passive observation erupts into aggressive exploitation, and when months of patient preparation culminate in hours of carefully orchestrated theft. This chapter examines perhaps the most audacious bank heist in history—not through vault doors or armed robbery but through the manipulation of the very systems designed to facilitate trusted financial transactions between institutions worldwide. What unfolded represents a masterclass in operational planning, where the convergence of technical sophistication, cultural understanding, and exquisite timing created a narrow window of opportunity that the attackers exploited with devastating effectiveness. The perfect storm, as it came to be known, demonstrates how modern financial crime has evolved beyond physical theft into something far more abstract yet infinitely more lucrative: the manipulation of digital trust itself.

### Thursday Night: Why Timing Mattered

The selection of Thursday evening as the initiation point for the heist was no accident, no casual choice made by attackers rolling dice to determine when they would strike. Instead, it represented the culmination of meticulous analysis of banking operations, international time zones, institutional workflows, and human behavior patterns that govern how financial institutions respond to anomalies. Understanding why this particular moment offered optimal conditions requires examining the intricate choreography of global banking operations, where the intersection of multiple calendars, time zones, and operational procedures creates brief windows of vulnerability that sophisticated adversaries can exploit with surgical precision. The attackers had studied their target institution not merely as a technical system to be breached but as a living organization with rhythms, routines, and predictable patterns that could be turned into advantages for those patient enough to observe and bold enough to act.

The timing selection reflected deep understanding of how financial institutions manage the transition from business hours to after-hours operations. Thursday evening in the target institution's time zone represented a moment when the organization's defensive posture inevitably weakened as day-shift security personnel handed responsibilities to smaller night crews, when managers and senior analysts departed for the evening, leaving junior staff to monitor automated systems, and when the natural tendency toward normalcy bias—the assumption that tonight would proceed like every other quiet night—reduced vigilance against unexpected anomalies. The attackers understood that human attention follows predictable patterns, that fatigue accumulates throughout the work week, and that Thursday night specifically occupies a psychological space where personnel are neither at the beginning of their work week with fresh attention nor at the weekend's edge with heightened awareness that significant incidents occurring on Friday often extend into unpaid weekend work. This particular evening offered the perfect combination of reduced staffing, accumulated weekly fatigue, and the natural human tendency to avoid discovering problems that would complicate the approaching weekend.

Beyond the target institution's internal rhythms, Thursday night positioning served crucial strategic purposes related to how fraudulent transactions would flow through the international banking system. Initiating the attack late on Thursday evening in the victim bank's time zone meant that fraudulent SWIFT messages would begin arriving at recipient banks in various time zones at moments calculated to maximize confusion and minimize immediate scrutiny. Some messages would arrive during overnight hours when receiving banks operated with skeleton crews ill-equipped to question unusual transactions. Others would land during business hours but at institutions in regions where the weekend was beginning, creating situations where transactions requiring verification or callbacks would face delays as key personnel became unavailable. The temporal orchestration demonstrated that the attackers thought not in terms of single transactions to single destinations but as conductors managing a symphony of fraudulent transfers, each timed to exploit specific weaknesses in how different institutions at different times with different operational procedures would process unusual requests.

The choice also reflected sophisticated understanding of investigation and response timelines. Fraud detected on a Thursday evening, particularly one occurring late enough that exhausted staff might delay deep investigation until the following morning, cascades into Friday—a day when the approaching weekend creates pressure to resolve issues quickly or accept that comprehensive response will require working through days typically reserved for personal time. The attackers gambled, correctly as it turned out, that institutional desire to avoid weekend emergency response would create hesitation in the initial hours after detection, providing crucial additional time for fraudulent transactions to progress through the banking system's clearing processes. Each hour of delay, each moment of uncertainty about whether observed anomalies represented genuine fraud or technical glitches, allowed money to move further from its origin point, passing through additional intermediate banks and becoming progressively more difficult to recall or freeze.

The psychological dimension of Thursday timing extended to how the attackers themselves managed operational risk. Launching on Thursday provided them with a full business week of observation before the strike, allowing final verification that security postures remained normal, that no unusual monitoring or heightened alert status had been implemented, and that the target environment matched their reconnaissance-based expectations. It positioned their active operational phase—when they would be most exposed to detection through their direct interactions with compromised systems—during a period when they themselves likely felt most alert and capable, avoiding the fatigue and diminished decision-making that might come from working through a weekend. The timing demonstrated that sophisticated attackers think holistically about operations, considering not just target vulnerabilities but their own human limitations and the psychological factors that influence both defender and attacker effectiveness.

Weather patterns, holiday schedules, and broader contextual factors also influenced the specific Thursday selection, though these elements rarely appear in post-incident reports. The attackers likely avoided periods surrounding public holidays when either heightened security or skeleton operations might disrupt their plans. They selected a week without major financial reporting deadlines or regulatory events that might have increased institutional vigilance around transaction monitoring. They ensured that no major system upgrades or security implementations were scheduled that might alter the environment they had so carefully mapped during reconnaissance. Every contextual factor received consideration, with the final Thursday selection representing the optimal convergence of multiple variables, creating a moment when institutional defenses were neither at their highest alert nor so reduced as to make unusual activity obviously suspicious. This was timing as both art and science, where deep understanding of organizational behavior combined with technical precision to create the perfect moment to strike.

## Weekend Banking Schedules and Time Zones

The global banking system operates on a framework of interlocking schedules, regional holidays, and time zone differentials that create a complex temporal landscape where money flows continuously around the world yet individual institutions experience distinct periods of high activity and reduced operations. The attackers' strategy demonstrated masterful exploitation of this temporal complexity, using the approaching weekend as both a weapon and a shield—a weapon to create confusion and delay response, and a shield to hide their activities within the reduced oversight and skeleton staffing that characterizes banking operations during non-business days. Understanding how they weaponized time zones and weekend schedules requires examining the intricate choreography of international finance, where the same characteristics that enable 24/7 global commerce also create vulnerabilities that sophisticated criminals can exploit with devastating effectiveness.

The fundamental challenge in global banking involves maintaining continuity across institutions that observe different business hours, weekends, and holidays according to local customs and regulations. While the SWIFT network itself operates continuously, the banks connected to it do not. Staff available to investigate unusual transactions, verify unexpected requests, or coordinate with counterparty institutions varies dramatically depending on time and location. The attackers studied these patterns with academic thoroughness, creating detailed maps of when each target institution would be operating with full staffing, when they would transition to reduced weekend operations, and crucially, when they would be in that liminal state between business and non-business operations where unusual transactions might be processed automatically but where human oversight capable of questioning anomalies would be minimal or absent entirely.

The exploitation began with the understanding that Friday in many Western countries represents the transition into weekend operations, when banks begin reducing staff, when managers depart early, and when the institutional focus shifts from proactive management to defensive maintenance—keeping systems running while avoiding new initiatives or complex problem-solving that might extend into personal time. Fraudulent SWIFT messages arriving at recipient banks on Friday morning or midday in European and American time zones landed in environments where personnel, facing the approaching weekend, exhibited predictable cognitive biases toward processing transactions routinely rather than scrutinizing them deeply. The psychology is subtle but powerful: questioning a transaction creates work, requires phone calls to verify details, might uncover problems that demand immediate attention, and could transform a normal Friday into an emergency situation preventing weekend plans. Absent obvious red flags, the path of least resistance involves processing transactions as requested, trusting that the SWIFT system's inherent security means that messages must be legitimate.

Time zone manipulation added additional layers of complexity that the attackers exploited ruthlessly. By routing fraudulent transactions through institutions scattered across multiple time zones, they ensured that no single bank's business hours coincided perfectly with all the other institutions involved in any particular transaction chain. Verification requests sent from New York banks reached Asian institutions during overnight hours when minimal staff were available. Follow-up questions from European banks arrived at American institutions during early morning hours before key personnel had arrived. The temporal fragmentation meant that comprehensive investigation requiring coordination across multiple institutions faced inherent delays measured in business days rather than hours, with each handoff between time zones introducing opportunities for information loss, miscommunication, or simply gaps in coverage where important questions went unasked because the right person wasn't available at the right moment.

The weekend itself functioned as a critical defensive barrier for the attackers, creating an approximately 60-hour period during which most banking institutions operated with drastically reduced capabilities. Transactions initiated late Thursday or early Friday that raised questions requiring investigation often found that investigation stalled at the weekend's edge, with concerned personnel leaving notes for Monday follow-up rather than working through days off to resolve ambiguities. This delay was not mere laziness but reflected realistic institutional constraints: weekend fraud investigation requires pulling in senior personnel on overtime, coordinating across institutions that might not have anyone available to respond, and often involves international calls during what would be overnight hours for at least one party. The barriers to effective weekend investigation are structural rather than individual, creating a systemic vulnerability that the attackers understood and exploited. By the time Monday arrived with its full staffing and renewed attention, fraudulent transactions had gained precious days of clearing time, moving through intermediate banks and approaching their ultimate destinations where recovery would become exponentially more difficult.

Regional variations in weekend definitions added further complexity that sophisticated attackers incorporated into their planning. While Western banks typically observe Saturday-Sunday weekends, institutions in Middle Eastern countries often follow Friday-Saturday schedules, and some Asian banking centers maintain different weekend patterns. The attackers routed transactions through this patchwork of schedules to maximize confusion and minimize periods when all involved institutions simultaneously maintained full operations. A transaction path that touched banks in New York, Dubai, Singapore, and Manila ensured that at any given moment, at least one institution was operating with reduced weekend staffing, creating weak links in the verification chain that prevented comprehensive, real-time investigation of the emerging fraud.

The exploitation of weekend schedules extended to regulatory and law enforcement coordination as well. Banking regulators in most countries operate on standard business schedules, with emergency contact procedures that, while available, create inherent delays compared to business-hours reporting. Law enforcement agencies, similarly, maintain reduced weekend staffing for financial crimes units, with serious investigations typically launched during business hours by specialized personnel who aren't continuously on call. The attackers understood that fraud discovered Friday afternoon or Saturday morning would face delayed regulatory reporting and law enforcement engagement, providing additional hours or days for money to flow through the pipeline before authorities with power to freeze accounts or block transactions could be effectively engaged. Every hour of delay multiplied the difficulty of recovery, transforming what might have been a contained incident if discovered immediately into a transnational financial crisis spanning multiple jurisdictions and requiring unprecedented international cooperation to address.

## The 35 Fraudulent SWIFT Messages

The sheer audacity of the attack crystallized in the flood of fraudulent payment instructions that began flowing from the compromised institution's systems once the attackers initiated their operation. Thirty-five separate SWIFT messages, each meticulously crafted to appear legitimate while directing the transfer of millions of dollars to accounts controlled by the attackers or their intermediaries, represented not just technical forgery but masterful understanding of how international wire transfers actually work, what makes transactions appear normal versus suspicious, and how to structure theft to maximize success rates while minimizing immediate detection. Each message stood as a carefully constructed fraud, balancing the need for sufficient transfer amounts to make the crime profitable against the reality that excessively large transactions would trigger additional scrutiny that might unravel the entire scheme. The volume and velocity of these messages, released in a concentrated burst rather than distributed over time, created a wave of financial activity that overwhelmed normal monitoring processes and exploited the natural tendency of banking systems to process routine transactions automatically when faced with high volumes.

The construction of each fraudulent message demonstrated intimate familiarity with SWIFT message formats, authentication procedures, and the specific conventions that the victim institution used in its legitimate international transfers. SWIFT messages follow standardized formats with specific field requirements, authentication codes, and structural elements that verify message integrity and sender authenticity. The attackers' ability to generate properly formatted messages that passed automated validation checks indicated they had either captured and studied legitimate message traffic during their reconnaissance phase or possessed insider knowledge about the institution's SWIFT operations. Every field was populated correctly, every required element present, and every authentication code valid—making the messages technically indistinguishable from legitimate transfer instructions unless human analysts examined not the format but the content, questioning whether the transactions themselves made operational sense for the institution to be executing.

The distribution of transfer amounts across the thirty-five messages revealed sophisticated thinking about how to maximize theft while managing detection risk. Rather than attempting a single massive transfer that would certainly trigger alerts, the attackers distributed their theft across multiple messages with varying amounts. Some transactions fell below threshold limits that automatically triggered enhanced review at receiving banks, designed to slip through as routine large transactions that nonetheless remained within normal operating parameters. Others pushed boundaries but remained plausible as legitimate high-value commercial transactions. The distribution pattern suggested that the attackers had studied not just the victim institution's transaction patterns but also the receiving banks' fraud detection systems, crafting a portfolio of transfers designed to exploit the gaps between what was large enough to matter and what was large enough to trigger immediate human review.

Timing gaps between the thirty-five messages also reflected careful orchestration. Rather than transmitting all fraudulent instructions simultaneously in a massive burst that might have appeared anomalous to monitoring systems designed to detect unusual transaction patterns, the attackers staggered the messages over several hours. This pacing made the fraudulent activity blend more naturally with the institution's normal evening and overnight processing of international transfers, spreading the volume across time in ways that prevented any single moment from appearing dramatically outside normal parameters. The staggered approach also hedged against total failure—if early transactions were detected and blocked, later messages might be halted before execution, but the reverse was also true: if early transactions succeeded, they validated that the attack was working and subsequent messages could proceed with confidence. The attackers essentially beta-tested their fraud in real-time, with each successful transaction providing intelligence that informed whether to continue or abort remaining transfers.

Recipient account details embedded in the messages revealed the carefully constructed money laundering infrastructure that supported the theft. The thirty-five messages directed funds not to obvious criminal accounts but to what appeared at first glance to be legitimate commercial entities, many positioned in jurisdictions where banking secrecy laws or limited regulatory cooperation would complicate recovery efforts. Account names suggested trading companies, money service businesses, and commercial enterprises that might plausibly receive large international wire transfers as part of normal business operations. The attackers understood that recipient bank compliance officers evaluating incoming wire transfers would compare transaction details against account profiles, and that transfers appearing consistent with an account's stated business purpose would face less scrutiny than payments to individuals or entities whose profiles didn't match the transaction narrative.

The technical achievement of generating thirty-five authenticated SWIFT messages from a compromised system cannot be understated. SWIFT's security architecture includes multiple layers of authentication and message integrity verification specifically designed to prevent exactly this type of fraud. The attackers needed not just access to the SWIFT terminal infrastructure but also the cryptographic credentials, authentication tokens, and operational procedures required to generate messages that the SWIFT network would accept and route. Their success indicated either comprehensive compromise of the institution's SWIFT operations infrastructure or sophisticated manipulation of the legitimate message generation process. They had essentially hijacked one of the most secure financial communication systems in the world, bending it to criminal purposes while maintaining the appearance of legitimate authorized activity. The technical sophistication required approached that of nation-state cyber operations, raising questions about the attackers' background, training, and possible state sponsorship or support.

The diversity of destination countries represented in the thirty-five messages demonstrated global operational reach and complex money laundering preparation. Funds flowed to accounts in the Philippines, Sri Lanka, and various other Asian countries, chosen not randomly but for specific characteristics that made them useful for this type of financial crime. These jurisdictions offered varying combinations of limited real-time banking coordination with Western institutions, time zone differences that complicated immediate investigation, banking secrecy traditions that made account holder identification difficult, and in some cases, regulatory frameworks that created delays in freezing accounts or responding to foreign law enforcement requests. The geographic distribution ensured that no single country's law enforcement or regulatory system could halt the fraud by freezing accounts within its jurisdiction, instead requiring unprecedented international coordination that would take days or weeks to fully orchestrate—time the attackers counted on to move money beyond recovery.

## Routing Money Through Multiple Countries

The path that stolen funds traveled after leaving the victim institution's accounts represented perhaps the most sophisticated aspect of the entire operation, transforming what could have been a simple theft-and-extraction scheme into an elaborate international shell game designed to frustrate investigation, complicate recovery, and obscure the ultimate beneficiaries of the crime. Money laundering at this scale requires not just moving funds but doing so through a carefully choreographed sequence of jurisdictions, institutions, and transaction types that progressively distance the stolen money from its origin while converting it into forms and locations that make seizure or reversal increasingly difficult. The routing strategy employed in this heist demonstrated that the attackers thought beyond the theft itself to the equally crucial challenge of actually keeping and using the stolen funds, recognizing that successfully stealing money proves worthless if that money can be immediately traced and recovered by law enforcement and banking authorities working in coordination.

The first-stage transfers from the victim institution to initial recipient accounts represented only the opening move in a complex multi-stage money laundering operation. Once fraudulent SWIFT messages triggered transfers to accounts in the Philippines and other countries, secondary movements began almost immediately, with funds rapidly redistributed to additional accounts held by different entities in different institutions. This rapid secondary movement served crucial purposes: it distanced the money from the initial fraudulent transaction, making each subsequent transfer appear to be a separate, unrelated transaction rather than part of an ongoing fraud; it multiplied the number of accounts, institutions, and jurisdictions involved in the overall scheme, exponentially increasing the coordination required for comprehensive investigation; and it started the clock on various legal and procedural timelines, with each new jurisdiction introducing its own rules about how quickly accounts can be frozen, under what circumstances funds can be seized, and what evidence standards must be met before authorities can take action.

The attackers demonstrated sophisticated understanding of correspondent banking relationships and how international transfers actually flow through the global banking system. Large international transfers rarely move directly from origin to destination but instead pass through intermediate correspondent banks that maintain relationships with institutions in regions where the sender and receiver lack direct banking connections. By carefully selecting destination accounts that would require transfers through specific correspondent banks, the attackers could influence the path their stolen funds traveled, routing money through institutions in jurisdictions they assessed as less likely to quickly freeze accounts or where they had additional prepared accounts ready to receive forwarded funds. This manipulation of correspondent banking networks turned what should have been a straightforward transaction trail into a labyrinth of intermediate steps, each additional hop creating new paperwork, new jurisdictional questions, and new delays in any recovery effort.

Conversion between transaction types and monetary instruments constituted another critical laundering technique. Funds that arrived via international wire transfer might be quickly converted to bank checks, cashier's checks, or other negotiable instruments that could be deposited into different accounts or cashed at various locations. Some portion of the funds flowed into prepaid cards, cryptocurrency purchases, or other monetary forms that provided additional anonymity and complicated tracing efforts. Each conversion created discontinuities in the transaction trail, points where the clear chain of electronic transfers gave way to ambiguity about what happened to the money next. Some funds entered foreign exchange transactions, being converted from dollars into local currencies and back again, with each conversion creating legitimate business justification for why the money moved and where it went next while simultaneously obscuring the connection to the original theft.

The exploitation of cash-intensive businesses represented a particularly clever aspect of the money laundering strategy, transforming electronic digits into physical currency that could be moved and used without creating the electronic transaction trails that enable modern financial investigation. Once funds reached certain destination accounts, rapid withdrawals converted electronic money into cash that could be physically transported, spent directly, or deposited into additional accounts in ways that severed the electronic chain connecting the cash to its fraudulent origin. Cash-intensive businesses like casinos, money service businesses, and remittance centers served as particularly useful tools for this conversion, as large cash transactions at these businesses appear routine rather than suspicious, and the businesses themselves handle sufficient legitimate cash volume that commingling stolen funds with legitimate proceeds creates nearly insurmountable challenges for investigation.

Shell company networks and seemingly legitimate business transactions provided cover for what were essentially just additional steps in moving stolen money. Funds transferred to commercial accounts then flowed outward as payments for purported goods or services, creating transaction narratives that appeared to justify the movement of money rather than revealing it as ongoing theft dispersal. Invoices, purchase orders, and shipping documents—all fabricated but sufficiently detailed to appear legitimate on casual inspection—provided paper trails that suggested normal business operations rather than money laundering. Investigators later faced the challenge of distinguishing genuine business transactions occurring in the same institutions and jurisdictions from the fraudulent transactions designed to look identical. The attackers essentially hid their money laundering within the massive volume of legitimate international trade and commerce, banking on the reality that authorities lack resources to investigate every transaction and must instead focus on those that appear obviously criminal.

The speed of the entire routing operation proved nearly as important as its complexity. The attackers understood that every hour counted once the theft was discovered, that international coordination would eventually freeze accounts and halt money movement, and that their window for successfully laundering stolen funds was measured in days at most before the weight of law enforcement and regulatory action would close in. The pre-positioned accounts, prepared shell companies, and pre-arranged extraction mechanisms all enabled rapid movement of funds through the laundering pipeline before detection and response could interdict the process. This velocity transformed what might have been a slowly unfolding money laundering operation extending over weeks or months into a compressed sprint where stolen millions moved through multiple countries and dozens of accounts within days of the original theft. The approach traded subtlety for speed, accepting that the rapid movement might itself appear suspicious but calculating correctly that by the time investigators unraveled the transaction chains, much of the money would already have reached its final destinations or been converted into forms that made recovery impossible.

## The Philippines Casino Connection

Among the many destinations where stolen funds flowed, the Philippines emerged as a particularly crucial node in the money laundering network, specifically through the exploitation of the country's casino industry—an industry that combines massive legitimate cash flows with regulatory frameworks that, at the time of this attack, provided unusual protections against financial crime investigation. The casino connection represented not opportunistic use of convenient money laundering facilities but rather evidence of sophisticated pre-planning that identified and prepared to exploit specific regulatory gaps that made Philippine casinos ideal for converting electronic transfers into untraceable assets. Understanding why casinos became the focal point requires examining the unique intersection of gambling industry characteristics, Philippine regulatory policy, and the specific challenges that casino transactions create for financial crime investigation—challenges that sophisticated money launderers have exploited across multiple operations worldwide.

Philippine casinos operated under a regulatory framework that, prior to the scrutiny this theft generated, excluded them from certain anti-money laundering reporting requirements that applied to other financial institutions. While banks in the Philippines were required to report suspicious transactions and large cash movements to regulators, casinos maintained greater operational privacy, with less stringent reporting requirements and substantial protection against external investigation of their customer transactions. This regulatory carve-out existed for legitimate policy reasons—protecting customer privacy in gambling activities, supporting the growth of a significant economic sector, and reflecting the reality that casinos had not been prominently featured in major money laundering cases in the Philippines prior to this incident. However, what policymakers intended as reasonable industry regulation created gaps that sophisticated money launderers could exploit, allowing funds to enter casinos through bank transfers and emerge as gambling proceeds with greatly diminished connection to their fraudulent origin.

The mechanics of casino-based money laundering followed patterns familiar to financial crime investigators but executed with scale and speed that overwhelmed detection capabilities. Stolen funds arriving at Philippine banks through the fraudulent SWIFT transfers were quickly moved to accounts held by individuals or entities with relationships to specific casinos. These accounts then transferred funds into the casinos, ostensibly to purchase casino chips for gambling. Once inside the casino financial ecosystem, the money's trail became dramatically more opaque. Casino patrons could engage in minimal gambling—playing a few hands of cards or spinning slot machines—before cashing out their chips, receiving payment in the form of checks or wire transfers that appeared to be gambling winnings rather than recycled stolen funds. The casinos, processing thousands of legitimate gambling transactions daily involving millions of dollars in chip purchases and redemptions, provided perfect cover for laundering operations that blended fraudulent funds with legitimate gambling activity.

The scale of funds flowing through Philippine casinos in the aftermath of the heist was staggering, with tens of millions of dollars moving through multiple establishments in rapid succession. This velocity should have triggered alarms, as the volume far exceeded normal patterns even for high-roller gambling. However, several factors combined to delay effective intervention. First, the regulatory framework meant that casinos weren't immediately reporting these transactions to authorities monitoring for financial crime. Second, the individuals conducting the transactions at casinos maintained at least surface plausibility as legitimate high-stakes gamblers, having established relationships with casino operators and presenting themselves as affluent individuals engaging in legal gambling activities. Third, the speed of the operation meant that by the time law enforcement became aware of the casino connection and sought to freeze assets, much of the money had already been converted to chips, minimally gambled, and paid out as winnings, creating completed transactions that were significantly harder to reverse than pending bank transfers.

The specific casinos involved found themselves at the center of international controversy and investigation, with questions about whether casino operators knew or should have known that funds being gambled represented proceeds of crime. The casinos themselves were not the masterminds of the theft but rather tools exploited by the money laundering network. However, the due diligence applied to high-value customers flowing massive amounts through their operations faced intense scrutiny after the fact. Had casino operators asked sufficiently probing questions about the source of funds? Had they noticed that gambling patterns seemed designed to move money through their systems rather than genuinely attempting to win? Had they observed coordination among multiple individuals who appeared to be working together rather than independently gambling? The answers to these questions proved complex, with some evidence suggesting inadequate customer vetting and anti-money laundering controls but stopping short of proof that casinos actively conspired in the fraud.

The international dimension of the casino connection highlighted significant challenges in cross-border financial crime enforcement. While the theft originated in one country and victim institution, and while early-stage money laundering occurred across multiple Asian jurisdictions, the casino phase concentrated activity in the Philippines—a country that maintained sovereign control over its regulatory frameworks and that could not be simply ordered by foreign governments to freeze assets or seize funds. International cooperation required formal requests through proper channels, diplomatic engagement, and complex legal procedures that unfolded over days and weeks while the laundering operation proceeded. The tension between national sovereignty and international financial crime enforcement emerged starkly, with victim countries and institutions frustrated by what they perceived as insufficient urgency in Philippine responses while Philippine authorities navigated their own legal frameworks and jurisdictional limitations.

Recovery of funds from casinos proved extraordinarily difficult once the money had been converted to chips and then paid out as winnings. Unlike frozen bank accounts where transfers could be reversed or funds held pending investigation, casino transactions that had completed created facts on the ground that were legally and practically difficult to undo. Individuals who had received casino checks or wire transfers as payouts claimed they were legitimate gambling winnings, forcing investigators to prove not just that the original funds were stolen but that the specific money paid out by the casino represented stolen funds rather than legitimate casino operational funds commingled with the illegal deposits. The burden of proof and the complexity of tracing specific dollars through casino operations created nearly insurmountable challenges for recovery efforts, with much of the money that reached casinos ultimately remaining beyond the reach of law enforcement and victim institutions.

The regulatory response to this exploitation of Philippine casinos demonstrated how major financial crimes drive policy changes that close identified loopholes. Following the international attention this case generated, Philippine authorities significantly strengthened anti-money laundering requirements for casinos, bringing them under the same reporting and customer due diligence requirements that applied to banks and other financial institutions. The case became a textbook example in international forums about the importance of comprehensive financial sector regulation that doesn't create carve-outs or exemptions that sophisticated criminals can exploit. However, these regulatory improvements came too late for the victims of this particular theft, who had already lost tens of millions of dollars that successfully laundered through casinos before the regulatory gaps were closed. The evolution highlighted a fundamental challenge in financial crime prevention: regulations often strengthen in response to demonstrated exploits rather than anticipating novel money laundering techniques, creating situations where criminals who identify and exploit gaps successfully benefit while their actions trigger reforms that prevent similar future operations.

## Conclusion

The perfect storm represented by this audacious heist demonstrates that modern financial crime operates at the intersection of technical sophistication, cultural understanding, and meticulous operational planning. The attackers' success stemmed not from any single element but from the seamless integration of multiple advantages: technical compromise of secure banking systems, timing that exploited institutional rhythms and international coordination challenges, transaction structuring that balanced ambition with plausibility, routing through jurisdictions and institutions selected for specific vulnerability characteristics, and exploitation of regulatory gaps that transformed stolen electronic funds into assets that could be physically dispersed and used. Each element was necessary but insufficient alone; only the combination of all factors created the conditions for theft at this scale to succeed even partially.

The thirty-five fraudulent SWIFT messages that initiated the operation represented merely the visible tip of an operational iceberg that extended deep into the infrastructure of international finance. Beneath those messages lay months of reconnaissance, compromise, and preparation. Supporting them was an elaborate money laundering network spanning multiple countries and dozens of institutions. Enabling their partial success were regulatory gaps, coordination challenges, and timing exploits that demonstrated how the same characteristics that make the international financial system efficient and accessible also create vulnerabilities that sophisticated adversaries can exploit with devastating effect. The operation as a whole served as a wake-up call for financial institutions worldwide about the evolution of cyber-enabled financial crime, forcing uncomfortable recognition that traditional perimeter security and fraud detection systems were inadequate against adversaries who thought holistically about the entire attack lifecycle from initial compromise through successful money laundering.

For the victims, the perfect storm proved costly both financially and reputationally. While some funds were eventually recovered through extraordinary international cooperation and legal proceedings, much of the stolen money disappeared into the complex laundering network, converted into forms and distributed to locations where recovery became impossible. The reputational damage extended beyond the immediate victim institution to raise questions about the security of the SWIFT system itself and the reliability of international banking infrastructure that the global economy depends upon. The incident catalyzed significant changes in how financial institutions approach cybersecurity, moving from treating it as primarily an IT problem to recognizing it as a fundamental risk management challenge requiring board-level attention and enterprise-wide response capabilities.

The timing element—that Thursday night initiation, the exploitation of weekend schedules, the careful orchestration across time zones—proved as crucial as the technical compromise itself. This recognition has driven changes in how financial institutions staff their security operations centers and respond to potential fraud, with many implementing follow-the-sun monitoring where multiple regional centers provide continuous expert coverage rather than accepting reduced capability during overnight and weekend hours. The realization that attackers specifically time operations to exploit reduced staffing has forced uncomfortable questions about the true cost of security, where savings from minimal staffing during off-hours potentially create vulnerabilities worth billions to sophisticated adversaries.

The casino connection, particularly, highlighted regulatory gaps that exist at the intersection of different financial sectors and national jurisdictions. The case became instrumental in driving enhanced anti-money laundering requirements for casinos globally, with major jurisdictions recognizing that exemptions or lighter regulation for any significant financial sector create opportunities for money laundering that sophisticated criminals will inevitably identify and exploit. The lesson transcends casinos specifically, applying to any financial service or institution that moves, stores, or converts significant value—all must be comprehensively regulated with robust anti-money laundering and know-your-customer requirements, or they will become tools for financial crime.

As we move forward to examine the detection and response to this breach, the perfect storm serves as a reminder that defense requires thinking like attackers, understanding not just individual vulnerabilities but how multiple factors can be combined to create windows of opportunity that no single defensive measure can close. The sophistication demonstrated here represented capabilities previously associated primarily with nation-state actors, forcing recognition that the line between cyber espionage and cyber crime has blurred as criminal organizations achieve technical and operational sophistication that rivals government intelligence services. Financial institutions found themselves facing adversaries as capable as those targeting national security systems, requiring corresponding evolution in defensive capabilities, threat intelligence, and incident response procedures. The perfect storm passed, but it revealed a permanently altered threat landscape where the stakes of inadequate cybersecurity extend to the stability of international financial systems themselves.

# Chapter 5: 81 Million Reasons to Panic

The discovery of catastrophic security breaches rarely announces itself with clarity or certainty. Instead, it emerges through fragments of confusion, anomalies that don't quite make sense, and the gradually dawning horror as scattered pieces coalesce into recognition of disaster. Friday morning at Bangladesh Bank began like countless other mornings, with routine checks of overnight transactions and standard reconciliation of accounts—mundane administrative work that forms the backbone of banking operations worldwide. Yet within hours, this ordinary day would transform into a nightmare of unprecedented proportions as staff discovered that their institution had become the victim of one of history's most sophisticated cyber heists. The eighty-one million dollars successfully stolen represented only a fraction of what the attackers attempted, with the ultimate damage mitigated not by security measures or rapid response but by something far more prosaic and accidental: a simple typographical error that triggered scrutiny where careful planning had intended to create none. This chapter examines the critical hours when theoretical compromise became discovered reality, when confusion yielded to panic, and when the race to minimize damage began against adversaries who had already gained a substantial head start.

## Friday Morning Discovery at Bangladesh Bank

The morning of February 5, 2016, began with deceptive normalcy at Bangladesh Bank's headquarters in Dhaka, with staff arriving for their shifts, systems powering up for another day of operations, and the institution's rhythms proceeding along familiar paths that had been worn smooth by countless repetitions. The bank's operations staff, responsible for monitoring international transactions and reconciling accounts, initiated their routine morning procedures—checking overnight message traffic, reviewing transaction logs, and ensuring that the institution's accounts with correspondent banks around the world remained properly balanced. These tasks, performed thousands of times before without incident, created an expectation of normalcy that made the initial anomalies difficult to properly contextualize. The human mind resists disruption of established patterns, preferring to interpret unexpected data as errors or glitches rather than signs of catastrophic compromise. This cognitive bias, while normally beneficial in preventing panic over routine technical issues, created crucial delays in recognizing and responding to the disaster that had unfolded during the overnight hours.

The first indications of trouble emerged not as obvious alarms but as confusing discrepancies that didn't immediately suggest their true cause. Staff reviewing overnight SWIFT message traffic noticed an unusually high volume of outgoing payment instructions, far exceeding normal patterns for the bank's international transactions. However, the messages themselves appeared properly formatted and authenticated, passing the technical validation checks that normally confirm legitimacy. The initial response reflected the natural tendency to assume technical issues rather than security breaches—perhaps a system glitch had duplicated messages, or maybe routine transactions had been processed incorrectly. These explanations, while ultimately wrong, seemed far more probable than the reality that hackers had compromised the bank's most secure systems and spent the night orchestrating massive theft. The psychology of normalcy bias worked powerfully against rapid recognition, with each staff member's training and experience suggesting that technical problems were common while successful breaches of SWIFT infrastructure were essentially theoretical threats rather than practical realities.

As staff began deeper investigation of the anomalies, the true scale of the disaster started crystallizing through fragmentary discoveries that accumulated into horrifying comprehension. Account balances for Bangladesh Bank's foreign exchange reserves held at the Federal Reserve Bank of New York showed massive unauthorized debits. Dozens of transfer instructions bore proper authentication codes yet directed funds to recipients that made no operational sense for the central bank. The transactions had executed during overnight hours when minimal staff were present to question them, and they targeted accounts scattered across multiple countries in what appeared to be a coordinated pattern rather than random errors. Each new discovery added weight to the emerging realization that this was not a technical glitch or isolated mistake but rather a systematic, sophisticated attack that had successfully bypassed security measures specifically designed to prevent exactly this scenario.

The institutional response to these discoveries reflected the shock and confusion that inevitably accompanies recognition of catastrophic security failures. Initial reactions focused on verification—checking and rechecking the data, confirming that account balances were actually debited, ensuring that the transactions were real rather than display errors or reporting glitches. This verification phase, while necessary, consumed precious time during which fraudulent transfers continued progressing through the international banking system's clearing processes. Simultaneously, staff struggled with the practical challenge of whom to notify and how to explain what they were seeing when they themselves didn't fully understand the situation. The bank's senior management needed to be alerted, but with what message? That the institution might have been hacked? That millions of dollars were missing? That SWIFT systems appeared compromised? Each potential message carried enormous implications, and the instinct to avoid false alarms or premature panic clashed with the growing evidence that something terrible had occurred.

Communication challenges compounded the crisis, with the physical and hierarchical distance between operational staff who first noticed anomalies and senior executives who needed to authorize emergency responses creating delays that the attackers had likely anticipated and planned for. Bangladesh Bank's organizational structure, like many large institutions, featured multiple layers of management and approval processes designed to ensure proper oversight and prevent rash decisions. These same structures, however, became obstacles when situations demanded rapid, decisive action. Staff discovering the anomalies needed to brief supervisors, who needed to brief department heads, who needed to alert senior management—and at each level, questions arose about the accuracy of information, the appropriate response, and who held authority to make critical decisions like contacting international partners, freezing accounts, or notifying law enforcement. The very hierarchies that provided order and accountability during normal operations became sources of delay and confusion during crisis.

The Friday morning discovery also faced the challenge of coordinating with international partners across time zones and weekend schedules. The Federal Reserve Bank of New York, which held Bangladesh Bank's accounts that had been debited, operated in a time zone more than ten hours behind Dhaka. Friday morning in Bangladesh meant Thursday evening in New York, with key personnel potentially unavailable and the approaching weekend threatening to create additional delays in coordination and response. This temporal mismatch meant that Bangladesh Bank staff discovering the theft could not immediately engage in real-time conversation with counterparts at the Federal Reserve who could provide additional information, freeze accounts, or take other actions to limit damage. Instead, communications occurred through formal channels with inherent delays, with each message and response consuming hours rather than minutes while stolen funds continued their journey through the international financial system.

The psychological impact on staff members who first discovered the breach cannot be understated. These were professionals who had devoted careers to banking operations, who took pride in maintaining the integrity and security of their institution's finances, and who now faced the devastating realization that their systems had been comprehensively compromised under their watch. The emotional response combined professional humiliation with genuine fear about implications for their careers, their institution, and potentially their personal safety if they became scapegoats for the failure. Some experienced paralysis, struggling to process the magnitude of what they were seeing and unsure how to proceed. Others shifted into crisis mode, recognizing that every minute counted and driving forward with investigations and notifications despite incomplete information and uncertain authority. The human dimension of discovering institutional catastrophe often gets lost in technical post-mortems, yet the emotional reactions of those first responders significantly influenced how rapidly and effectively the institution mobilized its response.

## The Typo That Saved $870 Million

Among the many fraudulent SWIFT messages that the attackers dispatched during their overnight operation, one transaction stood apart not because of its sophistication or successful execution but because of a seemingly trivial error that would ultimately prevent the vast majority of the intended theft from succeeding. A single typographical mistake—the kind of error that occurs countless times daily in communications worldwide—transformed what should have been a routine transaction approval into an anomaly that triggered scrutiny, raising questions that unraveled a significant portion of the attack before the stolen funds could be successfully laundered beyond recovery. The story of this typo serves as a reminder that even the most meticulously planned operations can be undone by the smallest oversights, and that the difference between catastrophic loss and partial recovery sometimes hinges on details so minor that they might seem insignificant until they prove decisive.

The fraudulent transaction in question directed funds to a Sri Lankan non-profit organization, with the transfer instruction ostensibly sending money for legitimate charitable or operational purposes. The message included all the proper technical elements—correct authentication codes, proper formatting, valid account details—and should have processed automatically like the dozens of other fraudulent instructions the attackers had dispatched. However, the organization's name had been misspelled in the payment instruction, containing a subtle but significant error that transformed what should have been an invisible transaction into one that stood out to human reviewers. This seemingly minor mistake became the thread that, when pulled, began unraveling the entire operation, triggering questions that led to discovery of the broader pattern of fraudulent transactions and enabling response efforts that, while ultimately inadequate to prevent all losses, succeeded in stopping the majority of the attempted theft.

The specific nature of the error involved confusion between similar-sounding words in the organization's name, a type of mistake that suggests the message may have been created through dictation, automatic speech recognition, or simply careless typing rather than careful copying from verified sources. Such errors are remarkably common in normal business communications, typically corrected without incident when noticed or simply processed despite the minor misspelling if the intended recipient remains clear. However, in this case, the error occurred at a particularly unfortunate moment—from the attackers' perspective—when a transaction reviewer at an intermediate bank happened to notice the misspelling and, rather than simply processing the payment despite the minor error, flagged it for additional review. This decision, which might easily have gone the other way with a different reviewer or at a different time, initiated a chain of events that would expose the attack.

The reviewer's decision to flag the transaction for additional scrutiny reflected training and institutional culture around payment verification. Banking staff receive instruction to watch for anomalies that might indicate fraud, with particular emphasis on payments to unfamiliar recipients, unusual transaction patterns, or details that don't appear professionally prepared. A misspelled organization name, while minor, suggested that the transaction might not have received the careful attention that large international transfers should command. This led to additional questions: Who authorized this payment? What was its business purpose? Did the recipient organization actually exist, and did it actually use this misspelled version of its name? Each question led to additional review, and as reviewers dug deeper, they discovered inconsistencies and red flags that had nothing to do with the typo but everything to do with the fraudulent nature of the underlying transaction.

The amount involved in this particular transaction—representing a substantial portion of the overall attempted theft—meant that blocking it had enormous financial consequences. Had this single payment processed successfully along with the others, the total successful theft would have reached into hundreds of millions of dollars rather than the eighty-one million that ultimately escaped. The magnitude transformed what might have been dismissed as a lucky catch of one fraudulent transaction into a success story that prevented catastrophic losses. Banking security professionals often note that fraud prevention relies on defense in depth, where multiple layers of security controls and verification procedures each catch some percentage of fraudulent activity. In this case, one of those layers—human review of transaction details—caught an anomaly that automated systems had missed, demonstrating why institutions continue to rely on human oversight despite sophisticated automated fraud detection capabilities.

The broader implications of this typo extended beyond the immediate financial impact to raise questions about the attackers' operational security and quality control. Sophisticated cyber operations typically involve extensive planning, attention to detail, and verification processes to ensure that technical execution doesn't fail on mundane errors. The presence of this typo suggested either that the attackers were not as professionally organized as their technical sophistication implied, or that the pressure of executing thirty-five separate fraudulent transactions in rapid succession created conditions where quality control failures became inevitable. Some analysts speculated that different individuals or teams within the attacking group might have been responsible for different transactions, with varying levels of care and attention resulting in inconsistent quality across the fraudulent messages. Others suggested that the late-night timing, while strategically important, may have contributed to fatigue-induced errors that more leisurely operation might have avoided.

The discovery of this flagged transaction became the catalyst that prompted broader investigation of Bangladesh Bank's overnight SWIFT activity. Once reviewers at the intermediate bank raised questions about one transaction, they naturally examined others from the same source institution occurring during the same timeframe. This wider review revealed the full pattern of fraudulent activity—dozens of suspicious transactions, all bearing proper authentication but directing funds to unusual recipients through routing that didn't match the bank's normal patterns. The initial typo became, in essence, the loose thread that revealed the entire tapestry of fraud. By the time investigators finished tracing all the connections, they had mapped out an operation far more extensive than anyone initially suspected, with the scale of the attempted theft dwarfing what had actually succeeded in clearing.

## "Fundation" versus "Foundation"

The specific typographical error that triggered enhanced scrutiny and ultimately prevented hundreds of millions in additional losses involved the misspelling of the word "Foundation" as "Fundation" in the name of the intended recipient organization. This single missing letter transformed what should have been a properly spelled organization name into something that immediately appeared unprofessional and potentially suspicious to reviewers examining the transaction. The error exemplified how attention to detail in criminal operations can make the difference between success and failure, and how even the most sophisticated technical execution can be undone by human factors and quality control failures in operational tradecraft.

The misspelled word appeared in a payment instruction directing funds to the Shalika Foundation, a legitimate Sri Lankan non-profit organization whose name and account details had been appropriated by the attackers for their money laundering operation. However, the instruction spelled the organization as "Shalika Fundation," with the missing "o" creating an obvious red flag to English-speaking reviewers at international correspondent banks processing the transaction. The error was particularly glaring because "foundation" is a common word in organizational names worldwide, especially for non-profit entities, making its misspelling immediately noticeable to professionals accustomed to processing international charitable transfers. Had the attackers simply spelled the organization name correctly by copying it from publicly available sources, the transaction would likely have processed without additional scrutiny, allowing the funds to flow through to accounts controlled by the money laundering network.

The linguistic aspect of this error provides insight into possible characteristics of the attackers or the specific individuals responsible for crafting this particular fraudulent message. The "fundation" spelling suggests someone whose first language may not be English, or who was working under conditions that prevented careful proofreading of the transaction details before submission. English speakers, especially those with professional banking experience, typically catch this type of error automatically because the correct spelling has been internalized through repeated exposure. The error pattern—confusing similar-sounding vowels in an unstressed syllable—is consistent with mistakes made by non-native speakers or by speech recognition systems that process phonetic input into text without human verification. These clues, while not definitive, contributed to investigative profiles of the attackers and their operational characteristics.

The discovery of the "fundation" error occurred at Deutsche Bank in New York, which served as a correspondent institution through which the fraudulent transfer would have passed before reaching its ultimate destination in Sri Lanka. Staff reviewing the payment instruction noticed the misspelling and, following established procedures for verifying unusual transactions, reached out to Bangladesh Bank to confirm the payment details and ensure that the transaction was legitimate. This inquiry—which should have been routine verification that Bangladesh Bank confirmed the payment and corrected the spelling error—instead reached an institution that was simultaneously discovering the full scope of the overnight attack. The timing meant that the verification request arrived just as Bangladesh Bank was beginning to understand that something was terribly wrong, transforming what might have been a routine spelling correction into a crucial data point confirming that fraudulent transactions were actively progressing through the international banking system.

The amount involved in this particular transaction made its prevention especially significant. Various sources report the transaction as attempting to move between twenty and thirty million dollars—a substantial portion of the overall theft attempt. Blocking this single payment materially reduced the attackers' take, demonstrating how even partial fraud prevention can have major financial consequences. The scale also explains why Deutsche Bank's staff felt compelled to verify the transaction despite only minor concerns about the spelling error. Large transfers naturally receive more scrutiny than smaller ones, with banks implementing escalating review procedures based on transaction amounts. Had this been a smaller payment, reviewers might have processed it despite the misspelling, assuming that the slight error didn't materially affect the transaction's legitimacy. The large amount triggered more thorough review, which combined with the spelling error to create sufficient concern to pause the payment pending verification.

The public attention that this typo received following the attack's disclosure generated widespread discussion about the role of human oversight in fraud prevention. Some commentators pointed to the incident as evidence that automated systems cannot fully replace human judgment in identifying suspicious transactions, since computers might process a misspelled organization name without questioning it if all technical validation checks pass. Others noted that the same human factors that led to the misspelling—fatigue, language barriers, lack of attention to detail—affected both attackers and defenders, with the outcome depending on which side made more or more consequential errors. The incident became a case study in security training, illustrating how seemingly minor anomalies can indicate major problems and how cultivating institutional cultures that encourage staff to raise questions about details that seem off can prevent fraud that technical controls miss.

The "fundation" typo entered the lexicon of cybersecurity professionals as shorthand for how operational security failures in execution can undermine sophisticated technical capabilities. The attackers demonstrated extraordinary sophistication in compromising SWIFT infrastructure, maintaining persistent access for months, and timing their attack to exploit institutional vulnerabilities. Yet this technical mastery could not compensate for a simple spelling error that a proofreader would have caught in seconds. The lesson transcended this specific case, applying to offensive and defensive operations across cybersecurity: technical capability must be matched with operational discipline and attention to detail at every level of execution. The most sophisticated exploit in the world fails if delivered to the wrong target or accompanied by social engineering materials filled with errors that alert targets to the attack's illegitimacy.

## Federal Reserve Flags Suspicious Transactions

While Deutsche Bank's discovery of the "fundation" typo prevented one major fraudulent transaction, the Federal Reserve Bank of New York played an equally crucial role in detecting and blocking additional suspicious transfers that lacked such obvious errors but nonetheless raised red flags through behavioral and pattern analysis. The Federal Reserve's intervention demonstrates how correspondent banking relationships create opportunities for fraud detection at multiple points in the transaction chain, with each institution serving as a potential checkpoint that might catch what others missed. The Fed's role also highlights the importance of established relationships and institutional knowledge in identifying anomalous activity, as reviewers familiar with a client institution's normal transaction patterns are best positioned to recognize when something deviates from expected behavior.

The Federal Reserve Bank of New York served as the correspondent bank for Bangladesh Bank's foreign exchange reserves, maintaining accounts that the central bank used for international transactions and foreign currency operations. This relationship meant that the fraudulent SWIFT messages, even though they originated from compromised systems at Bangladesh Bank, needed to pass through Federal Reserve systems for execution since they directed transfers from Bangladesh Bank's accounts held at the Fed. This correspondent relationship created a critical control point where the fraudulent transactions faced scrutiny from an institution with no stake in processing them quickly and every incentive to verify their legitimacy before releasing funds from accounts it held in trust for the client.

Federal Reserve staff reviewing overnight payment instructions from Bangladesh Bank noticed multiple red flags that, even absent the Deutsche Bank typo discovery, suggested something was seriously wrong. The sheer volume of transfer instructions exceeded Bangladesh Bank's normal patterns by a significant margin, with dozens of high-value transactions clustered in a short timeframe rather than distributed across business hours as legitimate transfers typically would be. The destinations for these transfers included entities and accounts that had never previously received payments from Bangladesh Bank, raising questions about why the central bank would suddenly be sending substantial funds to these recipients. The amounts involved were large enough to be individually significant, and collectively they represented a substantial portion of Bangladesh Bank's foreign exchange reserves—the kind of massive movement that would normally be accompanied by advanced notice, explanatory documentation, and confirmation through multiple communication channels rather than appearing suddenly through overnight SWIFT messages.

The timing of the transactions also raised suspicions, as they arrived during periods when Bangladesh Bank's business hours had ended, making real-time verification with senior officials impossible. Experienced Fed staff recognized that central banks typically conduct large transfers during business hours when senior management and treasury officials are available to authorize and oversee such significant movements. The overnight timing suggested either an emergency situation requiring immediate fund transfers—which had not been communicated in advance—or potentially unauthorized activity. This timing red flag, combined with the other anomalies, created sufficient concern that Federal Reserve staff decided to pause several transactions pending verification with Bangladesh Bank before releasing the funds.

The Federal Reserve's institutional culture and risk management framework supported staff decisions to question unusual transactions despite potential frustration from client institutions who might view such scrutiny as slow or excessive. The Fed operates with the understanding that its primary obligation is to the integrity and security of the financial system rather than to processing transactions as quickly as possible. This institutional priority means that staff are empowered and expected to flag concerns about unusual activity, even when doing so creates delays or challenges client relationships. The culture contrasts with commercial banks where pressure to provide fast, seamless service might create incentives to process transactions without excessive questions. The Federal Reserve's different mandate and institutional structure created space for the careful review that detected multiple fraudulent transactions before they could clear.

Communication between the Federal Reserve and Bangladesh Bank on Friday morning proved challenging due to the time zone differences and the chaos unfolding in Dhaka as staff there were simultaneously discovering the scope of the breach. When Fed staff attempted to reach Bangladesh Bank contacts to verify the suspicious transactions, they encountered delays, confusion, and difficulty getting clear answers about whether the transfers were legitimate. This communication difficulty itself served as an additional red flag, as legitimate large transactions would normally be accompanied by clear communication channels and designated contacts who could quickly confirm authorization. The inability to reach appropriate Bangladesh Bank officials who could verify the transactions strengthened the Federal Reserve's decision to hold funds pending resolution rather than releasing them based solely on the properly authenticated SWIFT messages.

The scale of what the Federal Reserve prevented from clearing represents a substantial success in limiting the damage from the attack. While precise figures remain disputed, estimates suggest that Federal Reserve actions blocked between $850 million and $900 million in fraudulent transfers that would have cleared had the transactions not been flagged and held. This prevention occurred not through technical detection of the SWIFT system compromise—the Federal Reserve's systems had no way to know that the messages came from attackers rather than legitimate Bangladesh Bank personnel—but through behavioral analysis, pattern recognition, and institutional knowledge about what normal activity looks like versus what appears suspicious. The success demonstrates the continuing importance of human expertise and judgment in fraud prevention, even in highly automated systems.

The Federal Reserve's role in the incident also raised complicated questions about the responsibilities of correspondent banks in preventing fraud versus their obligations to execute properly authenticated instructions from client institutions. The SWIFT system operates on the principle that properly authenticated messages can be trusted, with correspondent banks expected to execute instructions that pass authentication checks. However, correspondent banks also have some obligation to exercise reasonable care in protecting both their own institutions and the broader financial system from fraud. The Bangladesh Bank case tested the boundaries of these sometimes-conflicting obligations, with the Federal Reserve's decision to question suspicious transactions ultimately proving correct but also raising questions about what would have happened if the transactions had been legitimate but unusual and the delays had caused problems for Bangladesh Bank. These questions about correspondent bank responsibilities continue to influence policy discussions about financial crime prevention and the appropriate balance between facilitating legitimate transactions and preventing fraud.

## Chaos in Dhaka

As the scale of the breach became clear throughout Friday morning and into the weekend, chaos erupted at Bangladesh Bank's headquarters in Dhaka, with the institution scrambling to understand what had happened, contain the damage, and coordinate response efforts across multiple time zones with partners who were just beginning to comprehend that one of the world's most secure financial communication systems had been successfully compromised. The chaos reflected both the unprecedented nature of the attack—central banks simply didn't experience successful cyber heists at this scale—and the practical challenges of managing a complex international crisis involving technical systems, law enforcement coordination, diplomatic communications, and financial recovery efforts that needed to occur simultaneously under intense time pressure.

The immediate crisis management priorities centered on determining the scope of the breach and stopping any ongoing fraudulent transactions before additional funds could be stolen. This required Bangladesh Bank staff to verify which transactions were legitimate versus fraudulent among the dozens of SWIFT messages that had been sent overnight, a task complicated by the fact that the attackers had generated properly authenticated messages that technical systems could not distinguish from legitimate instructions. Staff needed to contact recipient banks in multiple countries to request holds on incoming transfers, but this required navigating international calling procedures, time zone differences, language barriers, and institutions with varying levels of responsiveness to urgent requests from an unfamiliar foreign central bank claiming that incoming funds were stolen. Some recipient banks cooperated immediately while others required more persuasion or formal documentation before agreeing to freeze funds.

The technical investigation began in parallel with operational response efforts, with Bangladesh Bank's IT staff attempting to understand how the SWIFT systems had been compromised and whether attackers maintained ongoing access that could enable additional theft. This investigation faced the fundamental challenge that the attack was extraordinarily sophisticated, with malware that had successfully hidden from security systems for months now requiring forensic analysis to identify and remove. The bank lacked in-house expertise for an investigation at this level, requiring engagement of international cybersecurity firms with experience in advanced persistent threat response. However, procuring and deploying these resources took time, with initial hours relying on bank staff who, while competent in normal IT operations, found themselves far beyond their experience in dealing with nation-state-level cyber compromise.

Communication became both critical and challenging as the crisis unfolded. Senior bank officials needed to notify Bangladesh's government and central bank leadership about the breach, requiring careful messaging that conveyed the severity without creating broader panic about the security of the nation's financial reserves. International coordination required contacting counterpart institutions like the Federal Reserve, SWIFT organization headquarters, and law enforcement agencies in countries where stolen funds had been sent. Media inquiries began almost immediately once rumors of problems at Bangladesh Bank started circulating, requiring decisions about what information to disclose publicly while investigations remained ongoing. Each communication channel demanded attention from senior officials who were simultaneously trying to manage operational response, coordinate with law enforcement, and understand the technical details of how their systems had been compromised.

The institutional culture and capabilities at Bangladesh Bank influenced how effectively the chaos could be managed. As a central bank in a developing nation, the institution maintained sophisticated capabilities for monetary policy and banking oversight but had not historically faced sophisticated cyber threats requiring advanced technical response capabilities. The sudden need to coordinate a complex international incident involving cutting-edge cyber attack techniques, international law enforcement cooperation, and recovery of funds scattered across multiple jurisdictions pushed the institution beyond its normal operational comfort zone. Staff demonstrated remarkable dedication and effort in responding to the crisis, but the gap between the sophistication of the attack and the institution's preparation for such incidents created inevitable confusion and delays that better-resourced institutions might have avoided.

Political pressures added additional complexity to the crisis management environment. Bangladesh's government and central bank leadership faced questions about how such a massive security breach could occur, who would be held accountable, and what it meant for the country's financial security and international reputation. The incident occurred against a backdrop of complex political dynamics within Bangladesh, with various factions seeking to use the crisis for their own purposes or to deflect blame toward opponents. These political undercurrents complicated the response effort, as decisions about disclosure, accountability, and corrective actions carried implications beyond pure crisis management into the realm of institutional and political survival for key officials. The result was sometimes-conflicting guidance about how to handle different aspects of the crisis, with operational necessities clashing with political considerations.

The weekend timing—with the theft discovered Friday morning in Dhaka—created additional challenges as many international partners operated with reduced staffing or had difficulty assembling the expertise needed to respond to complex fraud investigation requests. Bangladesh Bank found itself trying to coordinate urgent responses from institutions where key personnel had left for the weekend, where skeleton crews lacked authority to make significant decisions, and where the approaching Monday deadline created pressure but also recognition that comprehensive response might need to wait for full staffing to return. The temporal mismatch between the urgency Bangladesh Bank felt and the pace at which international partners could respond generated frustration and highlighted the challenges of managing global crises that don't respect weekend schedules or time zone boundaries.

The chaos extended to Bangladesh Bank's own staff, who found themselves working extended hours under extreme pressure with incomplete information about what had happened, uncertain guidance about what to do, and the knowledge that their careers and the institution's reputation hung in the balance. Some staff members, particularly those who discovered the breach or worked in IT and operations, faced implied or explicit accusations that they might have been complicit in the attack or negligent in their security practices. This atmosphere of suspicion, while perhaps inevitable given the magnitude of the breach, made cooperation and information-sharing more difficult as staff became defensive and reluctant to share information that might be used against them later. The human toll of the crisis—the stress, fear, and exhaustion that affected everyone involved—often gets lost in technical post-mortem analyses but significantly influenced how effectively the institution could respond during the critical early hours of the incident.

## Conclusion

The discovery of the Bangladesh Bank heist on Friday morning transformed a successful cyber operation into a revealed crime, initiating a race between the attackers seeking to complete their money laundering operation and defenders trying to freeze assets and recover stolen funds. The eighty-one million dollars that successfully escaped represented both a massive loss and a significant victory, as the amount stolen was dwarfed by the $870 million to $900 million that various interventions prevented from clearing. The typo that saved hundreds of millions demonstrated how even the most sophisticated operations remain vulnerable to simple human errors, while the Federal Reserve's behavioral analysis showed that technical authentication alone cannot prevent fraud when accompanied by pattern recognition and institutional knowledge about normal versus suspicious activity.

The chaos that erupted in Dhaka reflected the unprecedented nature of the attack and the challenges of managing complex international crises involving technical, legal, diplomatic, and financial dimensions simultaneously. Bangladesh Bank's response, while imperfect, ultimately succeeded in containing what could have been a catastrophic loss that threatened the nation's foreign exchange reserves and economic stability. The incident exposed gaps in institutional preparedness for advanced cyber threats, highlighting the need for central banks and financial institutions to invest not just in technical security but in crisis management capabilities, international coordination procedures, and staff training for responding to incidents that exceed normal operational experience.

The "fundation" typo entered financial security lore as a reminder that sophisticated technical operations require matching sophistication in operational execution and quality control. The attackers demonstrated remarkable technical capabilities in compromising SWIFT systems and maintaining persistent access for months, yet failed to apply the same care to proofreading their fraudulent transaction instructions. This mismatch between technical and operational excellence suggests possible conclusions about the attackers' organization, priorities, or expertise, and serves as a warning that defenders can still achieve successes against sophisticated adversaries who make mistakes in execution.

The Federal Reserve's role highlighted the importance of correspondent banking relationships as fraud prevention checkpoints where institutions with institutional knowledge and no pressure to facilitate transactions can apply skeptical scrutiny to unusual activity. The Fed's actions prevented massive additional losses not through technical detection of the compromise but through human expertise, pattern recognition, and willingness to delay transactions pending verification despite the operational friction such delays create. This success vindicated the value of human oversight in highly automated financial systems and demonstrated that behavioral analysis remains effective even against attackers who successfully forge technical authentication.

As investigations and recovery efforts intensified over the following weeks, the full scope of the operation would emerge, revealing connections to other cyber attacks, identifying likely perpetrators, and exposing the sophisticated infrastructure that supported the money laundering operation. However, the critical hours on Friday morning determined how much could be recovered versus how much was irretrievably lost. The chaos in Dhaka, while painful for those experiencing it, represented the institution's attempt to respond to an unprecedented challenge with inadequate preparation and resources. The lessons learned would ultimately drive changes in how financial institutions approach cybersecurity, how SWIFT enhances its security architecture, and how international cooperation on financial crime prevention evolves to address threats that transcend national boundaries and traditional categories of criminal activity.

# Chapter 6: The Money Trail

The successful theft of eighty-one million dollars represented only half of the attackers' challenge—the harder half, in many ways, involved transforming stolen electronic funds into usable assets that could be spent, invested, or enjoyed without leading law enforcement directly to the perpetrators. Money laundering at this scale requires sophisticated infrastructure, carefully cultivated relationships, and deep understanding of regulatory gaps across international jurisdictions. This chapter traces the journey of the stolen funds as they flowed from New York through Manila and beyond, illuminating the complex ecosystem of complicit institutions, exploitation of legal loopholes, and cash-intensive businesses that transformed digital theft into physical wealth. The money trail reveals not just where the funds went but how the modern financial system's complexity creates opportunities for criminals to obscure the origins of their ill-gotten gains, turning electronic digits into tangible riches while investigators struggle to follow a path deliberately designed to confound pursuit. What unfolds is a story of regulatory arbitrage, institutional failures, and the sobering reality that once money successfully enters certain channels, recovery becomes exponentially more difficult with each passing hour.

## Following the Stolen $81 Million

The journey of the successfully stolen funds began at the moment the fraudulent SWIFT transfers cleared from Bangladesh Bank's accounts at the Federal Reserve Bank of New York, sending money flowing through the international correspondent banking network toward destinations carefully selected during months of operational planning. Understanding how eighty-one million dollars moves through the global financial system requires recognizing that large international transfers rarely occur as single transactions but instead pass through multiple intermediate institutions, with each hop creating new opportunities for interception but also new challenges for investigators attempting to freeze or reverse the payments. The attackers' sophistication manifested not just in the initial theft but in the carefully orchestrated money laundering operation that began executing simultaneously with the fraudulent transfers themselves, ensuring that stolen funds immediately entered channels designed to obscure their origin and frustrate recovery efforts.

The initial transfers from the Federal Reserve accounts followed standard correspondent banking routes, with funds flowing to recipient banks in the Philippines and Sri Lanka where the attackers had established accounts to receive the stolen money. These initial hops occurred through trusted banking relationships and established payment networks, with the transfers appearing to be legitimate international transactions between recognized financial institutions. The recipient banks received properly formatted SWIFT payment messages directing credit to specific account holders, and absent real-time notification from Bangladesh Bank that the transfers were fraudulent, these institutions processed the incoming funds according to standard procedures. This initial phase of the money trail demonstrates how the same trusted relationships and automated processes that enable legitimate international commerce also facilitate financial crime when criminals successfully compromise the authentication mechanisms that underpin the system's security.

The speed with which the funds moved proved crucial to the operation's partial success. The attackers understood that their window of opportunity was measured in hours once the theft was discovered, and that every moment funds remained in easily identifiable banking channels increased the likelihood of freezing or recall. The money laundering operation therefore executed with remarkable velocity, with incoming transfers immediately triggering secondary movements that redistributed funds before Bangladesh Bank could coordinate effective holds with recipient institutions. This rapid redistribution transformed what began as a small number of large transfers into a much more complex web of smaller movements across multiple accounts, institutions, and jurisdictions—exponentially increasing the investigative challenge and creating situations where even successful freezes of some accounts left other portions of the funds already beyond reach.

Tracking the money required investigators to coordinate across multiple countries' law enforcement and regulatory agencies, each with different procedures, authorities, and responsiveness to international cooperation requests. The funds that successfully cleared to Philippine banks demanded engagement with Philippine authorities, while transfers to Sri Lankan institutions required parallel coordination with that country's regulatory and law enforcement systems. This jurisdictional fragmentation represented a deliberate strategic choice by the attackers, who understood that investigation and recovery efforts requiring coordination across multiple sovereign nations face inherent delays and complications that investigations within a single jurisdiction avoid. Each additional country involved introduced new legal frameworks, language barriers, and diplomatic procedures that slowed the response while money continued moving through the laundering pipeline.

The investigative tools available for following stolen funds operate under significant constraints that the attackers exploited in planning their money laundering operation. Banking privacy laws in many jurisdictions limit what information institutions can share with foreign law enforcement or other banks, creating blind spots in transaction tracking. Real-time payment monitoring across international borders remains limited, with investigators often receiving transaction data hours or days after movements occur rather than in the moment. Legal processes for freezing accounts, seizing funds, or compelling institutions to provide detailed transaction records require formal requests through official channels, introducing delays measured in days or weeks while criminal operations unfold over hours. These structural limitations meant that investigators following the money trail operated at a fundamental disadvantage, always learning about fund movements after they occurred and struggling to predict where money would go next in time to preemptively freeze accounts before funds arrived.

The digital trail left by electronic fund transfers, while comprehensive in theory, proved challenging to follow in practice due to the volume of legitimate international transactions among which the fraudulent transfers hid. Bangladesh Bank's initial notification to international partners that specific transfers were fraudulent needed to be disseminated to dozens of potentially affected institutions across multiple countries, each of which maintained thousands or millions of customer accounts and processed huge volumes of daily transactions. Identifying which specific incoming transfers represented stolen Bangladesh Bank funds versus legitimate transactions required matching transaction amounts, dates, and originating account details against the fraudulent SWIFT messages—a matching process that sounds straightforward but becomes complex when dealing with correspondent banking layers where multiple institutions might have handled the same funds. The practical challenges of tracking money through this complex system meant that even with full cooperation from all involved institutions, significant time elapsed between theft and comprehensive mapping of where the money went.

The human dimension of following the money trail involved investigators, compliance officers, and banking staff across multiple institutions and countries working extended hours under intense pressure to identify and freeze assets before they could be further laundered beyond recovery. These professionals faced the challenge of coordinating across time zones, language differences, and organizational cultures while racing against criminals who had prepared for exactly this response and built their money laundering operation to exploit the inevitable delays. Some institutions responded with immediate cooperation and urgent action, assigning senior staff to assist with the investigation and implementing holds on suspicious accounts with minimal procedural delays. Others responded more slowly, whether due to bureaucratic constraints, legal concerns about freezing assets without sufficient evidence, or simple lack of urgency about a crime that victimized a foreign institution rather than their own depositors. This variation in institutional responsiveness created a patchwork of effective and ineffective intervention, with some portions of the stolen funds successfully frozen while others slipped through gaps in the coordinated response.

## Manila's Rizal Commercial Banking Corporation

The Philippine banking system, specifically Rizal Commercial Banking Corporation (RCBC), emerged as the critical node through which the majority of successfully stolen funds flowed on their journey from electronic transfers to physical assets. RCBC's branch in Jupiter Street, Manila, became the focal point of what would evolve into a major scandal within Philippine banking, raising questions about institutional complicity, regulatory oversight failures, and the adequacy of anti-money laundering controls in an era where sophisticated criminals deliberately target institutions and jurisdictions where such controls are weakest. Understanding

RCBC's role requires examining not just what happened but how a respected Philippine banking institution became the conduit for one of history's largest cyber heists, and why the safeguards that should have prevented such massive money laundering proved inadequate when tested by determined, sophisticated adversaries.

The accounts at RCBC that received the fraudulent transfers belonged to individuals and entities that would later prove to be fronts for the money laundering operation, though at the time they appeared to be legitimate customers with plausible reasons for receiving international transfers. These accounts had been opened weeks or months before the heist, establishing banking relationships and building transaction histories that made the eventual large incoming transfers appear less anomalous than if they had arrived at brand-new accounts with no prior activity. This preparatory work demonstrated the sophistication of the operation, with the attackers understanding that successful money laundering requires not just moving money but creating contexts where those movements appear normal to compliance officers reviewing transactions for suspicious activity. The advance preparation also suggested that the Philippine component of the operation had been planned long before the actual theft occurred, with the attackers committing resources and effort to establishing infrastructure that would only become useful if and when the heist successfully executed.

The arrival of tens of millions of dollars at RCBC's Jupiter Street branch through multiple incoming international wire transfers should have triggered immediate scrutiny under the bank's anti-money laundering procedures. Philippine banking regulations required institutions to monitor for unusual transaction patterns, particularly large international transfers to individual or small business accounts that lacked obvious commercial justification. However, the controls that should have caught and questioned these transfers either failed to activate or were somehow circumvented, allowing the funds to be credited to the recipient accounts without the enhanced due diligence that such large, unusual transactions would normally trigger. The failure raised questions about whether RCBC's anti-money laundering systems were inadequately designed, whether they were circumvented through some form of insider complicity, or whether the institution simply failed to act on alerts that their systems did generate.

The speed with which funds moved after arriving at RCBC proved critical to the laundering operation's partial success. Rather than remaining in the recipient accounts where they could be easily frozen once Bangladesh Bank notified Philippine authorities of the fraud, the money immediately began redistributing through additional transfers, cash withdrawals, and conversions into other forms of value. This rapid secondary movement occurred over a weekend, when regulatory oversight operated with reduced capacity and when coordinating emergency freezes proved more difficult than during business hours. By the time Philippine authorities responded to Bangladesh Bank's notifications and implemented holds on the relevant RCBC accounts, significant portions of the funds had already departed, transformed into cash, casino chips, or transfers to additional accounts beyond the immediate investigation's reach. The timing demonstrated how the attackers exploited not just banking systems but the operational rhythms of regulatory oversight, structuring their laundering operation to move fastest during periods when defensive responses would be slowest.

The internal culture and procedures at RCBC, particularly at the Jupiter Street branch where the suspicious accounts were held, came under intense scrutiny following the revelation of the bank's role in the money laundering operation. Investigations revealed that a branch manager had been involved in facilitating the accounts and transactions, raising questions about whether this was individual misconduct by a corrupt employee or whether broader institutional failures enabled or even encouraged looking the other way when profitable deposits arrived regardless of their suspicious characteristics. The scandal that erupted destroyed careers and damaged RCBC's reputation, with the institution facing regulatory sanctions, management changes, and prolonged legal proceedings attempting to determine accountability for the failures that allowed the money laundering to succeed. The human drama of these internal investigations—employees accused of complicity, careers ruined by association with the scandal, families affected by the financial and reputational consequences—often gets overshadowed by the technical details of the money laundering but represents a crucial dimension of the story.

The relationship between RCBC and the casino operators who received transferred funds from the bank proved central to understanding how the laundering operation functioned. Funds that arrived at RCBC quickly flowed to casino-related accounts or were withdrawn in cash for delivery to casinos, converting the electronic transfers into gambling chips that would be minimally gambled before being cashed out as purported winnings. This casino connection exploited regulatory gaps that exempted gambling establishments from certain anti-money laundering reporting requirements, but it also required coordination between banking personnel and casino operators that suggested at least some level of institutional knowledge that something irregular was occurring. The precise nature of these relationships—whether they represented deliberate conspiracy, willful blindness, or exploitation of relationship banking culture where accommodating valued customers sometimes overrides suspicious transaction questioning—remained subject to investigation and dispute.

Philippine regulatory authorities faced criticism for both pre-incident supervision of RCBC's anti-money laundering controls and post-incident response speed in freezing accounts and preventing further fund movements. The country's central bank and financial regulators had responsibility for ensuring that Philippine banks maintained adequate safeguards against money laundering, yet RCBC had clearly failed to prevent being used for massive criminal fund transfers. The delayed regulatory response once the fraud was reported further compounded the problem, with crucial hours passing between Bangladesh Bank's notification and effective freezing of RCBC accounts—hours during which substantial funds completed their conversion into forms that made recovery impossible. The regulatory failures highlighted challenges facing financial oversight agencies in developing economies, where sophisticated international criminal operations sometimes exceed the expertise and resources available to supervisory authorities tasked with preventing exactly such abuses.

The international diplomatic complications arising from RCBC's role tested Philippine-Bangladesh relations and raised broader questions about cross-border financial crime enforcement. Bangladesh authorities and media expressed frustration at what they perceived as inadequate urgency from Philippine institutions in responding to the theft and freezing assets. Philippine officials, meanwhile, defended their adherence to legal procedures and noted the challenges of responding to complex international incidents over weekends with limited information. The tension reflected fundamental challenges in international cooperation on financial crimes, where victim countries often feel that host jurisdictions where stolen funds land don't treat recovery with sufficient priority, while those host jurisdictions note that they must balance foreign requests against domestic legal requirements and procedures. RCBC itself, while clearly having failed in its anti-money laundering obligations, could argue that it was victimized by sophisticated criminals who exploited its systems rather than being a willing participant in the theft—a distinction that mattered for determining liability and culpability.

## Casino Money Laundering Operations

The exploitation of Philippine casinos to launder the stolen funds represented the most innovative and effective component of the money laundering operation, taking advantage of regulatory gaps, the cash-intensive nature of gambling operations, and the cultural context where large-scale gambling by wealthy Asian patrons represented normal rather than suspicious activity. Understanding how casinos became such effective money laundering vehicles requires examining both the general characteristics that make gambling establishments attractive for criminals seeking to obscure the origins of illicit funds and the specific regulatory environment in the Philippines that made casinos there particularly vulnerable to exploitation by sophisticated money launderers. The casino phase of the laundering operation transformed electronic bank transfers into physical cash and legitimized gambling winnings, effectively severing the traceable connection between the stolen millions and their fraudulent origin.

The fundamental appeal of casinos for money laundering stems from the combination of massive legitimate cash flows, minimal regulatory oversight of individual transactions, and the cultural expectation of privacy around gambling activities. Casinos routinely handle enormous volumes of cash as patrons exchange currency for chips, play various games, and cash out their winnings. This legitimate activity provides perfect cover for money laundering operations, where illicit funds can be commingled with legitimate cash flows in ways that make distinguishing the criminal from the lawful nearly impossible without comprehensive investigation. The privacy traditionally afforded to casino patrons—casinos don't typically report individual gambling activities to authorities absent specific legal requirements—creates an environment where large cash movements draw less scrutiny than they would in conventional banking channels. These characteristics make casinos perennial favorites for money laundering operations worldwide, with sophisticated criminals understanding that the gambling industry represents a vulnerability in financial crime prevention systems.

The mechanics of casino-based money laundering in the Bangladesh Bank case followed patterns that investigators had seen in other cases but executed with scale and speed that overwhelmed detection capabilities. Funds that arrived at RCBC were quickly transferred to accounts controlled by individuals who then purchased large quantities of casino chips at multiple Philippine gambling establishments. These individuals—later revealed to be working for the money laundering operation—presented themselves as high-stakes gamblers, a role that's familiar to casino operators who regularly host wealthy Asian clientele known for extremely large bets. Once the chips were purchased, the laundering operation required only minimal actual gambling—playing a few hands, spinning some slots, perhaps participating in some table games—to create the appearance of legitimate gambling activity before cashing out the chips and receiving payment in the form of casino checks, wire transfers, or even cash that appeared to be gambling winnings rather than laundered theft proceeds.

The scale of gambling activity required to launder tens of millions of dollars might seem like it would attract immediate attention even in casinos accustomed to high-rollers. However, the operation distributed activity across multiple casinos and multiple individuals, reducing the concentration at any single establishment. Additionally, the gambling occurred over a relatively short period—essentially a long weekend—creating a compressed timeframe where casino operators might have noticed unusual activity but faced challenges coordinating any response before the laundering operation completed. Some accounts suggest that certain casino personnel were aware that something unusual was occurring, with rapid chip purchases and minimal gambling followed by immediate cashouts representing suspicious patterns that experienced casino staff would recognize. However, whether this recognition translated into action or merely private speculation varied across establishments, with some casinos proving more compliant with investigation requests than others.

The regulatory framework governing Philippine casinos at the time of the Bangladesh Bank heist contained a critical loophole that the money laundering operation exploited ruthlessly: casinos were explicitly exempted from certain anti-money laundering reporting requirements that applied to banks and other financial institutions. This exemption existed for multiple reasons, including privacy concerns around gambling activities, the political influence of the casino industry in Philippine economic policy, and perhaps insufficient recognition of casinos' vulnerability to money laundering exploitation. The practical effect was that casinos could accept enormous cash deposits, facilitate massive gambling transactions, and pay out huge winnings without the same suspicious activity reporting obligations that would have applied if the same transactions occurred through banks. This regulatory gap created an obvious vulnerability that sophisticated money launderers identified and exploited, using casinos as the bridge between traceable electronic banking transfers and untraceable physical assets.

The cultural context of gambling in Asian societies, where high-stakes gambling represents an accepted activity among wealthy individuals, provided additional cover for the money laundering operation. Philippine casinos regularly hosted affluent gamblers from China, Hong Kong, and other Asian markets, with individual patrons sometimes gambling millions of dollars during visits. This established pattern of extremely high-value gambling made the

Bangladesh Bank laundering operation's activities less anomalous than they would have appeared in jurisdictions where such gambling levels were rare. The money launderers essentially hid their criminal activity within the substantial legitimate high-roller gambling that Philippine casinos serviced, banking on the reality that casino operators would be reluctant to question or turn away customers whose gambling patterns, while perhaps unusual, remained within the broad spectrum of behavior seen among legitimate wealthy gamblers. The strategy succeeded because it exploited casino operators' business incentives—large gamblers generate substantial revenue—creating situations where economic interest potentially conflicted with due diligence obligations.

The speed of the casino laundering phase proved as critical as the speed of earlier banking transfers. The operation unfolded over the weekend following the Friday discovery of the theft, with chips purchased, minimally gambled, and cashed out before Philippine authorities could coordinate freezes or restrictions on the individuals involved. This velocity demonstrated sophisticated operational planning that understood exactly how long different phases would take and how much time would elapse before authorities could respond effectively. By the time law enforcement identified specific casinos where stolen funds had been laundered, the transactions had largely completed, with the funds converted into casino checks or cash that could be immediately moved beyond the casinos' reach. Some individuals allegedly walked out of casinos with millions in cash stuffed into bags, representing the physical conversion of electronic theft into tangible, moveable, and spendable assets.

The investigation of casino money laundering faced unique challenges that distinguished it from investigating conventional banking transfers. Casinos' partial exemption from anti-money laundering reporting meant that comprehensive transaction records might not exist or might not be maintained in formats that facilitated investigation. Casino operators, particularly those whose legal status might be ambiguous or who valued customer privacy as a competitive advantage, sometimes proved less than fully cooperative with investigation requests. The physical nature of casino transactions—chips exchanged for cash, gambling conducted in person, winnings paid in tangible forms—created discontinuities in the electronic transaction trails that investigators could normally follow, requiring different investigative techniques more akin to traditional criminal investigation than financial forensics. The net effect was that the casino phase of laundering proved far more difficult to fully investigate and unravel than the banking components where comprehensive electronic records existed.

## The Remittance Company Pipeline

Beyond casinos, the money laundering operation utilized remittance companies—businesses that facilitate international money transfers, particularly serving immigrant communities sending funds to family members in their countries of origin. These companies represent another node in the global financial system where regulatory oversight has historically been lighter than in traditional banking, where cash transactions are routine, and where the business model creates opportunities for criminals to inject illicit funds into legitimate transaction flows. The remittance pipeline in the Bangladesh Bank case demonstrated how money launderers exploit the entire spectrum of financial services, using each type of institution for the specific vulnerabilities it offers while shifting between systems to frustrate coordinated investigation and recovery efforts.

Remittance companies operate in a regulatory gray area in many jurisdictions, licensed and supervised but often facing less stringent requirements than banks, particularly regarding large-value transaction monitoring and beneficial ownership verification. These businesses handle enormous volumes of small-value transfers—workers sending modest amounts home to support families—but also process larger transactions and sometimes offer additional services like currency exchange and check cashing that make them versatile tools for money laundering. The legitimate business model involves accepting cash or electronic funds in one location and arranging for equivalent funds to be paid out in another country, often in a different currency. This service, while crucial for millions of legitimate users worldwide, also provides a mechanism for moving money across borders while obscuring the source of funds and the identity of ultimate beneficiaries.

The use of remittance companies in the Bangladesh Bank money laundering operation likely occurred during the phase where funds needed to move from initial laundering through casinos into forms that could be further distributed or moved to ultimate beneficiaries. Some portion of casino cashouts may have been converted to remittance transfers sent to additional accounts in other countries, adding another layer of jurisdictional complexity to the money trail. Other funds might have entered remittance channels directly from bank accounts before reaching casinos, with the remittance companies serving as alternatives to bank transfers for moving money between institutions or countries. The specific role of remittance companies in this case remained less publicized than the casino connections, partly because remittance operations occurred more discretely and partly because investigation of these channels faced challenges in obtaining cooperation and records from companies operating in multiple jurisdictions with varying regulatory oversight.

The challenges of investigating remittance company involvement in money laundering stem from both the fragmented structure of the industry and the cash-intensive nature of the business. Unlike banks where comprehensive electronic records facilitate investigation, remittance companies often maintain less detailed records, particularly for cash transactions where the business model doesn't require extensive documentation of fund sources. The industry's structure—with many small operators, complex networks of agents, and services that involve multiple companies in completing single transactions—creates investigative challenges as authorities attempt to trace money through systems designed for convenience and cost-efficiency rather than investigative transparency. Some remittance companies operate in jurisdictions with minimal financial services regulation, creating havens where due diligence standards remain extremely low and where money launderers can exploit the system with minimal risk of questioning.

The legitimate importance of remittance services for immigrant communities and developing economies creates political and social complexities around regulating these businesses more stringently. Policymakers recognize that excessive regulation or compliance requirements for remittance companies risk pricing out legitimate users who depend on these services for essential family support and economic lifelines. Yet inadequate oversight creates vulnerabilities that sophisticated criminals exploit, using remittance channels to launder criminal proceeds while hiding behind the massive volume of legitimate transactions these services handle. The Bangladesh Bank case highlighted this tension, with investigation of remittance connections needing to distinguish criminal money flows from legitimate transactions while respecting the privacy and dignity of ordinary users who had no connection to the money laundering operation.

The international dimension of remittance services—with companies facilitating transfers between countries that may have vastly different regulatory standards, enforcement capabilities, and cooperation with international law enforcement—creates opportunities for strategic exploitation by money launderers. Funds might enter remittance channels in a jurisdiction with strong oversight and exit in a country where remittance companies face minimal regulation, effectively allowing the money to wash through the international system's gaps. The Bangladesh Bank laundering operation's use of remittance channels, whether as primary or secondary money movement mechanisms, demonstrated sophisticated understanding of these vulnerabilities and willingness to exploit them as part of a comprehensive laundering strategy that used every available tool.

## Where the Money Disappeared

The ultimate destination of the stolen eighty-one million dollars represents perhaps the most frustrating aspect of the entire case for investigators and victims seeking to understand and potentially recover the stolen funds. Despite extensive investigation involving law enforcement agencies from multiple countries, banking institutions, casinos, and remittance companies, significant portions of the money effectively disappeared into forms and locations that made comprehensive accounting impossible and recovery impractical or impossible. Understanding where the money went requires examining not just specific destination accounts or individuals but the broader reality that successful money laundering transforms traceable electronic funds into untraceable physical assets that can be spent, invested, or hidden without creating the trails that modern financial investigation depends upon.

The most immediately apparent destination for substantial stolen funds was the Philippine casino system, where tens of millions were rapidly laundered through chip purchases and cashouts. However, even within this relatively well-documented phase, tracking precisely where every dollar went proved challenging. Some funds cashed out as casino checks that were then deposited into additional accounts, creating new paper trails that investigators could follow. Other portions left casinos as physical cash, carried away in bags by individuals working for the money laundering operation. This physical cash—millions upon millions of dollars in actual currency notes—entered the realm of complete untraceability, as cash movements leave no electronic records and can be physically transported across borders, stored in hidden locations, or spent through transactions that create no permanent documentation. The conversion of electronic money into physical cash represented the crucial moment where the digital trail went cold and investigation shifted from financial forensics to traditional law enforcement techniques like surveillance, informants, and physical evidence.

Some portion of the funds appeared to have been converted into real estate and other tangible assets that sophisticated money launderers favor for preserving and legitimizing wealth derived from criminal activity. Real estate purchases offer multiple advantages for money laundering: they convert liquid cash into stable assets, they can be structured through shell companies that obscure true ownership, and they create legitimate-appearing wealth that can be explained through purported business success or investment returns. Investigation into possible real estate purchases using stolen Bangladesh Bank funds faced the challenges of identifying which properties among millions in the Philippines and potentially other countries might have been purchased with laundered proceeds, proving the connection between specific properties and the stolen funds when ownership had been deliberately obscured through complex corporate structures, and overcoming legal protections for property owners that make seizure difficult even when suspicious circumstances exist.

Luxury goods purchases represented another likely destination for portions of the stolen funds, with jewelry, vehicles, art, and other high-value items offering portable wealth that can be easily transported, hidden, or sold in secondary markets without creating the paper trails that banking transactions generate. The luxury goods market, particularly in Asia, involves substantial cash transactions where due diligence on the source of funds varies widely depending on the seller and jurisdiction. Money launderers understanding this market's characteristics can convert millions in cash into jewelry, watches, or other portable valuables that can be physically carried across borders, gifted to associates or family members, or gradually sold through private transactions that avoid oversight. Investigation of luxury goods purchases using stolen funds faced challenges similar to those involving real estate, with the added difficulty that luxury items are far more portable and can be moved across borders or between owners with even less documentation than property transfers require.

Distribution to the individuals who actually conducted the money laundering operation consumed some portion of the stolen funds, representing payment for the significant risk these operatives took in serving as the public faces of the laundering scheme. The individuals who opened accounts at RCBC, purchased casino chips, and physically transported cash were compensated for their role, though investigators never fully established how much they received versus how much moved on to higher-level organizers of the operation. Some of these individuals were arrested and faced legal proceedings in the Philippines, but others disappeared or proved difficult to locate, and even those who were detained provided limited cooperation in explaining where the money went. The threat of prosecution encouraged some cooperation but also incentivized others to protect information about funds they might have retained or higher-level conspirators they might have feared more than Philippine law enforcement.

The masterminds behind the operation—the sophisticated actors who planned and executed the SWIFT compromise, coordinated the money laundering infrastructure, and ultimately controlled the stolen funds—remained largely shadowy figures who successfully maintained distance from the laundering operation's visible components. These individuals or groups likely retained the majority of the stolen funds, but their identity and location remained subject to speculation and investigation that produced theories but limited definitive evidence. Attribution analysis suggested possible connections to North Korean state-sponsored hacking operations, with technical indicators in the malware and operational patterns matching known North Korean cyber operations. If correct, this attribution suggested that the stolen funds ultimately flowed to a nation-state actor rather than conventional criminal organization, with the money potentially funding government operations, weapons programs, or other state priorities rather than individual enrichment. However, proving such attribution definitively and recovering funds from a sovereign nation presented challenges far beyond conventional money laundering investigation.

The portion of funds successfully frozen and eventually recovered—estimated at perhaps fifteen to twenty million dollars from various sources—represented partial success in a largely unsuccessful recovery effort. Philippine authorities, working with international partners, managed to freeze some accounts before funds fully dissipated, claw back some casino-laundered money, and recover assets from individuals charged with participating in the money laundering. However, the majority of the stolen eighty-one million disappeared beyond recovery, converted into forms or moved to locations where Philippine, Bangladeshi, or international law enforcement lacked authority or practical ability to seize assets. This reality—that successful money laundering, despite leaving some traces, ultimately achieves its objective of making stolen money usable by criminals while placing it beyond victims' reach—represents the fundamental challenge in combating financial crime. Technical success in theft proves worthless if money can be easily recovered, but successful laundering transforms electronic theft into permanent loss.

The years following the heist saw continuing investigation and occasional developments as new information emerged about funds' movements or individuals' involvement. Some previously unknown accounts or asset purchases came to light, leading to additional recovery efforts. Various legal proceedings in the Philippines and other jurisdictions attempted to determine liability and compensation for victims. The SWIFT organization and international banking community implemented new security measures and monitoring procedures designed to prevent similar thefts. Yet despite all these efforts, the central reality remained unchanged: most of the money disappeared, successfully laundered through a system that investigators mapped in considerable detail after the fact but could not effectively interdict in the critical hours when recovery remained possible. The vanished millions stand as testament to both the sophistication of the laundering operation and the fundamental challenges facing financial crime investigation in a globalized world where money moves instantly across borders while law enforcement cooperation occurs at the pace of bureaucracy and diplomacy.

## Conclusion

The journey of the stolen eighty-one million dollars from Bangladesh Bank's Federal Reserve accounts through Philippine banks, casinos, and remittance channels to ultimate destinations that remain partially unknown represents a masterclass in modern money laundering and a case study in the challenges facing international financial crime investigation. The money trail illuminated fundamental vulnerabilities in the global financial system, where regulatory gaps between jurisdictions create opportunities for criminals, where some types of financial institutions face less stringent oversight than others, and where the speed of electronic fund movement dramatically exceeds the pace at which international cooperation can effectively respond. The trail also demonstrated how criminals have evolved beyond simply stealing money to developing sophisticated capabilities for laundering it, recognizing that theft without successful laundering represents failure.

RCBC's role as the primary conduit for laundered funds highlighted risks that correspondent banking relationships create when institutions in jurisdictions with weaker regulatory enforcement become linked to the international financial system. The bank's failures in detecting and preventing the money laundering generated a major scandal within Philippine banking and prompted regulatory reforms, but only after damage was done. The case demonstrated that financial systems are only as secure as their weakest links, and that sophisticated criminals deliberately identify and exploit institutions and jurisdictions where those weak links exist. RCBC's experience serves as a cautionary tale for banks worldwide about the reputational and financial consequences of inadequate anti-money laundering controls and the importance of viewing compliance not as regulatory burden but as fundamental risk management.

The casino connection exposed regulatory gaps that had existed for years but received limited attention until exploited so dramatically and publicly. The revelation that tens of millions in stolen funds could be laundered through casinos with minimal detection prompted substantial reforms in Philippine law, with casinos brought under comprehensive anti-money laundering requirements similar to those governing banks. However, these reforms came too late for Bangladesh Bank's recovery efforts, demonstrating the recurring pattern where financial crime regulation strengthens in response to demonstrated exploits rather than proactive risk assessment. The casino phase also revealed how cultural context and legitimate business patterns can provide cover for money laundering, with criminal activity hiding within the substantial legitimate high-roller gambling that Asian casinos regularly service.

The remittance company connections, while less publicized than banking and casino channels, highlighted another vulnerability in the global financial system where services essential to immigrant communities and developing economies operate with oversight inadequate to prevent criminal exploitation. Balancing the legitimate needs these services meet against the risks they create remains an ongoing policy challenge, with solutions requiring nuanced approaches that enhance security without making services inaccessible to the populations that depend on them. The Bangladesh Bank case added urgency to international efforts to strengthen remittance company oversight while maintaining these crucial services.

The ultimate destinations of the money—spanning frozen accounts, converted assets, individual compensation, and unknown ultimate beneficiaries—reflect both partial successes and fundamental limitations in financial crime recovery. The fifteen to twenty million dollars eventually recovered represents approximately twenty-five percent of the stolen amount, a recovery rate that might be considered successful in complex international money laundering cases but remains deeply unsatisfying to victims who lost the remaining sixty-plus million dollars irretrievably. The case demonstrated that sophisticated, well-executed money laundering can succeed despite intensive investigation, and that once funds successfully enter certain channels—particularly conversion to physical cash or movement to uncooperative jurisdictions—recovery becomes effectively impossible regardless of how much investigators learn about where the money went.

As we move forward to examine the investigation, attribution, and response to this unprecedented cyber heist, the money trail provides crucial context for understanding why such attacks prove so attractive to sophisticated criminals. The technical challenge of compromising secure systems, while substantial, pales beside the operational challenge of successfully laundering enormous sums. The Bangladesh Bank attackers demonstrated mastery of both dimensions—technical penetration and operational money laundering—marking them as among the most sophisticated financial criminals of the modern era. Their partial success, despite eventual detection and substantial international response, validates their approach and provides a template that other sophisticated actors have studied and potentially adapted for future operations. The money trail they blazed through the international financial system remains visible years later as both a map of what they accomplished and a guide for defenders seeking to close the vulnerabilities that made their success possible.

# Part Three: The Aftermath

## Chapter 7: The Investigation

The discovery of the Bangladesh Bank heist triggered what would become one of the most complex and politically charged cybersecurity investigations in history, spanning multiple continents, involving dozens of agencies, and ultimately pointing toward conclusions that transformed the incident from a criminal case into a matter of international diplomacy and national security. The investigation required not just following the money trail but also conducting deep forensic analysis of compromised systems, attributing the attack to specific threat actors, and navigating the treacherous waters of international cooperation where national interests, political considerations, and technical evidence sometimes aligned and sometimes diverged dramatically. This chapter examines how investigators from multiple countries worked to understand what happened, who was responsible, and what could be done about it—efforts that produced remarkable technical insights, controversial attributions, and sobering lessons about the limitations of international law enforcement when adversaries operate from hostile or uncooperative nations. The investigation revealed not just the mechanics of a sophisticated cyber heist but also the profound challenges facing the international community in responding to state-sponsored cybercrime that exploits the borderless nature of digital networks while hiding behind the very real borders that constrain law enforcement authority.

# FBI Involvement and International Cooperation

The Federal Bureau of Investigation's engagement with the Bangladesh Bank case reflected both the United States' central role in international banking—with the theft occurring from accounts at the Federal Reserve Bank of New York—and the FBI's established position as a lead agency for investigating major cybercrimes affecting American financial infrastructure. The Bureau's involvement began almost immediately after the theft's discovery on Friday morning, with Bangladesh Bank's notification to the Federal Reserve triggering concurrent alerts to law enforcement agencies responsible for protecting the integrity of U.S. financial institutions and investigating crimes involving them. What followed represented a massive mobilization of investigative resources that would eventually span continents and involve coordination among law enforcement agencies, intelligence services, banking regulators, and private sector cybersecurity firms across dozens of countries.

The FBI's Cyber Division, headquartered in Washington with field offices maintaining specialized cyber squads across the country, took primary responsibility for the U.S. investigation. These agents brought specialized training in digital forensics, malware analysis, and the increasingly crucial discipline of cyber threat attribution—determining who conducted sophisticated attacks when the attackers deliberately obscure their identities and locations. The New York field office played a particularly central role given the Federal Reserve Bank of New York's location within its jurisdiction and the office's existing relationships with major financial institutions throughout the city. Within hours of notification, FBI agents were conducting interviews with Federal Reserve staff, reviewing transaction logs, and beginning the process of understanding exactly what had happened and how stolen funds had been routed through U.S. financial systems.

International cooperation proved essential from the investigation's earliest hours, as the transnational nature of the crime meant that no single country's law enforcement possessed all the evidence or authority needed for comprehensive investigation. The FBI immediately engaged with counterparts in Bangladesh, where the initial compromise had occurred and where forensic examination of Bangladesh Bank's infected systems would provide crucial evidence about the attack's technical characteristics. Philippine law enforcement became critical partners as investigations revealed that stolen funds had primarily flowed through Manila's banking and casino systems. Investigators in Sri Lanka, where some fraudulent transfers had been directed, provided additional cooperation. Each country's involvement required navigating different legal systems, investigative procedures, and levels of capability in handling sophisticated cybercrime investigations.

The coordination challenges involved in managing this multi-country investigation proved immense and at times overwhelming. Time zone differences meant that real-time communication required investigators to work irregular hours or accept delays as queries and responses passed across boundaries during different countries' business days. Language barriers necessitated translation services and created opportunities for miscommunication or nuance loss. Different legal frameworks meant that evidence collection, witness interviews, and other investigative procedures that would be routine in one jurisdiction required special procedures or permissions in another. Perhaps most significantly, varying national priorities meant that while Bangladesh viewed the case as a crisis demanding maximum urgency and resources, other countries treated it as one investigation among many competing for limited law enforcement attention.

Formal mechanisms for international law enforcement cooperation—primarily mutual legal assistance treaties and Interpol coordination—provided frameworks for requesting evidence, interviewing witnesses, and pursuing leads across borders. However, these mechanisms operated at bureaucratic speeds that frustrated investigators racing to freeze assets and identify perpetrators while evidence remained fresh. Mutual legal assistance requests typically require formal diplomatic channels, legal review to ensure compliance with both countries' laws, and approval processes that can consume weeks or months. Interpol coordination facilitates information sharing and coordination but lacks enforcement authority, depending entirely on member nations' willingness and ability to act on shared intelligence. The gap between the speed at which cybercriminals operate and the pace of formal international law enforcement cooperation represented a structural disadvantage that investigators struggled to overcome throughout the investigation.

Informal cooperation among investigators often proved more effective than formal channels, with law enforcement personnel in different countries developing direct relationships and sharing information through unofficial networks that bypassed bureaucratic delays. FBI agents cultivated contacts with Philippine National Police cyber units, Bangladeshi investigators, and cybersecurity professionals in private firms across Asia who possessed knowledge relevant to the case. These informal channels allowed rapid exchange of technical information, investigative leads, and situational awareness that formal processes would have delayed. However, informal cooperation had limitations—it couldn't compel unwilling witnesses to testify, couldn't authorize official evidence collection procedures, and sometimes created tensions when information shared informally needed to be formalized for prosecution purposes, requiring that the same information flow through official channels that added weeks of delay.

The private sector's role in the investigation demonstrated how cybersecurity has evolved beyond purely governmental responsibility to involve commercial firms that often possess greater technical expertise in analyzing sophisticated malware than government agencies command. Bangladesh Bank engaged FireEye's Mandiant division, a leading cybersecurity firm specializing in incident response and threat intelligence, to conduct forensic analysis of compromised systems and help understand the attack's technical characteristics. Other security firms contributed analysis of malware samples, indicators of compromise, and threat intelligence about the attackers' tools and techniques. These private sector contributions proved invaluable, bringing cutting-edge technical capabilities to the investigation, but also created coordination challenges as commercial firms balanced their investigative work with business considerations, client confidentiality obligations, and competitive pressures that sometimes complicated information sharing with government investigators or other companies.

The political dimension of international cooperation added layers of complexity beyond technical and legal challenges. Bangladesh's government, facing domestic pressure about the massive theft and international embarrassment about security failures at its central bank, demanded aggressive investigation and pushed international partners for rapid results. Philippine officials, sensitive to their country's reputation and concerned about perceptions that weak financial sector oversight had enabled money laundering, sought to demonstrate effective law enforcement response while navigating actual limitations in their legal system and investigative capabilities. U.S. authorities balanced their support for the investigation against broader diplomatic relationships and priorities, recognizing that the Bangladesh Bank case, while significant, represented one concern among many in complex bilateral relationships with both Bangladesh and the Philippines.

These political currents influenced resource allocation, public messaging, and sometimes the vigor with which different aspects of the investigation were pursued.

## Forensic Analysis of the Malware

The technical investigation of the Bangladesh Bank compromise centered on forensic examination of malware discovered on the bank's systems—sophisticated software that had enabled attackers to monitor operations, manipulate SWIFT messaging, and cover their tracks during the heist. This malware analysis represented one of the most crucial aspects of the entire investigation, as the code's characteristics, capabilities, and similarities to malware from other incidents would ultimately provide the strongest evidence for attribution to specific threat actors. Understanding what investigators discovered requires examining not just what the malware did but how it was designed, what that design revealed about the attackers' capabilities and priorities, and how forensic analysts pieced together the attack's technical narrative from artifacts left behind on compromised systems.

The initial discovery of malware on Bangladesh Bank's systems occurred during the early investigation phase when FireEye's Mandiant team, brought in to understand how the compromise occurred, began examining systems involved in SWIFT operations. The malware had been carefully designed to avoid detection by standard antivirus and security software, using sophisticated evasion techniques that allowed it to operate undetected for months while attackers conducted reconnaissance, tested their access, and ultimately executed the heist. Forensic analysts discovered multiple components serving different functions—some focused on maintaining persistent access to compromised systems, others designed to monitor legitimate SWIFT operations and capture credentials, still others engineered to manipulate SWIFT software and cover the attackers' fraudulent transactions. This modular architecture demonstrated advanced development capabilities and operational security awareness, with each component designed to minimize detection risk while maximizing functionality.

One of the malware's most sophisticated capabilities involved its manipulation of SWIFT's Alliance Access software, which Bangladesh Bank used to generate and transmit payment messages. The attackers had developed custom code that could inject fraudulent messages into the SWIFT network while simultaneously hiding those messages from the transaction logs and records that bank staff used to monitor operations. This dual functionality—executing fraudulent transactions while concealing them from oversight—required intimate knowledge of how SWIFT software operated, including undocumented features and internal database structures that weren't part of public documentation. The sophistication suggested either extensive reverse engineering of SWIFT software, possible insider knowledge about system architecture, or access to information about SWIFT operations that most criminal groups wouldn't possess. The capability to manipulate SWIFT software specifically marked the malware as highly specialized rather than general-purpose, indicating that the attackers had invested substantial resources into developing tools tailored for targeting banking infrastructure.

The malware's data destruction capabilities proved equally sophisticated and more destructive in some ways than its fraud functionality. Once the attackers completed their heist, portions of the malware executed wiping routines designed to destroy evidence and complicate forensic investigation. These wipers targeted log files, system records, and other artifacts that would normally allow investigators to reconstruct attack timelines and understand exactly what the attackers had done. The wipers operated with precision, destroying specific types of files while leaving others intact to avoid completely crippling systems in ways that would have triggered immediate investigation. Some wiping operations disguised themselves as legitimate system maintenance, overwriting files in ways that appeared to be routine cleanup rather than deliberate evidence destruction. The sophistication of these anti-forensic capabilities indicated that the attackers anticipated eventual discovery and had prepared specifically to complicate the investigation that would follow.

Code analysis revealed stylistic elements and technical approaches that experienced malware analysts could compare against other known threat actor tools. The programming languages used, the specific techniques employed for certain functions, the structure of configuration files, and even commenting styles in source code all provided indicators that could potentially link the malware to other samples. Analysts discovered similarities to malware used in previous incidents, including the 2014 Sony Pictures Entertainment breach and other attacks attributed to North Korean threat actors. These similarities weren't perfect matches—sophisticated actors often modify their tools between operations to complicate attribution—but the shared characteristics proved numerous and specific enough to suggest common authorship or at least shared tool development.

Network infrastructure analysis complemented code examination by mapping the command-and-control servers that the malware communicated with for receiving instructions and exfiltrating data. Investigators traced these servers' digital footprints, examining registration records, hosting providers, and network routing to understand the infrastructure supporting the attack. Many servers proved to be compromised legitimate systems rather than infrastructure directly controlled by the attackers, a common technique that adds layers of obfuscation to hide true origins. However, careful analysis of server locations, setup timing, and configuration patterns revealed operational security failures where the attackers had left traces linking different components of their infrastructure. These linkages eventually connected Bangladesh Bank attack infrastructure to servers used in other incidents, strengthening attribution to specific threat actors.

The timeline reconstruction from forensic evidence painted a picture of patient, methodical compromise extending over many months before the actual heist. The earliest malware infections appeared to have occurred eight to nine months prior to the February 2016 theft, indicating an extraordinarily long operational preparation period. During these months, the attackers had conducted extensive reconnaissance of Bangladesh Bank's systems, networks, and procedures. They tested their access repeatedly, learned how SWIFT operations functioned, identified security monitoring capabilities they needed to evade, and rehearsed their attack procedures. Evidence suggested that the actual heist itself—when fraudulent SWIFT messages flooded out over the course of hours—represented perhaps one percent of the total operation time, with the remaining ninety-nine percent devoted to preparation that made those critical hours successful.

The forensic investigation also revealed what the malware couldn't do, which proved as informative as understanding its capabilities. The code showed no signs of attempting data exfiltration beyond what was necessary to execute the heist, suggesting that the attackers were focused specifically on financial theft rather than espionage or intellectual property theft that characterizes many nation-state cyber operations. The malware targeted Bangladesh Bank specifically rather than demonstrating worm-like capabilities for spreading to additional victims, indicating a focused operation against a specific target rather than opportunistic infection seeking any available victims. These characteristics helped investigators understand the operation's objectives and scope, ruling out certain threat actor types while narrowing focus on others whose known tactics and priorities matched the observed malware behavior.

## Attribution to North Korea

The question of who conducted the Bangladesh Bank heist evolved from pure speculation in the immediate aftermath to increasingly confident attribution to North Korean state-sponsored threat actors as technical evidence accumulated and intelligence assessments matured. Attribution in sophisticated cyberattacks always involves probabilistic reasoning rather than absolute certainty—attackers deliberately obscure their identities and locations, sometimes engage in false flag operations to mislead investigators, and operate through layers of proxies that complicate tracing attacks to ultimate sources. However, the combination of technical indicators from malware analysis, operational patterns matching known North Korean tactics, and intelligence community assessments eventually built a compelling case that the heist represented yet another operation by a threat actor group U.S. intelligence designated as "Lazarus," associated with North Korea's government. Understanding this attribution requires examining the evidence supporting it, the confidence levels investigators assigned to various conclusions, and the broader context of North Korean cyber operations that made Bangladesh Bank consistent with established patterns.

The technical evidence linking the Bangladesh Bank malware to North Korean threat actors centered on code similarities with malware used in previous attacks attributed to the same actors. The most significant connection involved similarities to malware from the 2014 Sony Pictures Entertainment breach, which U.S. intelligence agencies had publicly attributed to North Korea with high confidence. The Sony attack, conducted in apparent retaliation for a comedy film depicting North Korea's leader, involved malware that shared multiple characteristics with code discovered at

Bangladesh Bank—similar programming approaches, comparable command-and-control infrastructure, and overlapping tools for data destruction and evidence manipulation. While no two malware samples were identical—sophisticated actors routinely modify their tools—the similarities proved numerous and specific enough that coincidental development by unrelated actors seemed extremely unlikely.

Additional technical connections emerged through analysis of infrastructure the attackers used. The command-and-control servers communicating with Bangladesh Bank malware showed connections to servers used in other incidents attributed to Lazarus Group, including attacks against financial institutions in multiple countries throughout 2015 and 2016. These connections weren't always direct—sophisticated actors deliberately compartmentalize infrastructure—but careful mapping revealed relationships suggesting common management of attack resources. The timing of infrastructure setup, patterns in how servers were configured, and stylistic elements in configuration files all provided indicators that linked diverse attacks to what appeared to be a coordinated campaign by a single threat actor group.

The operational patterns observed in the Bangladesh Bank attack matched North Korean tactics from previous incidents in ways that complemented technical indicators. The combination of lengthy reconnaissance, patient operation over months, focus on financial theft rather than espionage, and willingness to deploy destructive wipers matched the established Lazarus modus operandi. North Korean cyber operations had evolved over years from primarily espionage and propaganda-focused attacks to increasingly include financially motivated operations as international sanctions intensified pressure on the regime's finances. The Bangladesh Bank heist fit this pattern, representing a logical progression where sophisticated technical capabilities developed for intelligence operations were redeployed toward generating revenue to circumvent sanctions and fund regime priorities.

Intelligence community assessments provided classified and sometimes public evaluations of the attack's origins based on information beyond what technical forensics revealed. The U.S. intelligence community, drawing on signals intelligence, human intelligence, and classified technical sources, assessed with high confidence that North Korean actors conducted the attack. Similar assessments emerged from intelligence services in allied countries, creating consensus among nations with sophisticated cyber intelligence capabilities. These assessments carried weight beyond technical evidence because they incorporated information about North Korean cyber organizations, personnel, capabilities, and targeting that provided context for interpreting forensic findings. The convergence of technical forensics and intelligence assessment strengthened attribution confidence beyond what either source would support independently.

The attribution also considered alternative explanations and potential false flag scenarios where attackers might deliberately plant North Korean indicators to mislead investigators. Sophisticated adversaries understand that investigators look for technical signatures and might intentionally use tools or techniques associated with other threat actors to deflect blame. However, the depth and consistency of North Korean indicators across the Bangladesh Bank attack made false flag explanations increasingly implausible. Creating convincing false flags requires not just planting obvious signatures but consistently maintaining the deception across all technical indicators, operational patterns, and infrastructure elements—a level of commitment that, while theoretically possible, becomes exponentially more difficult to sustain across all aspects of a complex operation. The assessment concluded that while false flags couldn't be entirely ruled out, the weight of evidence pointing to North Korea was substantially stronger than any alternative explanation.

The broader context of North Korean cyber operations provided additional support for attribution by demonstrating that Bangladesh Bank fit within documented patterns of North Korean cyber activity. Intelligence agencies had tracked North Korean cyber operations for years, observing the regime's development of sophisticated capabilities, establishment of cyber units within military and intelligence organizations, and deployment of those capabilities for espionage, disruption, and increasingly financial crime. Other financially motivated attacks attributed to North Korea included attempted heists against banks in multiple countries throughout 2015 and 2016, suggesting Bangladesh Bank represented one operation in a sustained campaign. The Sony Pictures attack had demonstrated North Korea's willingness to conduct destructive cyber operations even when they would clearly be attributed back to the regime, indicating a level of boldness or calculation that risks international condemnation in pursuit of operational objectives.

The confidence levels in attribution varied across the investigation's participants and evolved over time as evidence accumulated. Initial assessments immediately after the breach were necessarily tentative, with multiple potential explanations receiving consideration. As forensic analysis progressed and technical indicators accumulated, confidence increased that the attack involved sophisticated state-sponsored actors rather than conventional cybercriminals. The specific attribution to North Korea emerged more gradually, building from possibilities to probability to eventually high confidence conclusions endorsed by multiple intelligence agencies. Some uncertainty remained—attribution in cyber operations rarely achieves absolute certainty—but by the time official statements were made, the collective assessment represented intelligence community consensus based on comprehensive evidence.

## Political Implications and Denials

The attribution of the Bangladesh Bank heist to North Korean state-sponsored actors transformed the incident from a criminal investigation into an international diplomatic crisis with profound implications for cybersecurity policy, financial system security, and the broader challenge of responding to state-sponsored cybercrime. North Korea's involvement meant that the heist represented not just theft but an act of economic warfare, where a nation-state employed sophisticated cyber capabilities to circumvent international sanctions and generate revenue through outright theft from foreign financial institutions. The political dimensions of attribution extended beyond simply naming the responsible party to encompass questions about appropriate responses, the precedents being set for state conduct in cyberspace, and the adequacy of existing international frameworks for addressing state-sponsored financial crime in the digital age.

North Korea's predictable and vehement denial of involvement followed the pattern the regime had established in response to previous cyber operation attributions. Official statements dismissed the accusations as baseless propaganda, suggesting that hostile nations fabricated evidence to damage North Korea's reputation and justify continued sanctions and isolation. These denials served multiple purposes: maintaining plausible deniability even when evidence made involvement obvious, reinforcing domestic propaganda narratives about external enemies conspiring against the nation, and creating at least surface ambiguity that some nations could point to in avoiding strong responses. The denials convinced few outside observers—the evidence was too strong and the operational patterns too consistent with known North Korean behavior—but they demonstrated the regime's unwillingness to acknowledge responsibility or change behavior in response to attribution.

The diplomatic response to the attribution proved complicated by existing tensions on the Korean Peninsula and the broader geopolitical context surrounding North Korea's nuclear weapons program and international sanctions regime. The Bangladesh Bank heist occurred during a period of elevated tensions following North Korean nuclear tests and ballistic missile launches, with the international community already engaged in sustained diplomatic pressure to curb these programs. Adding cyber financial crime to the list of North Korean transgressions requiring response created challenges in prioritizing which behaviors demanded most urgent attention and coordinating responses across issues when some nations remained focused primarily on nuclear proliferation while others viewed cyber operations as equally significant threats.

The United Nations became a forum for discussing North Korea's cyber operations and potential international responses. Discussions explored whether existing sanctions could be enhanced to specifically target North Korean cyber capabilities, whether new international norms or agreements might constrain state-sponsored financial cybercrime, and how the international community could more effectively cooperate in defending against and responding to such attacks. However, the UN's ability to take decisive action remained limited by geopolitical divisions, with China and Russia often protecting North Korea from the strongest proposed sanctions and expressing skepticism about attribution claims they viewed as potentially motivated by political considerations rather than pure technical evidence. The result was diplomatic statements condemning cybercrime and incremental sanctions enhancements rather than dramatic new approaches to addressing state-sponsored financial theft.

The U.S. response combined diplomatic pressure, enhanced sanctions targeting North Korean cyber capabilities, and strengthened cooperation with allies on cybersecurity and financial sector protection. The Treasury Department's Office of Foreign Assets Control designated specific North Korean entities and individuals associated with cyber operations for sanctions, targeting the regime's ability to benefit from cyber operations by making it more difficult to move money through international financial systems. The State Department engaged in diplomatic outreach encouraging nations to strengthen defenses against North Korean cyber operations and deny safe haven to North Korean cyber personnel operating abroad. The FBI and other law enforcement agencies intensified investigation and intelligence collection focused on North Korean cyber capabilities, seeking to understand the threat more comprehensively and develop more effective countermeasures.

The political implications extended beyond immediate diplomatic responses to influence broader policy debates about cybersecurity, financial system resilience, and the adequacy of existing international frameworks for addressing cyber threats. The incident demonstrated that even sophisticated financial institutions and secure payment networks remained vulnerable to determined state-sponsored attackers, raising questions about what level of security was achievable and what additional measures might be necessary. Some advocates pushed for mandatory cybersecurity standards for critical financial infrastructure, arguing that voluntary approaches had proven inadequate. Others emphasized the need for international cooperation and information sharing, suggesting that improved defensive coordination might matter more than prescriptive requirements. Still others focused on deterrence, arguing that states engaging in cyber financial crime needed to face consequences severe enough to make such operations too costly to continue.

The attribution's impact on cybersecurity industry practices and threat intelligence sharing proved significant and largely positive. The detailed technical information released about the attack—while redacted to protect sensitive sources and methods—provided the security community with indicators of compromise, malware signatures, and behavioral patterns that could help detect and prevent similar attacks. Financial institutions worldwide reviewed their SWIFT security, implemented enhanced monitoring for the specific techniques the attackers had used, and generally elevated their assessment of threat levels following the demonstration that even central banks could be successfully compromised. The case study became a staple of cybersecurity training and threat briefings, illustrating how sophisticated state-sponsored attacks unfold and what indicators might provide warning of compromise before damage occurs.

The question of precedent and what the international community's response signaled to other potential state-sponsored cyber attackers remained a source of concern for cybersecurity strategists and policymakers. If North Korea could steal tens of millions of dollars from international financial institutions with relative impunity—facing diplomatic condemnation and incremental sanctions but avoiding consequences that fundamentally changed the cost-benefit calculation—what message did that send to other nations facing financial pressure or simply seeking to generate revenue through cyber operations? The concern wasn't purely theoretical, as intelligence agencies documented other nations developing similar capabilities and appearing to study North Korean operations as potential models. The adequacy of international response to Bangladesh Bank thus had implications extending far beyond that specific incident to the broader question of whether the international system could effectively constrain state-sponsored cybercrime or whether such operations would proliferate as states recognized opportunities and faced limited consequences.

## Obstacles in Recovering Funds

The investigation's ultimate objective—beyond understanding what happened and who was responsible—involved recovering the stolen eighty-one million dollars and returning it to Bangladesh Bank. This recovery effort faced obstacles so substantial that, despite years of legal proceedings and international coordination, the majority of stolen funds remained unrecovered, demonstrating painful lessons about the limitations of international law enforcement and the challenges of clawing back successfully laundered money. Understanding why recovery proved so difficult requires examining the legal, jurisdictional, and practical barriers that investigators encountered, the sometimes-conflicting interests of different parties involved in recovery efforts, and the broader reality that modern money laundering techniques, when well-executed, achieve their intended objective of making stolen funds practically irrecoverable.

The jurisdictional fragmentation that complicated the investigation proved even more problematic for recovery efforts, which required not just understanding where money went but actually seizing and repatriating it through legal processes in multiple countries. Philippine law governed most recovery proceedings since the majority of stolen funds had flowed through Manila's banking and casino systems. However, Philippine legal procedures for asset forfeiture differed substantially from those in Bangladesh or the United States, creating situations where actions that would be straightforward in one jurisdiction became complex and time-consuming in another. The Philippine court system, while ultimately cooperative, moved at its own pace based on local procedures and standards of evidence, frustrating Bangladeshi officials who viewed the slow proceedings as inadequate urgency given the scale of the theft and their country's significant losses.

The conversion of stolen funds into cash and their dispersal through casino operations created perhaps the most insurmountable obstacle to comprehensive recovery. Once money laundering operations converted electronic transfers into physical cash carried away from casinos, the trail went cold in ways that made recovery effectively impossible. Physical cash leaves no electronic traces, can be easily transported across borders, and can be spent or invested through transactions that create minimal documentation. Even when investigators strongly suspected that specific individuals had received stolen funds in cash form, proving it to evidentiary standards required for asset seizure proved extraordinarily difficult without cooperation from those individuals—cooperation they had every incentive to withhold. The transformation of digital money into physical assets represented the successful culmination of the laundering operation and the point where recovery efforts faced their greatest challenges.

The limited frozen assets represented only a small fraction of the stolen total, with estimates suggesting perhaps fifteen to twenty million dollars successfully frozen across various accounts and assets in the Philippines and elsewhere. Even these partial successes faced legal challenges, with account holders and their attorneys contesting seizure attempts, claiming that funds were legitimate business proceeds or gambling winnings rather than stolen money. Philippine courts needed to weigh evidence that funds were traceable to the Bangladesh Bank theft against property rights protections and due process requirements for individuals claiming legitimate ownership. These legal proceedings extended over months and years, with frozen assets remaining inaccessible to Bangladesh Bank during extended litigation even when eventual recovery seemed likely.

The question of priority among competing claims on recovered funds created additional complications. Bangladesh Bank, as the direct victim, claimed obvious entitlement to recovered money. However, other parties argued for claims—RCBC suggested it had been victimized by the money laundering operation and deserved compensation for reputational damage and regulatory sanctions it faced. Some individuals caught up in the scandal argued they were unwitting pawns who should be compensated for assets seized despite their claims of legitimate ownership. Philippine authorities suggested that funds recovered within their jurisdiction might be subject to penalties or forfeiture under local laws before any repatriation to Bangladesh. Sorting out these competing claims required additional legal proceedings that further delayed actual recovery and distribution of whatever funds could be seized.

The practical challenges of proving that specific assets represented stolen Bangladesh Bank funds—rather than legitimate wealth that happened to exist in the same institutions and timeframes—created evidentiary burdens that complicated recovery even in cases where common sense suggested obvious connections. Asset forfeiture and recovery typically require proving by clear legal standards that specific assets are traceable to criminal activity. When money has passed through multiple accounts, been commingled with other funds, converted between electronic and physical forms, and distributed across multiple individuals and entities, establishing the chain of custody for specific dollars or assets becomes extraordinarily challenging. Defense attorneys exploited these evidentiary challenges, arguing that prosecutors had failed to conclusively prove that their clients' specific assets were traceable to the theft rather than representing legitimate funds that happened to move through similar channels at similar times.

International cooperation on asset recovery, while more developed than in previous decades, remained inadequate for the scale and complexity of the Bangladesh Bank case. Repatriating seized funds from one country to another requires formal legal assistance, bilateral agreements, and procedures that ensure compliance with both countries' laws while protecting the rights of all parties involved. These procedures, designed for legitimate purposes of ensuring due process and preventing abuse, created substantial delays between when funds were frozen and when they could actually be returned to Bangladesh. Some frozen assets remained in legal limbo years after the theft, with proceedings continuing through Philippine courts while Bangladesh Bank struggled to maintain institutional memory and sustained attention to recovery efforts even as personnel changed and immediate crisis faded into historical incident.

The role of attorneys and legal expenses in consuming portions of recovered funds represented an unfortunate but inevitable aspect of complex international asset recovery. Bangladesh Bank engaged law firms in multiple countries to pursue recovery, with these firms charging substantial fees for their work. RCBC hired attorneys to defend against claims that it should compensate Bangladesh Bank for its role in facilitating money laundering. Individuals and entities accused of participating in the laundering operation retained defense counsel. Courts appointed administrators to manage frozen assets pending resolution of competing claims. All these legal services consumed resources, with the result that even successful recovery efforts saw portions of recovered funds diverted to legal expenses rather than full restitution to the victim institution. While these expenses were necessary costs of pursuing recovery through legal channels, they represented additional losses from Bangladesh Bank's perspective.

The diminishing returns of continued recovery efforts created difficult decisions about how much additional time, money, and diplomatic capital to invest in pursuing remaining stolen funds. As years passed from the initial theft, the likelihood of recovering additional significant amounts decreased while the costs of continued legal proceedings remained substantial. Bangladesh Bank needed to weigh the expected value of continued recovery efforts against alternative uses for resources and the institutional toll of remaining focused on past trauma rather than moving forward. Some participants in recovery efforts advocated for settlements that would recover partial amounts immediately rather than continuing to pursue maximum recovery through proceedings that might extend indefinitely with uncertain outcomes. These pragmatic calculations competed with justice considerations that questioned whether settling for partial recovery sent the wrong message to criminals about the consequences of successful theft.

## Conclusion

The investigation into the Bangladesh Bank heist represented one of the most comprehensive and technically sophisticated cyber incident responses ever undertaken, mobilizing resources from dozens of agencies and private firms across multiple continents to understand an attack that pushed the boundaries of what the security community had previously observed in financially motivated cyber operations. The FBI's central role in coordinating U.S. involvement, combined with international cooperation that overcame substantial obstacles, demonstrated both the capabilities that law enforcement and intelligence agencies can bring to bear on major cyber incidents and the profound limitations they face when adversaries operate from hostile nations beyond the practical reach of arrest or prosecution. The investigation succeeded admirably in understanding what happened and building a compelling attribution case, but struggled to achieve the ultimate objective of recovering stolen funds and bringing perpetrators to justice.

The forensic analysis of malware discovered on Bangladesh Bank's systems provided crucial technical insights that informed not just this specific investigation but broader understanding of North Korean cyber capabilities and tactics. The detailed mapping of malware functionality, infrastructure, and similarities to other incidents contributed to a growing body of knowledge about Lazarus Group operations that has helped the cybersecurity community detect and respond to subsequent attacks. The technical documentation produced through this forensic work continues to serve as reference material for security professionals and threat intelligence analysts working to defend against similar threats. However, the sophistication of the malware and the attackers' operational security also demonstrated the substantial capabilities that well-resourced nation-state actors can deploy, raising sobering questions about whether even sophisticated defenses can reliably prevent determined, patient adversaries from eventually succeeding in compromise.

The attribution to North Korea, while controversial in some quarters and vehemently denied by the regime, represented a significant development in cyber threat intelligence and international response to state-sponsored cybercrime. The public attribution, backed by technical evidence and intelligence community assessments, established a precedent for naming states responsible for cyber operations and attempting to impose costs for such behavior through diplomatic pressure and sanctions. However, the limited impact of these responses on North Korean behavior—the regime continued conducting cyber operations despite attribution and sanctions—highlighted gaps in deterrence and the challenges of modifying state behavior when adversaries face limited practical consequences for cyber aggression. The Bangladesh Bank case became part of a broader pattern where attribution proved achievable but effective response remained elusive.

The obstacles to fund recovery illustrated perhaps the most frustrating dimension of sophisticated financial cybercrime: successful money laundering, despite leaving extensive evidence, achieves its objective of converting stolen electronic funds into assets beyond victims' reach. The partial recovery of perhaps twenty percent of the stolen amount represented meaningful success in limiting losses but profound failure in making the victim whole. The majority of the eighty-one million dollars remained beyond recovery years after the theft, successfully converted into cash, assets, or other forms that moved beyond the reach of international law enforcement. This reality provides sobering context for cybersecurity's limitations—preventing compromise proves crucial because recovery after successful theft and laundering remains extraordinarily difficult regardless of how much is known about what happened and who was responsible.

As we move forward to examine the broader implications and lessons learned from the Bangladesh Bank heist, the investigation phase provides essential context for understanding both what the international community can accomplish in responding to sophisticated cyber threats and where critical gaps remain that adversaries continue to exploit. The technical capabilities demonstrated in the investigation were impressive, the international cooperation achieved despite substantial obstacles was commendable, and the attribution developed through comprehensive analysis was convincing. Yet the limited recovery and the continuation of North Korean cyber operations despite attribution and sanctions suggested that the international framework for responding to state-sponsored cybercrime requires fundamental strengthening if it is to effectively deter, prevent, and punish such attacks. The investigation answered the questions of what happened and who was responsible with impressive thoroughness, but struggled to answer the more important question of what could be done about it in ways that would prevent similar incidents in the future.

# Chapter 8: Global Wake-Up Call

The Bangladesh Bank heist sent shockwaves through the global financial community not merely because of the audacity of the theft or the sophistication of the technical execution, but because it shattered a fundamental assumption that had underpinned international banking for decades: that the SWIFT network, the secure backbone connecting thousands of financial institutions worldwide, represented an impregnable fortress against sophisticated cyber attacks. The revelation that determined adversaries could compromise SWIFT-connected systems, manipulate transaction flows, and steal tens of millions of dollars exposed vulnerabilities that no financial institution could afford to ignore. What followed represented one of the most comprehensive security transformations in banking history, as SWIFT itself underwent fundamental architecture changes, individual banks reassessed and upgraded their defenses, and the entire industry grappled with the sobering recognition that the threat landscape had evolved beyond what existing security measures could adequately address. This chapter examines how the global financial community responded to its wake-up call, implementing sweeping changes that reshaped how institutions approach cybersecurity, how they verify transactions, and how they prepare for the inevitable reality that determined attackers will continue probing for weaknesses. The transformation came at enormous cost and required cultural shifts that challenged institutional inertia, but the alternative—continuing with security postures proven inadequate—was simply unacceptable in a world where cyber threats to financial stability had moved from theoretical concerns to demonstrated realities.

## SWIFT's Security Overhaul

The Society for Worldwide Interbank Financial Telecommunication faced an existential crisis in the wake of the Bangladesh Bank heist, with the compromise threatening the trust and confidence that formed the foundation of its entire operation. SWIFT had built its reputation over forty-plus years as the secure, reliable backbone of international financial messaging, facilitating trillions of dollars in daily transactions among more than eleven thousand member institutions across two hundred countries. The revelation that attackers had successfully manipulated SWIFT-connected systems to execute fraudulent transfers struck at the heart of this value proposition, raising uncomfortable questions about whether the network's security architecture remained adequate for the modern threat environment. The organization's response needed to be swift, comprehensive, and convincing—demonstrating to skeptical member institutions and nervous regulators that SWIFT understood the severity of the challenge and was implementing fundamental improvements rather than cosmetic adjustments. What emerged was the Customer Security Program, a multi-year initiative that represented the most significant security transformation in SWIFT's history.

The immediate response focused on information sharing and threat intelligence, recognizing that the Bangladesh Bank compromise was not an isolated incident but potentially represented one visible example of a broader attack campaign. SWIFT established enhanced mechanisms for sharing indicators of compromise, attack patterns, and security best practices among member institutions. The organization created new communication channels specifically dedicated to security alerts, ensuring that when one institution detected suspicious activity or discovered evidence of attempted compromise, that intelligence could rapidly disseminate to other potentially targeted members. This information sharing represented a cultural shift for an organization and industry that had historically treated security incidents as sensitive matters to be handled discreetly rather than openly discussed. The recognition that shared threat intelligence benefited all institutions by enabling collective defense overcame traditional reticence about acknowledging vulnerabilities.

The Customer Security Program introduced mandatory security controls that SWIFT required all member institutions to implement as conditions of continued network access. These controls addressed the fundamental vulnerabilities that the Bangladesh Bank attack had exploited—inadequate network segmentation between SWIFT infrastructure and general banking networks, insufficient monitoring of SWIFT transaction activity, weak authentication mechanisms, and inadequate security update and patch management. The mandatory controls represented a significant assertion of SWIFT's authority over member institutions' internal security practices, moving beyond the organization's traditional role as a messaging service provider to become, in effect, an enforcer of minimum security standards across the global financial system. This expansion of role proved controversial, with some institutions resisting what they viewed as overreach into their sovereign security decisions, but the alternative—maintaining a purely advisory stance after a catastrophic breach—proved untenable.

The Customer Security Program established a tiered framework of security controls—mandatory requirements that all institutions must implement, and advisory controls representing best practices that SWIFT strongly recommended but did not absolutely require. The mandatory controls focused on fundamental security hygiene: secure network configuration isolating SWIFT infrastructure from less-trusted systems, comprehensive logging and monitoring of all SWIFT-related activity, multi-factor authentication for system access, regular security assessments and vulnerability scanning, and timely implementation of security patches and updates. These requirements, while basic from a cybersecurity perspective, represented substantial improvements over practices at many smaller or less sophisticated institutions where resource constraints and competing priorities had resulted in security gaps that sophisticated attackers could exploit. The advisory controls addressed more advanced security practices like threat intelligence integration, security operations center capabilities, and incident response procedures that larger institutions might implement but that SWIFT recognized were beyond the capabilities of smaller members.

The attestation and assessment framework that SWIFT implemented to verify compliance with security controls represented another significant innovation, creating accountability mechanisms where none had previously existed. Institutions were required to annually assess their compliance with mandatory security controls and attest to SWIFT that they had implemented required measures. Independent third-party assessments became mandatory for larger institutions, with qualified security firms conducting audits that verified claimed compliance. SWIFT reserved the right to disconnect institutions from the network for persistent non-compliance, though this ultimate sanction was applied cautiously given the disruption that cutting off financial institutions from international messaging would cause. The attestation framework transformed security from an internal institutional matter into a shared responsibility with external verification and potential consequences for failure.

The technical architecture enhancements that SWIFT implemented focused on providing better visibility into transaction patterns and enabling more sophisticated anomaly detection. The organization developed new tools that allowed institutions to establish baseline patterns for their normal SWIFT activity and receive alerts when transactions deviated from expected norms. These behavioral monitoring capabilities complemented traditional security controls by addressing the reality that sophisticated attackers who successfully compromise authentication mechanisms might generate technically valid but operationally suspicious transactions. Enhanced reporting capabilities gave institutions more comprehensive visibility into their SWIFT activity, making it harder for attackers to hide fraudulent transactions within legitimate message flows. The SWIFT network itself implemented additional monitoring for patterns consistent with known attack techniques, providing a network-level defense layer that complemented individual institutions' security measures.

The Customer Security Program's implementation timeline reflected the enormous scale of transforming security practices across thousands of institutions in dozens of countries with vastly different capabilities and starting points. SWIFT established multi-year roadmaps with progressive implementation milestones, recognizing that smaller institutions or those in developing markets would need time to acquire resources, develop capabilities, and implement required controls. The organization provided substantial support resources—technical guidance, implementation toolkits, training programs, and forums for institutions to share implementation experiences and solutions to common challenges. Despite this support, implementation proved challenging and uneven, with sophisticated institutions in developed markets generally adapting more quickly while smaller or less-resourced institutions struggled with the technical and financial demands of compliance. The variation in implementation pace created ongoing security gaps that SWIFT and regulators continued addressing years after the initial program launch.

The governance changes that accompanied the Customer Security Program strengthened SWIFT's organizational focus on security as a core institutional priority rather than a supporting function. The organization elevated security leadership within its management structure, created new security-focused roles and teams, and substantially increased investment in security technology, personnel, and programs. SWIFT's board of directors, composed of representatives from member institutions, received regular security briefings and maintained active oversight of the Customer Security Program's implementation. This governance elevation reflected recognition that security had become essential to SWIFT's value proposition and that inadequate security would ultimately threaten the organization's viability as the trusted backbone of international finance. The cultural transformation within SWIFT—from viewing security primarily through an operational risk lens to recognizing it as existential to the organization's mission—represented as significant a change as the technical and procedural enhancements.

## Banking Industry Responses Worldwide

The banking industry's response to the Bangladesh Bank heist extended far beyond compliance with SWIFT's new security requirements to encompass fundamental reassessment of cybersecurity strategies, substantial increases in security investment, and recognition that cyber threats represented risks requiring board-level attention and enterprise-wide response capabilities. Financial institutions worldwide recognized that the Bangladesh Bank compromise demonstrated vulnerabilities that existed throughout the industry—the specific techniques might vary, but the fundamental challenge of defending complex systems against determined, sophisticated adversaries was universal. What followed was a period of intense security enhancement across the global banking sector, with institutions racing to identify and remediate vulnerabilities before attackers exploited them. The response varied dramatically across institutions and regions, reflecting differences in capabilities, resources, and threat perceptions, but the overall trajectory pointed toward substantially elevated security investment and capabilities across the industry.

Large multinational banks with sophisticated security capabilities used the Bangladesh Bank incident as justification for security investments they had been advocating but struggling to fund through normal budget processes. The demonstrated reality of successful attacks on SWIFT systems provided the compelling business case that security teams needed to secure executive and board approval for substantial security budget increases. These institutions conducted comprehensive assessments of their SWIFT security posture, implemented enhanced monitoring and detection capabilities, strengthened network segmentation, and deployed additional security personnel focused specifically on protecting payment systems. Many large banks had already maintained relatively sophisticated security programs, but the Bangladesh Bank wake-up call enabled acceleration of planned improvements and initiation of new programs. that might otherwise have faced budgetary resistance. The incident demonstrated that cybersecurity spending represented not optional IT costs but essential investments in operational resilience and risk management.

Regional and mid-sized banks faced more substantial challenges in responding to elevated security requirements, often lacking the in-house expertise, dedicated security staff, or technology infrastructure that larger institutions had developed over years of investment. These institutions needed to rapidly build capabilities that their larger counterparts had developed gradually, creating challenges in recruiting scarce cybersecurity talent, selecting and implementing appropriate technologies, and developing organizational competencies in security operations. Many turned to managed security service providers, outsourcing threat monitoring, incident response, and security operations center functions to specialized firms that could provide capabilities that smaller institutions couldn't economically develop internally. Others formed collaborative partnerships with peer institutions, sharing security intelligence, best practices, and sometimes even security services through consortiums that allowed cost-sharing and collective capability development. The challenge for these mid-tier institutions involved achieving adequate security without incurring costs that would threaten their competitive position or financial viability.

Banks in developing markets faced particularly acute challenges in responding to the heightened security requirements that the Bangladesh Bank incident triggered. Many institutions in these markets operated with limited technology budgets, often running legacy systems that were difficult to secure, and served customer bases where advanced security features like multi-factor authentication faced adoption challenges due to limited digital literacy or technology access. The cost of implementing SWIFT's mandatory security controls represented substantial investments for institutions with limited resources and competing priorities around basic banking infrastructure, regulatory compliance, and service expansion. Some institutions in developing markets struggled to find qualified security personnel in local labor markets where cybersecurity expertise remained scarce, forcing difficult decisions about whether to recruit expensive international expertise or attempt to develop internal capabilities despite limited starting points. The result was uneven security enhancement across developing market institutions, with the most sophisticated achieving compliance relatively quickly while others struggled for years to meet minimum requirements.

The industry's collective response included development of new security standards, frameworks, and best practice guidance through various financial services industry organizations and regulators. The Financial Services Information Sharing and Analysis Center enhanced its threat intelligence sharing among member institutions, distributing indicators of compromise related to the Bangladesh Bank attack and subsequent similar incidents. Industry working groups developed guidance on secure SWIFT implementation, payment system security, and detection of sophisticated financial fraud. Regulatory agencies in major financial centers issued security guidance or requirements that complemented SWIFT's customer security program, ensuring that institutions under their supervision met minimum security standards regardless of their specific SWIFT compliance status. This ecosystem of overlapping requirements, standards, and guidance created a comprehensive web of security expectations that reinforced SWIFT's initiatives and extended security enhancements beyond just SWIFT-connected systems to broader payment and banking infrastructure.

The response also encompassed significant investment in security workforce development, recognizing that technology alone couldn't address the cybersecurity challenge without skilled personnel to operate security systems, analyze threats, and respond to incidents. Financial institutions expanded recruitment of cybersecurity professionals, often competing intensely for limited talent and driving significant salary increases in security roles. Many institutions developed internal training programs to up-skill existing IT personnel into security roles, recognizing that growing their own talent might be more sustainable than competing in tight external labor markets. Industry partnerships with universities and training organizations aimed to develop curriculum and programs that would produce more cybersecurity graduates with relevant financial services knowledge. The workforce challenge proved particularly acute because the Bangladesh Bank incident occurred during a broader surge in cybersecurity staffing needs across all industries, creating a competitive talent market where financial services competed with technology companies, consulting firms, and other industries for the same limited pool of qualified candidates.

The cultural transformation within banking regarding cybersecurity proved as significant as technical and procedural changes. The Bangladesh Bank heist demonstrated that cybersecurity was not merely an IT concern but a fundamental business risk requiring executive leadership and board oversight. Financial institutions elevated cyber risk within enterprise risk management frameworks, establishing cybersecurity as a standing board agenda item and creating executive-level roles focused on information security and cyber resilience. This cultural shift acknowledged that defending against sophisticated cyber threats required organization-wide commitment rather than delegating responsibility to IT departments, and that business leaders needed to understand cyber risks even if they lacked technical expertise. The elevation of cybersecurity to strategic business priority represented a fundamental change from previous eras when security was viewed primarily as a technical or operational concern rather than an executive-level responsibility.

## New Protocols and Verification Systems

The Bangladesh Bank heist exposed critical gaps in transaction verification and approval processes that had evolved during an era when the primary fraud risks involved insiders with legitimate access rather than external attackers who could compromise authentication systems and generate seemingly legitimate transaction instructions. The successful execution of thirty-five fraudulent SWIFT messages demonstrated that authentication alone provided inadequate security when sophisticated attackers could compromise the systems that generated authenticated messages. What was needed were additional verification layers that could detect fraudulent transactions even when they passed authentication checks—systems that analyzed transaction patterns, verified business logic, and implemented multi-party approval requirements that made it substantially harder for compromised systems or insiders to execute unauthorized transfers. The development and implementation of these enhanced verification protocols represented a fundamental rethinking of how financial institutions validate that payment instructions represent legitimate business transactions rather than fraud or error.

Multi-party authorization requirements emerged as a cornerstone of enhanced verification protocols, implementing the principle that no single individual or compromised system should possess sufficient authority to execute large-value transactions independently. Institutions implemented requirements that large transfers above certain thresholds require approval from multiple authorized personnel, with approvers operating from different systems and ideally different physical locations to prevent compromise of a single system from bypassing controls. These multi-party requirements extended beyond simple dual authorization to encompass more sophisticated approval workflows where different parties verify different aspects of transactions—one person confirming that the recipient is a known business partner, another verifying that the transaction amount and purpose match expected business activity, still another reviewing the transaction against fraud indicators and patterns. The enhanced authorization requirements created friction in transaction processing, slowing down what had been relatively streamlined procedures, but institutions generally accepted this trade-off as necessary to prevent fraudulent transactions from executing with only compromised single-party approval.

Behavioral analysis and anomaly detection systems provided automated verification that complemented human approval processes by identifying transactions that deviated from established patterns even when they carried proper authentication and authorization. These systems analyzed historical transaction data to establish baselines for normal activity—typical transaction sizes, common recipients, standard processing times, usual geographic patterns—and flagged deviations for additional review before allowing transactions to process. Machine learning algorithms enhanced these systems' sophistication, identifying subtle patterns and correlations that rule-based systems might miss while reducing false positives that had plagued earlier anomaly detection attempts. The behavioral monitoring addressed a fundamental limitation of authentication-based security: that compromised credentials or systems could generate technically valid but operationally suspicious transactions that traditional security controls would pass through without question.

Out-of-band verification protocols required that transaction approvals for large or unusual transfers be confirmed through communication channels separate from the systems used to generate the transactions themselves. An institution receiving a SWIFT message directing a large transfer might require telephone confirmation through pre-established contact numbers, verification through alternative electronic messaging systems, or even in-person confirmation for especially large transactions. These out-of-band requirements created defense against attackers who had compromised primary transaction systems but lacked access to all communication channels that the institution used for verification. The protocols proved particularly valuable when correspondent banks received unusual transaction instructions from client institutions, enabling them to verify instructions without relying solely on the potentially compromised SWIFT channel. Implementation challenges included maintaining current contact information, managing verification processes across time zones and languages, and balancing security with operational efficiency when rapid transaction processing remained important for business purposes.

Transaction monitoring systems evolved from primarily focusing on anti-money laundering and sanctions compliance to incorporating fraud detection capabilities specifically designed to identify patterns consistent with cyber attack-enabled theft. These enhanced monitoring systems analyzed transaction flows for indicators that funds might be moving through money laundering channels—rapid distribution to multiple recipients, transfers to jurisdictions with weak regulatory oversight, payments to entities whose business profiles didn't match transaction patterns. The systems incorporated threat intelligence about specific fraud schemes and money laundering techniques observed in the Bangladesh Bank case and subsequent similar incidents. Real-time monitoring enabled institutions to potentially freeze suspicious transactions before they fully cleared rather than discovering fraud only during after-the-fact reconciliation. The enhanced monitoring required sophisticated analytics capabilities, substantial data processing infrastructure, and skilled analysts who could investigate alerts and make timely decisions about whether to block suspicious transactions.

Reconciliation procedures received enhanced attention following the discovery that Bangladesh Bank's reconciliation processes had failed to detect fraudulent transactions for hours after they executed. Institutions implemented more frequent reconciliation cycles, enhanced automated reconciliation tools that flagged discrepancies more quickly, and stronger controls ensuring that reconciliation was performed by personnel independent from those executing transactions. The recognition that attackers had manipulated confirmation messages and altered records to hide fraudulent transactions drove improvements in reconciliation systems' security and the integrity verification of data used for reconciliation. Some institutions implemented continuous reconciliation that verified account balances and transaction logs in near-real-time rather than waiting for end-of-day or end-of-week batch processes. These enhanced reconciliation procedures served as a last line of defense, providing opportunity to detect fraud that had bypassed authentication, authorization, and monitoring controls.

The implementation of enhanced verification protocols required substantial changes to operational procedures, technology systems, and personnel training. Institutions needed to redesign approval workflows, implement new software systems to support multi-party authorization and behavioral monitoring, integrate new verification requirements into existing transaction processing infrastructure, and train staff on new procedures and their security rationale. The operational impact proved significant, with enhanced verification adding time and complexity to transaction processing that had previously been relatively streamlined. Business units sometimes resisted additional verification requirements as creating unnecessary friction and slowing legitimate transactions, requiring security teams to balance fraud prevention against operational efficiency. The most successful implementations involved security and business teams collaborating to design verification protocols that provided necessary security while minimizing unnecessary operational impact—focusing enhanced verification on high-risk transactions while allowing more streamlined processing for routine payments that posed minimal fraud risk.

## The Cost of Upgrading Security

The transformation of financial sector cybersecurity following the Bangladesh Bank heist came with an enormous price tag that institutions across the industry struggled to quantify comprehensively but that clearly reached into the billions of dollars collectively. Understanding the true cost required looking beyond obvious technology purchases to encompass personnel expenses, operational impacts, opportunity costs, and the ongoing nature of security investment that never truly completes but rather continues indefinitely as threats evolve. For individual institutions, security upgrade costs varied dramatically based on starting points, institutional size and complexity, and regulatory jurisdiction requirements. Some sophisticated large banks that had already maintained strong security programs faced relatively modest incremental costs to comply with enhanced requirements. Other institutions, particularly smaller or less technologically advanced banks, faced security investments that represented substantial percentages of their annual technology budgets and required multi-year implementation programs. to achieve compliance without overwhelming their operational capabilities.

Technology infrastructure investments represented the most visible component of security upgrade costs, encompassing purchases of security tools, systems, and platforms needed to meet enhanced requirements. Institutions acquired or upgraded firewalls, intrusion detection and prevention systems, security information and event management platforms, endpoint protection solutions, network access control systems, and numerous other security technologies. Many institutions implemented security operations center capabilities if they lacked them, requiring substantial technology investments in monitoring platforms, threat intelligence feeds, case management systems, and supporting infrastructure. Network segmentation requirements drove costs for institutions that needed to redesign network architectures, install additional network equipment, and reconfigure connectivity to properly isolate SWIFT infrastructure from less-trusted systems. For some institutions, meeting enhanced security requirements necessitated wholesale replacement of legacy systems that could not be adequately secured, driving costs far beyond incremental security tool purchases into fundamental infrastructure modernization.

Personnel costs for security upgrades encompassed both recruiting new security staff and training existing personnel on new systems and procedures. The competitive market for cybersecurity talent drove significant salary increases, with institutions competing intensely for skilled professionals in security operations, threat intelligence, incident response, and specialized domains like payment system security. Many institutions created entirely new security roles—chief information security officers at institutions that previously lacked executive security leadership, security operations center analysts, threat hunters, security architects, and compliance personnel focused on security standard adherence. Training costs included not just security personnel but also broader workforce education on security awareness, recognizing that sophisticated social engineering attacks required that all employees understand basic security principles and their role in institutional defense. Ongoing personnel costs extended indefinitely, as security teams required continuous training to maintain skills against evolving threats and institutions faced ongoing recruiting and retention costs in competitive talent markets.

Compliance and assessment costs became significant line items as institutions needed to demonstrate adherence to SWIFT's mandatory security controls and various regulatory requirements. Third-party security assessments by qualified firms represented recurring expenses, with annual audits costing substantial amounts especially for larger, more complex institutions. Internal compliance programs required dedicated staff to manage assessment processes, coordinate with external auditors, track control implementation, and report to SWIFT and regulators on security posture. Some institutions engaged consulting firms to help design security enhancements, develop implementation roadmaps, and provide expertise that they lacked internally. The consulting and professional services costs proved particularly significant for institutions with limited internal security expertise that needed substantial external support to understand requirements, design appropriate solutions, and implement complex security programs.

Operational costs from enhanced security procedures impacted institutions in ways that were difficult to quantify precisely but nonetheless real and ongoing. Additional verification requirements and approval workflows added processing time to transactions, requiring more staff hours and potentially creating customer service challenges when payment processing slowed. The friction that enhanced security introduced into operational processes sometimes required business process redesign, additional staffing, or technology investments to maintain operational throughput despite enhanced security controls. Some institutions experienced temporary or ongoing business disruption during security implementation, with system changes requiring maintenance windows, testing periods, or phased rollouts that impacted normal operations. The opportunity costs of security investment—representing alternative uses for capital and personnel resources that were instead directed toward security—remained largely invisible but nonetheless significant, especially for institutions where security investments crowded out other strategic initiatives or technology modernization efforts.

The varying costs across different types of institutions created equity concerns and competitive implications within the banking industry. Large multinational banks, while facing the highest absolute costs due to their scale and complexity, generally possessed resources to absorb security investments without threatening their competitive position or financial stability. These institutions could amortize security costs across large customer bases and transaction volumes, making per-transaction security costs manageable. Smaller and mid-sized banks faced more challenging cost dynamics, with security investments representing substantially larger percentages of their overall budgets and potentially requiring difficult trade-offs against other priorities. Institutions in developing markets often struggled most acutely with security investment costs, facing requirements calibrated to global standards while operating in markets where fee structures, customer bases, and revenue models made absorbing substantial security costs particularly challenging. The disparate impact of security costs raised questions about whether enhanced requirements might inadvertently drive consolidation in banking, with smaller institutions unable to economically meet security standards potentially forced to merge with larger banks or exit certain businesses.

The ongoing nature of security investment meant that the costs of responding to the Bangladesh Bank wake-up call extended far beyond initial implementation to encompass perpetual security operations, continuous improvement, and adaptation to evolving threats. Security was not a one-time project with defined completion but rather an ongoing operational requirement that would continue consuming resources indefinitely. Threat landscapes evolved continuously, requiring that institutions regularly update security tools, refresh threat intelligence, adjust monitoring rules, and implement new controls as new attack techniques emerged. Technology depreciation and refresh cycles meant that security infrastructure investments made in response to Bangladesh Bank would require replacement and upgrading on regular schedules. Personnel costs would continue and likely grow as institutions competed to retain security talent in competitive markets. The perpetual nature of security investment created challenges for budgeting and resource allocation, requiring that institutions commit to sustained security spending rather than treating it as a temporary response to a specific incident.

## Lessons from Bangladesh

The Bangladesh Bank heist provided painful but invaluable lessons that extended far beyond the immediate victims to inform cybersecurity practices, risk management approaches, and strategic thinking across the global financial sector and indeed across all industries dependent on digital systems for critical operations. The incident served as a masterclass in what sophisticated attackers could accomplish when organizations failed to implement adequate security controls, and equally as a case study in how swift organizational and industry response could mitigate future risks even after catastrophic breaches demonstrated vulnerabilities. Understanding these lessons required looking beyond surface-level observations about specific technical failures to examine deeper patterns about organizational security culture, the challenges of securing complex global systems, and the evolution of threats that continue accelerating ahead of defensive capabilities. The lessons learned proved sufficiently important that the Bangladesh Bank case became required study in cybersecurity training programs, executive risk management education, and banking security professional development worldwide.

The fundamental lesson about defense in depth emphasized that no single security control, however sophisticated, provides adequate protection against determined adversaries. Bangladesh Bank's compromise succeeded despite SWIFT system authentication because attackers breached the underlying systems that generated authenticated messages, demonstrating that authentication only provides security when the systems performing authentication remain trustworthy. The lesson drove home the necessity of layered security controls where compromise of any single layer doesn't result in total security failure. Effective defense required combining network security, endpoint protection, access controls, monitoring and detection, incident response capabilities, and organizational processes in ways that created multiple opportunities to prevent, detect, or respond to attacks. The concept of assuming breach—designing security architectures on the assumption that adversaries will eventually penetrate perimeter defenses—gained renewed emphasis following Bangladesh Bank, with institutions focusing more attention on detection and response capabilities that could identify and contain breaches before they culminated in catastrophic damage.

The importance of security basics emerged as another crucial lesson, with the Bangladesh Bank compromise succeeding partly because fundamental security hygiene had been inadequate. The attackers exploited missing security patches, poor network segmentation, insufficient monitoring, and weak access controls—not sophisticated zero-day vulnerabilities but rather well-known security weaknesses that proper security practices should have addressed. The lesson challenged the tendency to focus security investment on advanced technologies while neglecting fundamentals, demonstrating that sophisticated attackers readily exploit basic security failures when they exist. Institutions learned that before implementing cutting-edge threat intelligence platforms or advanced behavioral analytics, they needed to ensure fundamentals were solid—systems patched regularly, networks properly segmented, access appropriately controlled, logging comprehensive, and monitoring actually reviewed and acted upon. The unglamorous work of security hygiene proved more important than exotic security technologies in preventing the majority of breaches.

The lesson about third-party and supply chain risk highlighted that institutional security depends not just on internal practices but on the security of every connected partner, vendor, and service provider. While Bangladesh Bank's compromise occurred on their own systems, the broader pattern of financial sector attacks included incidents where attackers compromised smaller institutions or service providers as stepping stones to larger targets. The interconnected nature of financial services meant that institutions were only as secure as their weakest connection, requiring that security programs extend beyond organizational boundaries to encompass third-party risk management, vendor security assessment, and supply chain security verification. The lesson drove increased attention to third-party security requirements, with institutions implementing more rigorous vendor security assessments, contractual security requirements, and ongoing monitoring of partner security postures.

The critical importance of incident detection and response capabilities became painfully clear through Bangladesh Bank's delayed discovery of the breach, with fraudulent transactions executing for hours before detection and successful money laundering occurring partly because response was too slow to freeze assets before they dispersed. The lesson emphasized that prevention, while important, would never be perfect against sophisticated adversaries, making rapid detection and effective response equally critical components of security programs. Institutions learned they needed to invest in security operations center capabilities, develop incident response plans and teams, conduct regular response exercises, and establish relationships with law enforcement and external experts before incidents occurred. The ability to quickly detect anomalies, investigate alerts, make decisions about suspicious activity, and coordinate response across organizational boundaries proved as important as preventing initial compromise.

The organizational and cultural dimensions of cybersecurity emerged as lessons equal in importance to technical controls. Bangladesh Bank's security failures stemmed partly from organizational culture where security was viewed as IT's responsibility rather than an enterprise-wide priority, where security staff lacked authority and resources to implement necessary controls, and where business pressures to maintain operational efficiency overrode security considerations. The lesson drove recognition that effective security required executive and board-level leadership, adequate resources and authority for security programs, and organizational cultures where security was everyone's responsibility rather than relegated to a single department. The incident demonstrated that institutions couldn't simply purchase security but needed to build security-conscious organizational cultures where personnel at all levels understood risks, recognized their roles in defense, and prioritized security alongside other business objectives.

The lesson about international cooperation and information sharing highlighted both the necessity and the challenges of collective defense against sophisticated cyber threats. The banking industry's relatively slow recognition that Bangladesh Bank represented one incident in a broader campaign of similar attacks demonstrated the costs of inadequate information sharing about threats and breaches. Institutions learned that sharing threat intelligence, indicators of compromise, and incident details benefited the entire financial sector by enabling collective defense against common adversaries. However, the lesson also revealed challenges in information sharing—concerns about reputational damage, legal liabilities, regulatory consequences, and competitive implications that made institutions reluctant to disclose breaches even when sharing information would benefit others. The balance between protecting institutional interests and contributing to collective security remained an ongoing challenge that industry organizations, regulators, and institutions themselves continued working to address through trust frameworks, legal protections for information sharing, and cultural change emphasizing that acknowledging and sharing breach information represented responsible behavior rather than embarrassing failure.

The geopolitical dimensions of cyber threats constituted a lesson that extended beyond cybersecurity technology to encompass national security strategy and international relations. The attribution to North Korea transformed Bangladesh Bank from a crime story to a national security incident, demonstrating that financial institutions faced not just criminal threats but state-sponsored adversaries with substantial capabilities and potential immunity from prosecution. The lesson drove recognition that defending critical financial infrastructure required not just institutional security measures but also government involvement in threat intelligence, diplomatic responses to state-sponsored attacks, and potentially cyber deterrence strategies that would impose costs on nations conducting cyber attacks against financial systems. The incident contributed to broader policy discussions about cyber norms, appropriate responses to state-sponsored cyber attacks, and the role of financial sanctions and other diplomatic tools in addressing nation-state cyber threats.

## Conclusion

The global response to the Bangladesh Bank heist represented one of the most comprehensive security transformation efforts in financial services history, touching every aspect of how institutions approached cybersecurity from technical controls to organizational culture to industry cooperation. SWIFT's Customer Security Program and the broader industry's security enhancements substantially improved the defensive posture of financial institutions worldwide, implementing mandatory security controls, enhancing monitoring and detection capabilities, and elevating cybersecurity to strategic priority status deserving executive and board attention. The transformation came at enormous cost measured in billions of dollars across the industry, with institutions making substantial investments in technology, personnel, processes, and ongoing security operations that would continue indefinitely as threats evolved.

The uneven nature of security enhancement across institutions and regions remained a concern, with sophisticated banks in developed markets generally achieving strong security postures while smaller and less-resourced institutions continued struggling to meet enhanced requirements. The financial sector's security posture improved substantially but not uniformly, creating ongoing risks that sophisticated adversaries might identify and exploit lagging institutions as paths to broader financial system compromise. The challenge of maintaining and continuously improving security in the face of evolving threats meant that the work initiated in response to Bangladesh Bank would never truly complete but rather require perpetual attention and investment.

The protocols and verification systems implemented following Bangladesh Bank addressed critical gaps that the heist had exposed, adding multiple layers of verification and control that made successful fraud substantially more difficult. Multi-party authorization, behavioral analysis, out-of-band verification, enhanced monitoring, and improved reconciliation created defense in depth that could detect fraudulent transactions even when attackers successfully compromised authentication systems. However, these enhanced protocols came with operational costs and complexity that institutions continued working to optimize, seeking the right balance between security and operational efficiency that protected against fraud without unnecessarily impeding legitimate business.

The lessons learned from Bangladesh Bank influenced cybersecurity thinking across industries beyond just financial services, demonstrating that sophisticated adversaries could compromise even secure systems through patient operation and exploitation of basic security weaknesses. The emphasis on security fundamentals, defense in depth, rapid detection and response, organizational culture, and international cooperation proved applicable far beyond banking to any sector dependent on digital systems for critical operations. The incident became a defining case study in cybersecurity education and professional development, teaching generations of security professionals about sophisticated attacks, effective defenses, and the organizational and international dimensions of cybersecurity beyond purely technical considerations.

As we move forward to examine the regulatory and policy responses that followed the Bangladesh Bank heist, the industry's transformation provides essential context for understanding how institutions, regulators, and policymakers sought to prevent similar incidents while balancing security imperatives against operational efficiency, competitive concerns, and the practical challenges of securing complex global systems against determined adversaries. The wake-up call that Bangladesh Bank provided prompted substantial improvements but also revealed continuing challenges and gaps that would require ongoing attention. The heist demonstrated both how far institutions had to go in achieving adequate security and how much could be accomplished when the industry collectively recognized the severity of threats and committed resources to addressing them. The transformation represented progress rather than completion, an important step forward in the perpetual challenge of defending critical systems against adversaries who continue evolving their capabilities and seeking new vulnerabilities to exploit.

# Chapter 9: Vulnerabilities Exposed

The Bangladesh Bank heist accomplished something that countless security audits, penetration tests, and threat assessments had failed to achieve: it exposed with brutal clarity the fundamental vulnerabilities that persist across the global financial system despite decades of security investment and increasingly sophisticated defenses. The attack succeeded not through exploitation of exotic zero-day vulnerabilities or deployment of revolutionary new attack techniques, but rather through methodical exploitation of weaknesses that cybersecurity professionals had warned about for years—weaknesses rooted more in human nature, organizational dynamics, and economic trade-offs than in technological limitations. This chapter examines the categories of vulnerability that the Bangladesh Bank case illuminated with painful specificity, exploring why these weaknesses persist despite widespread awareness of the risks they create and what their continued existence reveals about the profound challenges facing any organization attempting to achieve comprehensive security in complex digital environments. Understanding these vulnerabilities requires looking beyond specific technical flaws to examine the deeper structural, psychological, and economic factors that create and perpetuate security gaps even in institutions with strong motivation and substantial resources to defend themselves. The vulnerabilities exposed were not unique to Bangladesh Bank but rather reflected systemic challenges facing the entire financial sector and indeed all organizations dependent on digital infrastructure for critical operations.

## The Human Factor in Cybersecurity

The most persistent and perhaps most exploitable vulnerability in any security system remains the human beings who operate, manage, and interact with technology—individuals whose cognitive limitations, behavioral patterns, and susceptibility to manipulation create security gaps that no amount of technical sophistication can fully eliminate. The Bangladesh Bank attack exploited human vulnerabilities at multiple stages, from initial compromise through phishing and social engineering to delayed detection by personnel who failed to recognize anomalies that should have triggered investigation. Understanding the human factor in cybersecurity requires examining not just isolated mistakes or individual failures but the systematic ways in which human cognition, organizational behavior, and social dynamics create vulnerabilities that sophisticated adversaries understand deeply and exploit ruthlessly. The sobering reality is that humans represent both the ultimate defense against cyber threats and simultaneously the weakest link that attackers most frequently exploit to circumvent technical security controls.

The psychology of security decision-making reveals why even well-intentioned, intelligent individuals make choices that compromise security in ways they would recognize as risky if given time for careful reflection. Cognitive biases shape security-relevant decisions in predictable ways that attackers exploit systematically. Normalcy bias leads individuals to assume that the current moment will resemble the immediate past, making them slow to recognize that unusual patterns might indicate ongoing attacks rather than benign anomalies. This bias contributed to Bangladesh Bank staff initially interpreting suspicious transaction patterns as technical glitches rather than fraud, creating crucial delays before appropriate response began. Optimism bias causes individuals to believe that security threats affect others but not themselves or their organizations, leading to risk underestimation and inadequate security practices. Authority bias makes people more likely to comply with requests from apparent authority figures without sufficient verification, enabling social engineering attacks where adversaries impersonate executives or trusted parties to manipulate targets into compromising security.

The attention and awareness limitations that characterize human cognition create fundamental challenges for security operations that depend on personnel identifying subtle indicators of compromise among vast quantities of normal activity. Security operations center analysts reviewing thousands of alerts daily face inevitable attention fatigue, where the combination of high volume, time pressure, and predominantly false positives degrades their ability to identify the genuine threats hidden among the noise. The challenge mirrors the proverbial needle in a haystack but with the added complication that the haystack continually grows while the analyst's attention and energy deplete. Studies of security operations demonstrate that even highly trained analysts miss indicators of compromise at troubling rates, particularly when those indicators are subtle or when analysts work under conditions of fatigue, stress, or distraction. The human brain simply was not evolved to maintain hyper-vigilance indefinitely while processing large volumes of complex technical data—yet effective security monitoring requires exactly this impossible cognitive feat.

The behavioral patterns and habitual practices that individuals develop around security-relevant activities often prioritize convenience and efficiency over security, creating systematic vulnerabilities even when people intellectually understand risks. Password reuse across multiple accounts remains endemic despite universal security guidance against the practice, driven by the cognitive burden of remembering multiple complex passwords and the friction that strong authentication creates for routine access. The tendency to click links in emails without carefully examining their legitimacy persists despite widespread phishing awareness, as people process hundreds of emails under time pressure and develop automatic response patterns that attackers exploit. The practice of sharing credentials or leaving systems unlocked continues in many organizations, enabled by trust in colleagues and frustration with security procedures that impede workflow. These behavioral vulnerabilities reflect not ignorance or malice but rather the natural human tendency to develop efficient habits that minimize cognitive load and friction—tendencies that security protocols must work with rather than simply trying to override through policy and training.

The social engineering exploitation of interpersonal trust, authority relationships, and helpful impulses represents perhaps the most successful attack vector for compromising human elements of security systems. Sophisticated social engineers understand organizational dynamics, exploit cultural norms around responding to authority or helping colleagues, and craft scenarios where targets feel psychological pressure to comply with requests that compromise security. The Bangladesh Bank compromise likely began with phishing attacks that exploited these psychological principles, presenting scenarios where ignoring the request felt more awkward or risky than complying with it. Social engineering succeeds because it exploits fundamental aspects of human social behavior—the desire to be helpful, the tendency to trust apparently legitimate authority, the discomfort of confrontation, and the cognitive efficiency of making quick decisions based on surface characteristics rather than deep analysis. Training users to resist social engineering requires changing deeply ingrained social behaviors, a challenge far more difficult than implementing technical security controls.

The insider threat dimension of human vulnerability encompasses not just malicious insiders who deliberately compromise security but also the far more common scenario of well-intentioned personnel who inadvertently create security gaps through mistakes, oversights, or shortcuts taken under operational pressure. The vast majority of insider-related security incidents involve no malicious intent but rather human error—clicking the wrong button, misconfiguring a system, falling for a phishing attack, or failing to follow security procedures. These non-malicious insider threats prove particularly challenging to address because they cannot be prevented through background checks or monitoring for suspicious behavior that characterizes approaches to malicious insiders. Instead, addressing inadvertent insider threats requires systems that remain resilient to human error, procedures that reduce cognitive load and opportunities for mistakes, and organizational cultures where individuals feel comfortable reporting errors and near-misses without fear of punishment. The Bangladesh Bank case demonstrated how compromised user credentials enabled the attack, whether through phishing, malware, or other means—highlighting how insider access, even when not maliciously provided, creates vulnerabilities that external attackers exploit.

The challenge of maintaining security awareness and vigilance over time compounds human factor vulnerabilities, as security education and training demonstrate frustrating decay patterns where knowledge and behavioral changes fade without constant reinforcement. Organizations invest substantially in security awareness training, conducting regular sessions that educate personnel about phishing, social engineering, password security, and other fundamental security practices. However, research consistently demonstrates that training effects fade rapidly without reinforcement, with personnel reverting to less secure but more convenient behaviors within weeks or months of training. The forgetting curve for security knowledge proves steep, requiring that training be continuous and reinforced through multiple channels rather than consisting of annual or semi-annual classroom sessions. Moreover, training competes for attention with numerous other priorities, messages, and demands on personnel time and attention, often receiving lower priority than more immediately pressing operational concerns.

The organizational and cultural factors that shape how institutions approach security create systematic human vulnerabilities that transcend individual psychology. Organizations with cultures that prioritize operational efficiency over security create environments where personnel face pressure to circumvent security controls that impede productivity. Security awareness suffers when executives and managers fail to model secure behaviors, sending implicit messages that security policies represent suggestions rather than requirements. The allocation of resources to security versus other priorities reflects organizational values and creates real constraints on what security programs can accomplish. Institutions that treat security primarily as IT's responsibility rather than an organization-wide concern fail to create the distributed defense that sophisticated threats require. The Bangladesh Bank case revealed organizational culture challenges where security apparently lacked sufficient priority, resources, and authority to implement necessary controls—a pattern common across institutions where security must compete for attention and resources against more directly revenue-generating or operationally focused priorities.

## Legacy Systems and Outdated Infrastructure

The technology infrastructure that financial institutions depend upon often combines cutting-edge systems with decades-old legacy technology that predates modern security practices and challenges or completely lacks the security capabilities that current threat environments demand. These legacy systems persist not through preference but through the harsh economic and operational realities that make wholesale replacement extraordinarily expensive, disruptive, and risky when systems support critical business functions. The security implications of legacy infrastructure proved painfully relevant in the Bangladesh Bank case, where older systems and software presented vulnerabilities that sophisticated attackers exploited systematically. Understanding why legacy systems create such profound security challenges requires examining the technical limitations of older platforms, the business constraints that prevent their replacement, and the compromises that organizations make when they must defend technology that was never designed for current threat environments.

The fundamental technical limitations of legacy systems stem from their design during eras when security threats differed dramatically from current realities, when connectivity was limited, and when security was often an afterthought rather than a core design principle. Systems developed in the 1980s or 1990s often lack basic security capabilities that modern platforms include as standard features—capabilities like robust authentication mechanisms, comprehensive logging, encryption for data at rest and in transit, secure update mechanisms, and security monitoring interfaces. These limitations aren't defects that can be patched but rather fundamental architectural characteristics reflecting the assumptions and constraints of their development era. Retrofitting modern security capabilities onto platforms that never anticipated them proves somewhere between extraordinarily difficult and completely impossible, leaving organizations running legacy systems with fundamental security gaps that cannot be fully addressed without wholesale replacement.

The compatibility and integration challenges that legacy systems create compound their direct security limitations, as organizations struggle to connect older platforms that use outdated protocols and interfaces with modern security infrastructure designed for contemporary systems. Security monitoring tools that can comprehensively instrument and analyze modern platforms often provide only partial visibility into legacy systems that don't expose the necessary data or that require custom integration work to connect with security infrastructure. Multifactor authentication systems that can secure access to modern applications may not be compatible with legacy platforms that use older authentication mechanisms. Encryption technologies designed for current systems may not be implementable on legacy platforms without unacceptable performance impacts or compatibility breaks. These integration challenges create security architecture fragmentation where different systems receive inconsistent security controls based on technical capabilities rather than risk-based requirements—a situation that sophisticated attackers understand and exploit by targeting the least secure components of organizations' technology portfolios.

The vendor and support constraints for legacy systems create additional security vulnerabilities as original vendors discontinue support, stop releasing security patches, or cease to exist entirely through acquisition or business failure. Unsupported legacy systems present organizations with impossible security dilemmas: known vulnerabilities that will never be patched, security updates that are no longer available, and vendor expertise that may no longer exist when problems arise. Organizations running such systems face difficult choices between continuing to operate vulnerable platforms or undertaking disruptive and expensive migrations to newer alternatives. Some organizations maintain legacy systems through internal expertise developed over decades of operation, but this approach creates personnel dependencies and knowledge concentration risks while still failing to address fundamental security limitations of the underlying platforms. The Bangladesh Bank case involved systems where timely security patching apparently didn't occur consistently, whether due to vendor support issues, operational constraints, or simply inadequate patch management procedures—a vulnerability pattern common across institutions running complex combinations of current and legacy technologies.

The business constraints that prevent legacy system replacement reflect harsh economic realities about the costs, risks, and complexity of wholesale technology infrastructure modernization. Replacing critical systems that have operated reliably for decades requires enormous capital investment—not just purchasing or developing replacement technology but also migrating data, retraining personnel, integrating with other systems, and conducting extensive testing to ensure business continuity. The risk inherent in replacing systems that support core business functions creates understandable reluctance to undertake migrations where problems could disrupt operations in ways that pose existential threats to organizations. The opportunity cost of directing capital toward infrastructure replacement rather than new capabilities or business growth creates additional resistance to modernization projects that don't directly generate revenue or improve customer-facing capabilities. These economic and risk factors create strong institutional inertia favoring continued operation of legacy systems despite their security limitations—a rational response to real constraints that nonetheless creates persistent vulnerabilities that attackers exploit.

The operational dependencies and process integration that accumulate around legacy systems over their operational lifetimes create additional barriers to replacement beyond the systems themselves. Business processes evolve to work with and around specific system capabilities and limitations, embedding legacy platform characteristics deep into operational procedures. Personnel develop expertise in operating particular systems, with institutional knowledge about workarounds, operational procedures, and system quirks becoming organizationally valuable and difficult to replicate on new platforms. Integration with other systems creates dependency webs where replacing one legacy platform requires assessing impacts on and potentially replacing numerous connected systems. These operational and organizational dependencies mean that replacing legacy systems requires transforming not just technology but also processes, procedures, and organizational capabilities—a change management challenge that exponentially increases complexity beyond the technical work of system replacement itself.

The hybrid infrastructure patterns that result from incomplete or ongoing modernization efforts create some of the most challenging security environments, where organizations must defend combinations of modern and legacy systems with inconsistent security capabilities, different management interfaces, and varying levels of supportability. These hybrid environments force security teams to maintain expertise across multiple technology generations, implement security controls differently for different system categories, and manage the security implications of connections between modern and legacy platforms. The boundaries between legacy and modern systems often represent particular security risks, as attackers may compromise older, less secure systems and leverage their connections to newer platforms to pivot through environments. The Bangladesh Bank attack potentially exploited such hybrid environment characteristics, where connections between older systems and modern SWIFT infrastructure created attack paths that wouldn't have existed in more homogeneous environments.

The future trajectory of legacy system security presents concerning trends as systems age further and the gap between their security capabilities and current threat requirements continues widening. Financial institutions face growing numbers of systems approaching or exceeding end-of-support dates, with vendors discontinuing patches and updates even as threats evolve and new vulnerabilities are discovered. The pool of personnel with expertise in older technologies shrinks as practitioners retire, taking institutional knowledge with them and leaving organizations dependent on increasingly rare and expensive specialized expertise. The technical debt accumulated through years of patches, workarounds, and customizations makes systems progressively more brittle and difficult to modify or secure. These trends suggest that legacy system security challenges will intensify before improving, creating windows of vulnerability that sophisticated adversaries will continue exploiting until organizations successfully complete modernization efforts that remain years away for many institutions.

## Third-Party Vendor Risks

The interconnected nature of modern financial services means that no institution operates in isolation but rather depends on extensive networks of third-party vendors, service providers, and business partners—each of which represents a potential security vulnerability that could be exploited to compromise the primary organization. These third-party relationships create complex security challenges because organizations must extend trust to external parties over whom they exercise limited control, must secure connections that facilitate necessary business interactions while preventing misuse, and must manage risks from vendors whose security practices may not meet the standards that the organization maintains for its own systems. The Bangladesh Bank case, while primarily involving compromise of the bank's own systems, occurred within a broader context of financial sector attacks that frequently exploited third-party relationships and vendor connections as paths to ultimate targets. Understanding third-party vendor risks requires examining the business necessity that creates these relationships, the security challenges they introduce, and the limited effectiveness of current approaches to managing risks from partners and suppliers.

The business necessity of third-party relationships reflects the reality that modern financial institutions cannot economically or technically maintain internal capabilities for all functions they require, leading to extensive outsourcing and partnership relationships that introduce security dependencies. Core banking platforms, payment processing systems, cybersecurity tools, network infrastructure, cloud computing services, and numerous other critical functions often involve vendors and service providers who maintain direct access to institutional systems or data. These vendor relationships enable institutions to leverage specialized expertise, scale operations without proportional cost increases, and access capabilities that would be prohibitively expensive to develop internally. However, each vendor relationship creates a trust boundary that must be managed, monitored, and secured—a boundary where the organization's security practices meet the vendor's potentially different practices, creating gaps that sophisticated attackers understand and exploit.

The access and connectivity that third-party relationships require fundamentally challenge security architectures designed primarily to protect perimeters from external threats. Vendors often need network access to systems they manage or support, administrative privileges to perform their functions, access to sensitive data to deliver services, and integration between their systems and the client institution's infrastructure. These access requirements create paths through security boundaries that must accommodate legitimate vendor needs while preventing misuse by adversaries who compromise vendor systems or impersonate vendor personnel. The challenge intensifies as vendor relationships multiply, creating dozens or hundreds of external parties with various types and levels of access to institutional systems and data—far more than security teams can comprehensively monitor or manage with traditional perimeter-focused security approaches.

The security practices and capabilities of third-party vendors vary enormously, ranging from sophisticated security programs that meet or exceed client institutions' standards to minimal security at smaller vendors or those in industries where security hasn't traditionally received priority. Organizations must contend with the reality that their overall security posture depends not just on their own practices but on the weakest link among their vendors—a sobering recognition when vendor security often proves difficult to assess comprehensively before relationships are established and even more difficult to continuously monitor during ongoing partnerships. Vendor security failures that result in compromise create cascading risks where attacks on vendors become stepping stones to their clients, with attackers exploiting trusted vendor connections to infiltrate organizations whose own direct defenses might have resisted the same attacks.

The supply chain dimension of third-party risk extends beyond vendors that organizations directly contract with to encompass the vendors' vendors—the suppliers, subcontractors, and service providers that support the companies that institutions directly engage. These fourth-party risks create blind spots where organizations have minimal visibility and essentially no control over security practices of entities they don't directly contract with but that nonetheless influence their overall security posture. Software supply chain attacks, where adversaries compromise software development or distribution processes to embed malicious code in legitimate applications, demonstrate how risks can propagate through multiple tiers of supplier relationships. The Bangladesh Bank case occurred during a period when financial sector organizations were beginning to appreciate supply chain security challenges but before comprehensive supply chain risk management practices had been widely implemented—a gap that subsequent attacks would expose with even greater clarity.

The contractual and legal frameworks that govern third-party relationships often prove inadequate for comprehensively managing security risks, with contracts that specify service levels and basic security requirements but fail to address the full range of security considerations or provide effective mechanisms for enforcement. Standard vendor contracts may require that vendors maintain "industry standard" security practices without defining what those standards are or how compliance will be verified. Contracts often lack provisions for continuous security monitoring, regular security assessments, or customer rights to audit vendor security practices—leaving organizations dependent on vendors' self-assessments of their own security posture. The liability provisions in vendor contracts typically limit vendor financial responsibility for security breaches, leaving client organizations bearing most costs of vendor security failures while having limited ability to recover damages. These contractual limitations reflect power imbalances in vendor relationships, where vendors serving multiple clients often resist security requirements they view as overly burdensome or unique to individual customers.

The vendor risk management programs that organizations implement to address third-party security challenges face substantial practical limitations in their ability to comprehensively assess and continuously monitor vendor security at scale. Initial vendor security assessments often rely heavily on questionnaires and vendor self-attestation, which provide limited assurance when vendors have incentives to present their security practices favorably and when assessments lack independent verification. The resources required for thorough vendor security assessment—on-site audits, technical security testing, comprehensive documentation review, and expert evaluation—prove prohibitively expensive to apply to all vendors, forcing organizations to prioritize assessment efforts on highest-risk relationships while accepting lower assurance for the majority of vendor relationships. Ongoing monitoring of vendor security remains even more challenging than initial assessment, as organizations typically lack real-time visibility into vendors' security postures and must rely on periodic reassessments that may miss security degradation or compromise between assessment cycles.

The fourth-party and nth-party risk that extends beyond direct vendor relationships into complex webs of supplier dependencies creates security challenges that current vendor risk management approaches struggle to address effectively. Organizations often lack even basic visibility into their vendors' supply chains, unable to identify all the fourth-party entities that ultimately provide components of or access to services the organization depends upon. The cumulative risk from these extended supply chain relationships proves nearly impossible to comprehensively assess or manage, as the number of entities involved and the lack of direct relationships prevents effective oversight. Some organizations have begun requiring vendors to assess and report on their own supply chain security, essentially outsourcing fourth-party risk management to vendors themselves—an approach that provides some incremental improvement but leaves organizations dependent on vendors' ability and willingness to effectively manage risks in their own supply chains.

## Insider Threats and Social Engineering

The threat from insiders—individuals with legitimate access to organizational systems and data who might misuse that access either maliciously or inadvertently—represents a particularly challenging vulnerability because it operates within the trust boundaries that security architectures are designed to protect. Insider threats take multiple forms, from malicious insiders who deliberately steal data or sabotage systems for personal gain or ideological reasons, to negligent insiders who compromise security through carelessness or failure to follow procedures, to compromised insiders whose credentials or systems have been taken over by external attackers. The Bangladesh Bank case involved elements of insider threat through compromised credentials that enabled attackers to operate as apparent insiders within the bank's systems, generating fraudulent transactions that passed authentication checks because they originated from legitimate accounts. Understanding insider threats requires examining the diverse motivations that drive malicious insider activity, the psychological and organizational factors that enable negligent behavior, and the sophisticated social engineering techniques through which external attackers convert insiders into unwitting accomplices.

The malicious insider threat stems from the reality that some percentage of any organization's personnel will have motivations to misuse their access for personal benefit, revenge, ideology, or coercion by external parties. Financial gain motivates many malicious insiders in banking, where individuals with access to transaction systems or customer data recognize opportunities to steal funds, sell information, or assist external criminals in exchange for payment. Disgruntled employees facing termination, experiencing personal financial difficulties, or feeling mistreated by organizations may seek revenge through sabotage or data theft. Ideological motivations drive some insider threats, particularly in politically charged contexts where individuals might leak information or disrupt operations to advance causes they believe in. Coercion or compromise by foreign intelligence services represents another malicious insider vector, where individuals with access to valuable systems or information face pressure to cooperate through blackmail, threats, or exploitation of personal vulnerabilities. Detecting malicious insiders before they act proves extraordinarily difficult because their behavior must appear normal to maintain their access and position while they identify and plan exploitation of their privileges.

The psychological and behavioral indicators that might signal increased insider threat risk—financial stress, personal grievances, policy violations, unusual work patterns, unexplained affluence—provide imperfect predictive value and raise significant privacy and employee relations concerns when organizations attempt to monitor them. The vast majority of individuals exhibiting stress or dissatisfaction never become insider threats, creating high false positive rates for behavioral monitoring programs and ethical dilemmas about employee privacy and dignity. Organizations struggle to balance legitimate security concerns against invasive monitoring that could damage employee trust and morale, potentially creating the very alienation and resentment that sometimes motivates insider threats. The legal and regulatory frameworks governing employee monitoring vary across jurisdictions, further complicating organizations' ability to implement comprehensive insider threat detection programs. These practical and ethical constraints mean that malicious insiders with adequate operational security can often operate undetected until significant damage has occurred.

The negligent insider threat arguably represents a larger cumulative risk than malicious insiders, as vastly more security incidents result from employees' mistakes, shortcuts, and policy violations than from deliberate malicious action. Negligent insiders compromise security by clicking phishing links, using weak passwords, sharing credentials with colleagues, misconfiguring systems, mishandling sensitive data, or failing to follow security procedures—actions taken not with intent to harm but through inattention, insufficient training, prioritization of convenience over security, or simple human error. The Bangladesh Bank compromise, while ultimately executed by external attackers, likely began with phishing or social engineering that exploited negligent insider behavior—an employee who clicked a malicious link, opened an infected attachment, or provided credentials to a social engineering attack. Addressing negligent insider threats requires not just training and awareness programs but fundamental system designs that remain resilient to human error and organizational cultures where security procedures are actually followed rather than circumvented under operational pressure.

Social engineering represents the primary mechanism through which external attackers convert insiders into unwitting accomplices, exploiting psychological vulnerabilities and social dynamics to manipulate individuals into compromising security. The sophistication of modern social engineering has evolved far beyond obvious scam emails to encompass targeted campaigns that demonstrate deep understanding of target organizations, individuals, and psychological pressure points. Spear phishing attacks craft messages that appear to come from trusted colleagues or business partners, reference actual ongoing projects or concerns, and create scenarios where compliance feels more natural than skepticism. Pretexting involves attackers creating elaborate false narratives—posing as IT support personnel, business partners, or authority figures—that provide seemingly legitimate reasons for targets to provide information or take actions that compromise security. The psychological principles underlying effective social engineering—authority, scarcity, urgency, social proof, likability, and reciprocity—remain remarkably consistent across attacks because they exploit fundamental aspects of human psychology that training alone cannot override.

The vishing and smishing vectors that extend social engineering beyond email into voice calls and text messages demonstrate how attackers adapt to defensive measures by shifting to communication channels where targets may be less guarded. Voice phishing allows attackers to exploit the personal nature of phone communication and the difficulty of verifying caller identity, while also enabling real-time adaptation to targets' responses in ways that email phishing cannot match. SMS phishing bypasses email security filters entirely and exploits the immediacy and personal nature of text messaging, with messages often viewed on mobile devices where security indicators may be less prominent than on desktop computers. The multi-channel nature of sophisticated social engineering campaigns—combining email, phone, social media, and in-person contact—creates coordinated attacks where information gathered through one channel informs and enables exploitation through others, building credibility and trust over time before making critical requests.

The business email compromise phenomenon represents perhaps the most financially damaging application of social engineering, where attackers impersonate executives or business partners to authorize fraudulent wire transfers or divert legitimate payments to attacker-controlled accounts. These attacks combine technical compromise of email systems with social engineering of finance personnel, exploiting organizational hierarchies where staff feel pressure to comply with apparent executive directives without excessive questioning. The Bangladesh Bank case, while involving SWIFT system compromise rather than simple business email fraud, shared characteristics with business email compromise in exploiting institutional trust in apparently authorized transaction instructions. The common thread across these attacks involves social engineering that creates scenarios where questioning or verification feels more awkward or risky than compliance, exploiting the social dynamics of organizational life to circumvent security controls.

The convergence of insider threats and social engineering creates particularly dangerous scenarios where external attackers deliberately cultivate relationships with insiders to exploit their access more effectively than phishing or malware alone would enable. Sophisticated adversaries invest substantial time in relationship-building, sometimes spending months establishing rapport with targets through social media or professional networking before making exploitation attempts. Romance scams adapted for espionage or data theft involve attackers creating fake personas and developing romantic or close personal relationships with targets who have access to valuable systems or information. The recruitment of insiders by foreign intelligence services or organized crime often begins through innocent-seeming contact that gradually escalates to requests that compromise security, with individuals sometimes not fully recognizing they've crossed into criminal activity until they're deeply compromised. These sophisticated recruitment operations blur the lines between insider threats and external attacks, creating hybrid scenarios where the actual attack is executed by insiders who have been manipulated or coerced by external parties.

## The Security Versus Convenience Trade-Off

The fundamental tension between security and operational convenience represents perhaps the most persistent and challenging vulnerability facing organizations attempting to defend complex systems while maintaining the usability and efficiency that enable productive work. Every security control that organizations implement creates some degree of operational friction—requiring additional authentication steps, restricting access that would be convenient, slowing processes with verification requirements, or constraining activities that could be accomplished more easily without security considerations. The Bangladesh Bank case, while resulting from inadequate security, occurred in an institutional context where tensions between security requirements and operational efficiency likely influenced decisions about what controls to implement and how strictly to enforce them. Understanding the security-convenience trade-off requires examining why this tension exists, how organizations navigate competing pressures, and why the consistent pattern across institutions involves accepting some security degradation to maintain operational viability even when the risks are intellectually understood.

The usability challenges that security controls create stem from their fundamental purpose of constraining access and actions in ways that frustrate both legitimate users attempting productive work and attackers seeking unauthorized access. Strong authentication mechanisms that require multiple factors, complex passwords, or frequent re-authentication improve security but create friction every time users need system access, with that friction accumulating across dozens of daily authentication events. Network segmentation that isolates sensitive systems from less-trusted networks improves security architecture but impedes workflows that require information or functionality to flow across security boundaries. Verification requirements that mandate multi-party approval for large transactions reduce fraud risk but slow processing times and require coordination among multiple personnel. Access restrictions that limit what users can do based on least-privilege principles improve security but require users to request elevated privileges when tasks legitimately require capabilities beyond their baseline access. Each security control makes some legitimate activities harder or impossible, creating operational costs that must be weighed against security benefits.

The user resistance that security measures generate reflects rational individual responses to controls that impede productivity, create frustration, and are often poorly explained or implemented in ways that seem disconnected from actual risk. Users who face password requirements demanding frequent changes develop patterns of incremental modifications that satisfy technical requirements while undermining security benefits. Employees required to use multifactor authentication repeatedly throughout the workday may seek workarounds or leave authentication devices connected to circumvent requirements they view as excessive. Personnel facing cumbersome verification procedures develop informal workarounds—credential sharing, approval shortcuts, or policy violations—that restore operational efficiency at the expense of security. This user resistance doesn't reflect malice or ignorance but rather the natural human tendency to optimize for immediate personal efficiency when the security benefits of restrictions are abstract or not directly observable. Security programs that fail to account for this resistance and design controls that minimize unnecessary friction while preserving essential security create conditions where policy violations become normalized and security controls are systematically circumvented.

The organizational pressures that prioritize operational efficiency over security create institutional dynamics where security teams must constantly justify controls that impede business activities while facing little pressure to justify security gaps that haven't yet been exploited. Business units measure success through operational metrics—transaction volumes, processing times, customer satisfaction—that security controls potentially degrade. Budget pressures create incentives to minimize security spending that doesn't directly generate revenue. Competitive dynamics may punish organizations whose security-conscious approach results in slower, more cumbersome processes than competitors offer. Senior leadership, while generally supportive of security in principle, must ultimately prioritize the operational viability and competitive positioning that enable the organization to survive and thrive. These organizational realities mean that security teams operate in environments where they must demonstrate that every control provides benefits that justify operational costs, while risks from inadequate security remain abstract until they manifest through actual incidents.

The risk-based approach to security decisions attempts to navigate security-convenience tensions by calibrating controls based on assessed risks rather than implementing maximum security regardless of context or impact. This approach recognizes that different systems, data, and processes merit different security levels based on their criticality and the threats they face, allowing organizations to implement stringent controls where risks are highest while accepting more user-friendly but less secure approaches for lower-risk scenarios. Risk-based security can rationalize why highly sensitive financial transaction systems warrant friction-inducing security measures while lower-risk functions might use more convenient controls. However, risk-based approaches depend on accurate risk assessment—a challenging proposition when sophisticated threats may not be well understood, when attack techniques evolve faster than risk models are updated, and when low-probability but catastrophic events are systematically underweighted in risk calculations. The Bangladesh Bank case arguably resulted partly from risk assessments that failed to fully appreciate sophisticated state-sponsored threats targeting central banks, leading to security postures inadequate for the actual threat environment.

The technological solutions that attempt to improve security without proportionally increasing friction represent important but incomplete approaches to resolving security-convenience tensions. Single sign-on systems reduce authentication friction by allowing users to authenticate once and access multiple systems without repeated credential entry, improving user experience while potentially creating single points of failure if the authentication system is compromised. Behavioral biometrics that continuously verify user identity through typing patterns, mouse movements, or other characteristics can provide continuous authentication without explicit user actions, though with privacy implications and reliability challenges. Adaptive authentication that adjusts security requirements based on context—requiring stronger authentication for unusual access patterns while streamlining routine access—can optimize the security-convenience balance dynamically. However, these technical solutions add complexity, cost, and sometimes create new vulnerabilities of their own, and they cannot fully eliminate the fundamental tension between constraining access for security and enabling broad access for convenience.

The mobile and remote work trends that have transformed how banking and financial services operate create new dimensions to the security-convenience trade-off, with personnel expecting to work from anywhere using any device while organizations struggle to extend security controls to environments they don't fully control. Users working from home, coffee shops, or while traveling need access to systems and data that organizations must secure, yet the uncontrolled nature of remote work environments—potentially compromised home networks, shared devices, uncertain physical security—creates risks that institution-controlled offices don't present. Organizations face difficult choices between maintaining security requirements that may prevent or degrade remote work capabilities versus relaxing requirements to enable remote work at the cost of security. The pandemic-driven acceleration of remote work forced many institutions to rapidly enable capabilities they had previously restricted on security grounds, accepting increased risk as necessary to maintain business continuity—a shift that demonstrated how security requirements can bend or break when business necessity demands it.

The long-term sustainability of security programs depends on finding balances in the security-convenience trade-off that users and business operations can live with, as security approaches that create excessive friction will be circumvented, undermined, or eventually abandoned regardless of their theoretical security benefits. Security controls that make legitimate work impossible or unreasonably difficult face implementation resistance from users, pushback from business units, and eventual dilution or removal when operational pressures mount. The most successful security programs incorporate user experience considerations into security design, seeking to achieve security objectives through approaches that minimize unnecessary friction while accepting that some friction is inevitable and appropriate. This balanced approach requires security teams to understand business processes deeply, engage with users to identify pain points, prioritize where security friction is truly necessary versus where alternative approaches might achieve similar security with less operational impact, and continuously refine controls based on feedback about their operational effects. The goal is not convenience without security or security without regard for convenience, but rather thoughtful balancing that achieves adequate security through approaches that the organization can sustain operationally over time.

## Conclusion

The vulnerabilities exposed by the Bangladesh Bank heist painted an unflattering but accurate picture of systemic weaknesses that characterize not just the victim institution but the global financial sector and indeed most organizations dependent on digital infrastructure. The human factor emerged as the most persistent vulnerability—one that no amount of technology can fully address because it stems from fundamental aspects of human psychology, cognition, and social behavior that security systems must accommodate rather than simply trying to override. The recognition that security depends ultimately on fallible humans making countless daily decisions under imperfect conditions, facing cognitive limitations and psychological biases, and operating within organizational cultures that may or may not prioritize security appropriately provides sobering context for the challenge of defending complex systems against sophisticated adversaries who understand and exploit human vulnerabilities systematically.

Legacy systems and outdated infrastructure represent technical vulnerabilities that institutions understand clearly yet struggle to address due to harsh economic realities and operational constraints. The persistence of decades-old technology with fundamental security limitations reflects not ignorance or negligence but rather the extraordinary difficulty and expense of replacing critical systems that have become deeply embedded in business operations. The security implications of legacy infrastructure—limited security capabilities, integration challenges, vendor support constraints, and operational dependencies—create persistent risks that institutions must manage for years or decades until comprehensive modernization can be achieved. The challenge intensifies as systems age further and the gap between their security capabilities and current threat requirements continues widening.

Third-party vendor risks demonstrate how organizational security depends not just on internal practices but on the security of extensive networks of partners, suppliers, and service providers over whom institutions exercise limited control. The interconnected nature of modern financial services creates security dependencies that current vendor risk management approaches struggle to comprehensively address, particularly regarding supply chain security and fourth-party risks that extend beyond direct vendor relationships. The contractual frameworks, assessment limitations, and monitoring challenges that characterize current vendor risk management leave organizations exposed to risks from partners whose security failures can cascade into compromise of their clients.

Insider threats, whether malicious or negligent, and social engineering attacks that convert insiders into unwitting accomplices represent vulnerabilities that operate within the trust boundaries that security architectures are designed to protect. The difficulty of detecting malicious insiders before they act, the prevalence of negligent behavior that compromises security inadvertently, and the sophistication of social engineering that exploits psychological vulnerabilities and social dynamics create threat vectors that technical controls alone cannot fully address. The convergence of insider access and external attacker social engineering creates particularly dangerous scenarios where the boundary between internal and external threats blurs, with adversaries effectively operating as insiders through compromised credentials or manipulated personnel.

The security versus convenience trade-off represents perhaps the most fundamental and persistent vulnerability, as every security control creates operational friction that organizations must balance against security benefits. The user resistance, organizational pressures, and business realities that prioritize operational efficiency create constant tension where security teams must justify controls while facing limited pressure to justify security gaps. The challenge of finding sustainable balances that achieve adequate security through approaches that don't create excessive friction or face systematic circumvention reflects the reality that security programs must work with human nature and business requirements rather than attempting to override them through pure technical controls. The Bangladesh Bank case occurred within this context of competing pressures, where decisions about security investments and control implementation reflected not just risk assessments but also considerations of operational impact, cost, and organizational capacity.

The cumulative effect of these vulnerabilities—human factors, legacy systems, third-party risks, insider threats, and security-convenience tensions—creates security challenges that no single solution or approach can fully address. Each vulnerability category requires different mitigation strategies, yet all interact in ways that create emergent risks exceeding the sum of individual vulnerability risks. An organization might address human factors through training, legacy systems through modernization, vendor risks through assessment programs, insider threats through monitoring, and convenience tensions through user experience design, yet still face sophisticated adversaries who exploit the gaps, interactions, and trade-offs that inevitably persist in any real-world security program. The sobering lesson from Bangladesh Bank is that motivated, sophisticated attackers will find and exploit whatever vulnerabilities exist, making continuous security improvement essential but perfect security impossible.

The exposed vulnerabilities also highlight the asymmetry between attackers and defenders, where defenders must address all vulnerabilities comprehensively while attackers need find only one exploitable weakness to succeed. This fundamental imbalance means that even substantial security investment and sophisticated security programs cannot guarantee prevention of all successful attacks against determined adversaries. The recognition of this asymmetry has driven evolution in security thinking toward approaches that assume breach and focus on rapid detection and response rather than purely prevention-focused strategies. Organizations cannot realistically eliminate all vulnerabilities—human limitations, legacy constraints, vendor dependencies, insider risks, and operational requirements ensure that some weaknesses will always persist—but they can build capabilities to detect exploitation quickly and respond effectively before limited compromise escalates into catastrophic damage.

The persistence of these vulnerabilities despite widespread awareness and substantial security investment reveals deeper truths about the challenges of securing complex sociotechnical systems that involve intricate interactions between technology, human behavior, organizational dynamics, and business requirements. Security is not purely a technical problem that technology solutions can solve, nor purely a human problem that training and awareness can address, nor purely an organizational problem that policy and culture can remedy. Instead, security requires holistic approaches that address technical, human, and organizational dimensions simultaneously while recognizing that perfect security remains unattainable and that the goal must be adequate security that manages risks to acceptable levels rather than attempting to eliminate all vulnerability.

The Bangladesh Bank heist thus serves as an enduring case study not because it revealed previously unknown vulnerabilities but because it demonstrated with painful clarity how known vulnerabilities persist despite understanding of their risks, how sophisticated adversaries systematically exploit these persistent weaknesses, and how the consequences of inadequate security can be catastrophic despite institutions' best efforts. The vulnerabilities exposed were not unique to Bangladesh Bank but rather reflected challenges facing the entire financial sector and indeed all organizations operating in adversarial digital environments. The value of examining these vulnerabilities lies not in assigning blame for their existence but in understanding why they persist and what realistic approaches might reduce them to levels that, while not eliminating risk entirely, make successful sophisticated attacks sufficiently difficult that fewer adversaries possess the capabilities and resources to succeed. The perfect security that would eliminate these vulnerabilities remains impossible, but meaningfully better security that makes attacks substantially harder and enables more rapid detection and response when breaches occur represents an achievable goal that institutions must pursue continuously in the face of evolving threats.

# Chapter 10: The Broader Implications

The Bangladesh Bank heist transcended its immediate financial impact to reveal profound implications about the evolution of international conflict, the emergence of cyber operations as instruments of state policy, and the inadequacy of existing international frameworks for addressing digital-age threats that ignore traditional boundaries and challenge fundamental assumptions about sovereignty, attribution, and deterrence. What began as investigation into a sophisticated bank robbery gradually transformed into recognition of a broader pattern where nation-states facing international isolation and economic pressure increasingly turn to cybercrime as a mechanism for generating revenue, circumventing sanctions, and projecting power in ways that conventional military or diplomatic tools cannot achieve. This chapter examines how the Bangladesh Bank case illuminated the economics of state-sponsored cybercrime, the specific model that North Korea has pioneered in using cyber capabilities for financial gain, the emerging landscape of financial warfare where digital attacks threaten the stability of international financial systems, and the profound challenges facing international law and deterrence frameworks designed for different eras and different types of conflict. Understanding these broader implications requires looking beyond the specific incident to recognize the Bangladesh Bank heist as a harbinger of fundamental shifts in how states interact, compete, and pursue their interests in an increasingly digital world where the rules, norms, and enforcement mechanisms of previous eras prove inadequate for addressing threats that operate at the speed of light across borders that constrain response but not attack.

## State-Sponsored Cybercrime Economics

The emergence of state-sponsored cybercrime as a significant phenomenon in international relations reflects a fundamental economic reality: sophisticated cyber operations can generate substantial revenue while requiring relatively modest investment compared to conventional criminal enterprises or legitimate economic activities. Nation-states facing economic pressure from international sanctions, diplomatic isolation, or simple lack of natural resources and viable export industries increasingly view cyber operations as attractive tools for generating hard currency and accessing the international financial system despite efforts to exclude them. Understanding the economics of state-sponsored cybercrime requires examining both the cost side—what resources states must invest to develop and maintain sophisticated cyber capabilities—and the revenue side—what financial returns successful operations can generate. The calculation proves compelling for states with certain characteristics: authoritarian governments able to direct substantial state resources toward cyber operations without democratic accountability, technical educational infrastructure that can produce skilled cyber operators, willingness to accept international condemnation and potential retaliation, and limited alternative options for generating foreign currency or accessing international markets.

The investment required to develop sophisticated cyber operations capabilities, while substantial, proves dramatically lower than the costs of developing conventional military capabilities or building legitimate export industries that could generate equivalent revenue. A state-sponsored cyber operation requires recruiting and training skilled personnel—computer scientists, software developers, network specialists—but the global proliferation of computer science education means that most countries possess populations with the necessary technical skills. The infrastructure requirements involve computers, internet connectivity, and development environments—technologies available globally at modest cost compared to weapons systems, industrial facilities, or other traditional instruments of state power. The operational security requirements—maintaining covert communication channels, laundering stolen funds, obscuring attribution—add complexity but remain achievable for states with intelligence services and diplomatic networks. The total investment for a state to develop sophisticated cyber operations capabilities might range from tens to hundreds of millions of dollars over several years—substantial in absolute terms but minimal compared to conventional military programs or industrial development initiatives.

The potential returns from successful cyber operations dramatically exceed investment costs when operations target financial institutions or execute theft at scales that the Bangladesh Bank case demonstrated were achievable. A single successful operation stealing tens of millions of dollars can exceed the annual cost of maintaining the cyber units that executed it, creating favorable return-on-investment profiles that make cyber operations economically rational for states seeking revenue generation. The scalability of cyber operations—where additional attacks require minimal marginal cost once capabilities are developed—further improves economics, as state cyber units can conduct multiple operations targeting different victims without proportional cost increases. The ability to target victims worldwide from centralized locations means that cyber operations can access far more potential targets than geographically constrained conventional crime could reach. These economic characteristics make state-sponsored cybercrime attractive for nations seeking to generate revenue through means that conventional criminal enterprises or legitimate businesses cannot match in terms of return relative to investment and risk.

The sanctions evasion capabilities that cyber operations provide create additional economic value beyond direct theft, enabling states facing international financial restrictions to access foreign currency, conduct transactions, and move money through the international system despite efforts to exclude them. North Korea, facing some of the most comprehensive international sanctions in history, has found in cyber operations a mechanism for circumventing financial restrictions that would otherwise severely constrain its access to hard currency and international commerce. Cyber operations enable sanctions evasion through theft that generates currency outside the sanctioned banking system, through cryptocurrency operations that bypass traditional financial intermediaries, and through cyber-enabled trade that obscures the origin of goods or payments. The value of sanctions evasion capabilities to heavily sanctioned states may exceed the direct financial gains from theft, as maintaining any access to the international financial system and global commerce provides strategic value that pure revenue numbers don't fully capture.

The risk-reward calculation for state-sponsored cybercrime proves favorable from the perspective of nations willing to accept international condemnation, as the probability of suffering consequences that exceed gains remains low under current international frameworks. The likelihood of successful attribution to specific state actors, while increasing with improved forensic capabilities, remains imperfect enough that states can maintain plausible deniability even when intelligence communities possess high confidence about responsibility. Even when attribution succeeds and international condemnation follows, the consequences typically involve additional sanctions on already-sanctioned states, diplomatic criticism that authoritarian governments can dismiss as propaganda, and occasional legal actions against individuals who likely remain beyond the practical reach of prosecution. The expected cost of international response to cyber operations, when weighted by probability and discounted for states already facing maximum sanctions and diplomatic isolation, proves minimal compared to potential financial gains. This asymmetry creates incentive structures where state-sponsored cybercrime represents rational behavior for certain actors despite violating international norms and laws.

The workforce development and skills transfer that cyber operations programs provide create additional strategic value for sponsoring states beyond immediate financial returns. Developing sophisticated cyber capabilities requires training personnel in cutting-edge technical skills, building organizational expertise in complex operations, and creating infrastructure that has potential applications beyond criminal operations. The skills developed for cyber theft operations translate to cyber espionage capabilities that serve intelligence objectives, to cyber attack capabilities that could be employed for military or strategic purposes, and to defensive capabilities that help protect the sponsoring state's own systems. The infrastructure, procedures, and organizational knowledge developed for financially motivated cyber operations create capabilities that states can leverage for multiple purposes, multiplying the strategic return on investment beyond what pure financial accounting would suggest. This multi-use characteristic means that resources devoted to cyber operations serve multiple state interests simultaneously, improving the overall cost-effectiveness of investment.

The competitive dynamics among states pursuing cyber operations as revenue generation mechanisms create concerning trends toward sophistication increases and potential escalation. As more states recognize the economic potential of cyber operations and observe successful operations like the Bangladesh Bank heist, the number of actors developing such capabilities increases, intensifying competition for targets and potentially driving innovation in attack techniques as actors seek advantages over defenders and competing attackers. The success of pioneering states like North Korea demonstrates viability of the model, potentially encouraging emulation by other nations facing economic pressure or seeking alternative revenue sources. The diffusion of capabilities, techniques, and tools through cyber criminal ecosystems accelerates as state-sponsored actors sometimes collaborate with or provide tools to conventional criminal groups, creating complex relationships between state and non-state cyber threats. These competitive and diffusion dynamics suggest that state-sponsored cybercrime will likely increase rather than decrease in coming years, with more states developing capabilities and existing actors conducting more operations against more targets.

## North Korea's Cyber Operations Funding Model

North Korea represents the most developed and extensively documented case of a nation-state systematically employing cyber operations for revenue generation, having built sophisticated cyber capabilities over more than two decades and conducted numerous operations targeting financial institutions, cryptocurrency exchanges, and other sources of hard currency. Understanding North Korea's model provides crucial insights into how states can organize, fund, and employ cyber capabilities for financial gain while operating under severe international sanctions and diplomatic isolation. The North Korean approach demonstrates how authoritarian control, technical education investment, and willingness to accept international condemnation combine to create a sustainable cyber operations program that has successfully generated hundreds of millions of dollars while simultaneously serving intelligence and strategic purposes. The model proves particularly relevant because other nations facing similar circumstances—international sanctions, limited legitimate economic options, authoritarian governance structures—might seek to replicate North Korea's success in using cyber operations as economic and strategic tools.

The organizational structure of North Korea's cyber operations reflects the regime's prioritization of these capabilities and its integration of cyber programs within military and intelligence apparatuses. The primary organizational home for North Korea's cyber operations is believed to be Bureau 121, a unit within the Reconnaissance General Bureau—North Korea's primary intelligence organization. Bureau 121 operates with substantial resources relative to North Korea's overall economy, reportedly employing thousands of personnel organized into specialized teams focused on different operation types and targets. The organizational structure enables coordination between financially motivated operations, espionage activities, and strategic cyber attacks, allowing the regime to leverage capabilities across multiple missions. The military and intelligence integration means that cyber operations receive high-level political support and resources despite North Korea's severe economic constraints, reflecting leadership assessment that cyber capabilities provide asymmetric advantages that justify investment even when other sectors face resource shortages.

The personnel recruitment and training pipeline that North Korea has developed represents a crucial foundation for its cyber operations capabilities, with the regime identifying talented students early and providing specialized education that channels them into cyber roles. North Korea's educational system identifies students with aptitude for mathematics and computer science during primary and secondary education, selecting them for specialized schools like Pyongyang's Kim Il-sung University and the University of Automation where they receive advanced technical training. The most talented graduates are recruited into military and intelligence cyber units, where they receive additional specialized training in offensive cyber operations. This pipeline approach ensures a steady supply of technically skilled personnel for cyber operations despite North Korea's relative technological and economic backwardness. The regime's authoritarian control enables it to direct talented individuals into cyber operations roles regardless of personal preferences, providing a workforce development advantage that democratic societies cannot replicate.

The overseas deployment of North Korean cyber operators represents an innovative aspect of their model that addresses technical infrastructure limitations while providing operational security benefits. Many North Korean cyber operators work from locations outside North Korea—including China, Southeast Asian countries, and reportedly other regions—where they can access better internet connectivity and more sophisticated technical infrastructure than domestic North Korean networks provide. These overseas operators maintain cover identities as software developers, IT consultants, or other legitimate roles while conducting cyber operations under direction from Pyongyang. The overseas deployment model provides several advantages: accessing superior technical infrastructure, creating attribution challenges by obscuring the North Korean origin of attacks, generating legitimate income through software development and IT services that supplements direct cyber theft, and potentially providing intelligence collection opportunities in host countries. However, the model also creates security risks as operators living abroad experience freedoms unavailable in North Korea and might potentially defect, requiring the regime to maintain surveillance and control mechanisms even for personnel operating overseas.

The financial operations and money laundering infrastructure that supports North Korea's cyber theft demonstrates sophisticated understanding of international financial systems and cryptocurrency technologies. The regime has developed relationships with individuals and organizations worldwide who facilitate moving and laundering stolen funds, converting them from electronic transfers into usable assets that can benefit North Korea despite international sanctions. The extensive use of cryptocurrency in recent North Korean cyber operations reflects recognition that digital currencies provide advantages for sanctions evasion and money laundering that traditional banking cannot match. The regime has targeted cryptocurrency exchanges worldwide, stealing hundreds of millions in digital assets that can be moved and converted more easily than funds in traditional banking systems. The sophistication of North Korean money laundering operations, demonstrated through the Bangladesh Bank case and numerous other incidents, indicates substantial investment in understanding financial crime techniques and building networks that can execute complex laundering operations across multiple jurisdictions.

The strategic integration of financially motivated cyber operations with intelligence and military objectives creates multiplier effects that enhance the overall value of cyber programs to the North Korean regime. Operations targeting financial institutions for theft simultaneously provide intelligence about financial sector security practices, test cyber capabilities against sophisticated defenders, and maintain organizational skills through regular operational activity. The infrastructure developed for cyber theft—command and control networks, malware development capabilities, money laundering mechanisms—can be adapted for espionage or strategic cyber attacks if needed. The revenue generated through cyber operations helps fund not just the cyber units themselves but potentially broader military and intelligence programs, creating positive feedback loops where successful operations enable expanded capabilities. This integration means that assessing North Korean cyber operations purely through financial returns underestimates their total strategic value to the regime.

The sustainability and evolution of North Korea's cyber operations model demonstrates that the approach can persist and improve over time despite international attention and defensive improvements. North Korean cyber capabilities have evolved from relatively crude early operations to sophisticated attacks that challenge even well-defended institutions, reflecting organizational learning and continuous improvement. The regime has sustained its cyber operations despite increased international focus on North Korean cyber threats, attribution of major attacks, and sanctions targeting cyber infrastructure and personnel. The financial returns from cyber operations, estimated in the hundreds of millions to potentially over a billion dollars in recent years, demonstrate that the model generates substantial value that justifies continued investment. The persistence and evolution suggest that North Korea's cyber operations program has achieved sustainability, functioning as a self-supporting or even revenue-positive component of the state's overall activities rather than purely a cost center requiring subsidy from other revenue sources.

## The New Landscape of Financial Warfare

The Bangladesh Bank heist and the broader pattern of cyber attacks targeting financial institutions represent the emergence of a new form of conflict that blurs traditional boundaries between war and crime, between state and non-state actors, and between economic competition and military action. This new landscape of financial warfare involves nation-states employing cyber capabilities to target the financial systems of other countries with objectives ranging from simple theft to strategic destabilization, using techniques that existing international frameworks struggle to categorize or address effectively. Understanding financial warfare requires examining how cyber operations against financial systems differ from conventional military conflicts, how they create strategic advantages for certain actors while challenging traditional notions of deterrence and response, and how they potentially threaten the stability of the international financial system that underpins global commerce. The transformation of financial systems into battlegrounds where states pursue strategic objectives through digital means represents as significant a shift as any in the history of warfare and international competition.

The strategic objectives of financial warfare extend beyond simple monetary gain to encompass destabilization of adversary economies, undermining confidence in financial institutions, demonstrating capability to threaten critical infrastructure, and potentially preparing cyberspace battlegrounds for future conflicts. A successful attack against a major financial institution creates ripple effects throughout the economy as confidence in banking security erodes, financial transactions face increased scrutiny and delay, and capital flows shift away from institutions or countries perceived as vulnerable. The psychological impact of demonstrated vulnerability can exceed direct financial losses, as attacks reveal that even sophisticated institutions can be compromised and that the digital financial infrastructure that modern economies depend upon contains exploitable weaknesses. These psychological and confidence effects mean that financial warfare operations can influence behavior and create strategic advantages beyond what their direct financial impact might suggest, functioning as a form of economic coercion or deterrence that doesn't require kinetic military action.

The asymmetric advantages that financial warfare provides to smaller or less powerful states represent a significant shift in international power dynamics, enabling actors that cannot compete conventionally with major powers to nonetheless impose costs and threaten interests through cyber operations. North Korea, despite its severe economic and military disadvantages relative to potential adversaries like the United States or South Korea, can conduct cyber operations against financial institutions in those countries that create damage, generate revenue, and demonstrate capability in ways that conventional military or economic tools could not achieve. This asymmetry creates concerning incentives where states that would be severely disadvantaged in conventional conflicts can pursue objectives through cyber financial warfare with reduced risk of triggering responses they couldn't manage. The barriers to entry for conducting sophisticated cyber operations, while not trivial, prove dramatically lower than barriers to developing competitive conventional military forces or economic leverage, enabling medium and even small states to become significant actors in financial warfare despite limited traditional power.

The interconnectedness of the global financial system creates systemic vulnerabilities where attacks targeting individual institutions can cascade into broader disruptions affecting the international system that all nations depend upon for commerce and economic stability. The same integration that enables efficient international financial transactions creates dependencies where compromise of major institutions or critical infrastructure can ripple through the system, potentially triggering broader instability. The concentration of international financial transactions through relatively small numbers of major banks and payment networks means that successful attacks on these critical nodes could disrupt global commerce far beyond the immediate victims. The potential for escalation from isolated attacks against individual targets to broader systemic disruption creates risks that extend beyond bilateral conflicts between attacking and victim states to threaten interests of the entire international community. This systemic risk dimension means that financial warfare potentially creates catastrophic risks that conventional warfare, while more visibly destructive, might not produce in the same way.

The challenges of response and escalation management in financial warfare reflect the difficulties of applying concepts developed for conventional military conflicts to cyber operations that often occur in gray zones between crime and war. When a nation-state conducts cyber operations that steal money from banks, should victims respond as they would to crime—through law enforcement, judicial proceedings, and international cooperation mechanisms—or as they would to acts of war or economic aggression—through diplomatic, economic, or even military responses? The answer proves unclear because cyber financial operations combine elements of both crime and strategic action, creating ambiguities that existing frameworks don't adequately address. The risk of miscalculation or unintended escalation increases when states struggle to categorize attacks and calibrate appropriate responses, potentially leading to overreaction that escalates conflicts beyond what the initial attack warranted or under-reaction that encourages additional attacks by demonstrating that consequences are minimal.

The evolution toward offensive financial cyber capabilities development by multiple states creates arms race dynamics and increases the likelihood that future conflicts will include financial warfare as standard components rather than exotic exceptions. As more states observe successful operations like the Bangladesh Bank heist and recognize the strategic value of financial warfare capabilities, investment in offensive cyber programs increases worldwide. The development of capabilities tends to drive their eventual employment, as states that invest substantial resources in building cyber financial warfare tools face incentives to use them to justify investment, demonstrate capabilities, achieve objectives, or maintain operational readiness. The normalization of financial warfare as an accepted tool of state competition creates concerning trajectories where the international financial system faces persistent threats from multiple state actors pursuing various objectives through cyber operations against financial institutions and infrastructure.

The defense challenges against sophisticated financial warfare operations demonstrate that protecting critical financial infrastructure requires sustained investment, international cooperation, and continuous adaptation that many institutions and countries struggle to maintain. The sophistication of state-sponsored attacks exceeds what most financial institutions face from conventional criminals, requiring enhanced security capabilities that prove expensive and difficult to implement comprehensively. The persistence and patience that characterize sophisticated state-sponsored operations—where attackers may spend months or years positioning for attacks—challenges detection and response capabilities designed for faster-moving conventional cyber threats. The international nature of financial systems means that comprehensive defense requires coordination across countries and institutions with varying capabilities and priorities, creating collective security challenges where the system's overall resilience depends on its weakest links. These defense challenges suggest that some level of successful attacks will continue despite defensive improvements, making financial warfare a persistent feature of the international landscape rather than a temporary phenomenon that enhanced security can eliminate.

## International Law and Cyber Attribution

The application of international law to cyber operations, including financially motivated attacks like the Bangladesh Bank heist, reveals profound gaps and ambiguities that limit the effectiveness of legal frameworks in constraining state behavior or providing clear guidance about acceptable conduct in cyberspace. Traditional international law developed primarily to address conventional military conflicts between states, with clearly defined concepts of sovereignty, use of force, armed attacks, and appropriate responses that mapped relatively well to kinetic military actions but that prove far more ambiguous when applied to cyber operations. The challenges of attribution—determining with sufficient confidence which state is responsible for cyber operations that are deliberately designed to obscure their origins—further complicate the application of international law, creating situations where victims may strongly suspect or even possess intelligence indicating responsible parties but struggle to prove attribution to evidentiary standards that would support legal or diplomatic action. Understanding how international law addresses cyber financial warfare requires examining existing frameworks, their limitations when applied to digital operations, and the slow evolution of new norms and agreements that attempt to fill gaps in traditional law.

The sovereignty principles that form the foundation of international law create threshold questions about whether cyber operations that don't cause physical damage or cross physical borders nonetheless violate sovereignty in ways that international law should address. Traditional sovereignty concepts focus on territorial integrity and non-intervention in domestic affairs, with clear violations occurring when states use military force against others' territory or directly interfere with governmental functions. However, cyber operations like the Bangladesh Bank heist involve no physical border crossing—attackers never entered Bangladesh territory—and cause no physical damage despite creating substantial financial harm. Whether such operations constitute sovereignty violations under international law remains debated, with some experts arguing that the effects-based approach (if harmful effects occur, sovereignty is violated regardless of means) while others contend that cyber operations without physical manifestations occupy a different category that existing sovereignty frameworks don't clearly address. This ambiguity creates situations where states can conduct harmful cyber operations while arguing they haven't violated traditional sovereignty principles, exploiting gaps between international law developed for kinetic threats and the realities of digital-age capabilities.

The concept of "use of force" and "armed attack" in international law creates additional complications when applied to cyber operations, as these terms traditionally referred to military actions involving physical destruction or casualties but must now potentially encompass digital operations with financial or informational effects. The UN Charter prohibits the use of force against the territorial integrity or political independence of any state, while recognizing the right of self-defense against armed attacks. However, whether cyber operations that steal money or disrupt systems constitute "use of force" or "armed attacks" that would trigger these international law provisions remains unclear. Most experts agree that catastrophic cyber attacks causing physical destruction equivalent to military strikes would qualify, but the threshold for less destructive operations remains contested. The Bangladesh Bank heist, despite its substantial financial impact, almost certainly would not qualify as an armed attack or use of force under most interpretations, leaving it in a legal gray zone where traditional international law provides limited guidance about appropriate state responses or legal characterization of the attack itself.

The attribution challenge represents perhaps the most significant obstacle to applying international law to cyber operations, as legal frameworks generally require clear identification of responsible parties before remedies or responses can be justified. Cyber operations are deliberately designed to obscure origins through techniques like proxy servers, compromised infrastructure, false flag operations, and routing through multiple jurisdictions. While technical forensics and intelligence capabilities have improved and can often identify responsible states with reasonable confidence, the standards of proof required for legal proceedings or to justify significant responses exceed what cyber attribution typically provides. The gap between intelligence community confidence—often expressed in probabilistic terms like "high confidence"—and legal proof sufficient for court proceedings or definitive public attribution creates practical limitations on applying international law. States may know with reasonable certainty who conducted cyber operations against them but lack evidence that would satisfy legal standards for formal attribution, limiting their options for responses that require clear establishment of responsibility.

The existing international legal instruments that address cybercrime, primarily the Budapest Convention on Cybercrime, focus on cooperation in investigating and prosecuting cyber criminals rather than addressing state-sponsored cyber operations or providing frameworks for state responsibility. The Budapest Convention facilitates international cooperation on cybercrime investigations, evidence sharing, and extradition, but it was designed primarily for addressing non-state criminal actors rather than state-sponsored operations. Many countries, including major cyber powers and sources of state-sponsored threats, are not parties to the Convention, limiting its effectiveness as a global framework. The Convention's focus on criminal prosecution proves inadequate for addressing operations conducted by or on behalf of states that have no intention of prosecuting their own operators and that may be beyond the reach of foreign prosecution. These limitations mean that the primary international legal instrument for cybercrime provides minimal constraint on state-sponsored operations like those North Korea conducts.

The slow emergence of new international norms and agreements specific to cyberspace reflects recognition that existing international law proves inadequate but also demonstrates the profound challenges of achieving consensus on appropriate rules for state behavior in a domain where interests diverge widely. Various international efforts have attempted to develop cyber norms—the UN Group of Governmental Experts process, regional agreements, bilateral understandings—but progress proves slow and uneven. Some states advocate for comprehensive international treaties that would regulate cyber operations similarly to how treaties regulate other weapons or domains, while others prefer less formal norms that would allow greater flexibility. Disagreements about fundamental questions—whether existing international law applies in cyberspace, what activities should be prohibited versus allowed, how to verify compliance, what responses are appropriate to violations—prevent rapid consensus. The continuing evolution of technology and attack techniques also challenges norm development, as agreements that address current threats may prove inadequate for future capabilities that don't yet exist.

The state responsibility doctrine in international law provides some framework for holding states accountable for cyber operations, but application to cyber contexts involves significant uncertainties and limitations. Under traditional international law, states bear responsibility for internationally wrongful acts that are attributable to them, including actions by state organs or by non-state actors operating under state direction or control. However, establishing clear links between cyber operations and state responsibility proves challenging given attribution difficulties and the potential for states to employ proxies or conduct operations through informal relationships that obscure direct control. The evidentiary standards for establishing state responsibility are demanding, requiring clear proof of state involvement rather than suspicion or even high-confidence intelligence assessments. Even when state responsibility can be established, the remedies available under international law—primarily cessation of wrongful acts, reparations, and potentially countermeasures by victim states—may prove inadequate to address cyber operations that are completed before they're detected or that can be easily repeated regardless of legal findings.

## Why Traditional Deterrence Doesn't Work

The concept of deterrence—preventing adversary actions through credible threats of unacceptable retaliation—has formed a cornerstone of national security strategy and international relations for generations, yet its application to cyber financial warfare reveals fundamental challenges that limit effectiveness and create conditions where traditional deterrence frameworks prove inadequate for preventing state-sponsored cyber operations. Understanding why deterrence fails in the cyber financial context requires examining the assumptions underlying traditional deterrence theory, the ways in which cyber operations violate those assumptions, and the implications of deterrence failures for international security. The Bangladesh Bank case and the broader pattern of North Korean cyber operations demonstrate persistent state-sponsored attacks despite international condemnation, attribution to responsible parties, and threats of consequences—suggesting that something about the cyber domain or the specific characteristics of financially motivated operations makes them resistant to deterrence mechanisms that might work for other types of state aggression.

The attribution challenges that characterize cyber operations fundamentally undermine deterrence by creating uncertainty about whether retaliation will target the actual responsible party rather than innocent third parties or by enabling attacking states to maintain plausible deniability that weakens political support for strong responses. Traditional deterrence requires that adversaries clearly understand that specific actions will trigger specific responses from identified retaliators. However, when attribution remains ambiguous or contested, potential attackers may calculate that they can avoid retaliation by obscuring their involvement or maintaining sufficient uncertainty that response proves politically difficult for victim states. The intelligence-policy gap—where intelligence agencies may possess high confidence about attribution but cannot publicly share evidence without compromising sources and methods—creates situations where leaders know who is responsible but face public or international skepticism that limits response options. North Korea's cyber operations demonstrate how states can continue aggressive campaigns despite general international awareness of their responsibility, betting that the specific attribution challenges of individual operations combined with plausible deniability will prevent cohesive response.

The asymmetric nature of potential responses to cyber financial warfare creates additional deterrence challenges, as victim states struggle to identify retaliatory actions that would impose costs on attackers proportional to the damage caused without escalating to levels that would be inappropriate or that would harm the victim state's own interests. Military retaliation against cyber financial theft would likely be viewed as disproportionate and potentially illegitimate, escalating conflicts beyond what the initial operation warranted. Economic sanctions against states like North Korea that already face comprehensive sanctions provide limited additional deterrent value, as marginal increases in existing sanctions create minimal additional costs for already-isolated regimes. Cyber retaliatory operations face challenges around appropriate targets and proportionality, particularly when attackers are states with critical infrastructure that retaliatory attacks might target but where collateral effects could harm innocent civilians. The difficulty of identifying proportional, effective responses that would actually deter future operations without creating unacceptable escalation risks limits victims' options for imposing costs that would influence adversary decision-making about future operations.

The cost-benefit calculations that inform state decisions about cyber operations prove fundamentally different from traditional military operations in ways that make deterrence less effective. Conventional military operations require substantial visible preparations, involve significant risks to personnel and equipment, and typically pursue objectives of sufficient importance to justify these costs and risks. These characteristics create threshold effects where states conduct military operations only when objectives are sufficiently important and when the probability of success justifies risks. However, cyber operations can be conducted at relatively low cost, with minimal risk to personnel, and with failure costs limited primarily to exposure of techniques and tools rather than casualties or equipment loss. The low cost-benefit ratio means that states can conduct cyber operations for objectives that might not justify conventional military action, and can accept high failure rates as long as occasional successes provide sufficient returns. This economic dynamic makes cyber operations attractive for objectives across a broader spectrum than conventional military operations, reducing the effectiveness of deterrence that depends on adversaries concluding that costs and risks exceed potential benefits.

The sanctuary problem—where cyber operators conducting attacks from within their home countries face minimal direct risk and where victim states have limited ability to physically reach or threaten those operators—removes one of the traditional mechanisms of deterrence that works through risks to the personnel conducting operations. Conventional military operations put personnel at risk of capture, injury, or death, creating individual and organizational incentives for caution and selectivity about when operations are worth those risks. However, cyber operators conducting attacks from secure locations within their home countries face no such physical risks, particularly when operating on behalf of nuclear-armed states like North Korea where victim countries cannot practically launch military operations to target cyber units. The combination of personal immunity from consequence for individual operators and state protection from foreign retaliation creates conditions where the personnel conducting operations face minimal disincentives, weakening one of the traditional mechanisms through which deterrence influences behavior.

The collective action problems that limit international response to state-sponsored cyber operations weaken deterrence by ensuring that even when multiple states recognize threats and agree on responsible parties, coordinating effective response proves difficult. Individual victim states may lack sufficient bilateral relationships or leverage with attacking states to influence behavior unilaterally, requiring collective international response to impose meaningful costs. However, collective response requires diplomatic coordination among states with diverse interests, competing priorities, and varying assessments of threats and appropriate responses. Some states may sympathize with attackers, some may value their relationships with attacking states more than supporting cyber victims, and some may simply prioritize other issues over cyber threats that don't directly affect them. These collective action challenges mean that even clear attribution and consensus about state responsibility often fail to trigger coordinated international response sufficient to deter future operations, as attacking states correctly calculate that the international community's response will be fragmented and limited.

The regime characteristics of major state-sponsored cyber threat actors further limit deterrence effectiveness, as authoritarian governments that face minimal domestic accountability can accept international criticism and reputational damage that might influence democratic governments more significantly. North Korea's regime faces no meaningful domestic political consequences for international condemnation of its cyber operations—if anything, defying international pressure may strengthen the regime's domestic legitimacy by demonstrating independence from foreign influence. The regime's priorities emphasize regime survival and maintaining military and security capabilities over international reputation or diplomatic relationships beyond those with a small number of key partners. This means that forms of deterrence that work through reputational costs or diplomatic isolation prove largely ineffective, as the regime has already sacrificed international reputation and diplomatic relationships in pursuit of other objectives and views additional condemnation as acceptable costs of conducting operations that serve its interests.

The evolving nature of cyber capabilities and techniques creates deterrence instability, as rapid technological change means that what might be effectively deterred today may become feasible through new techniques tomorrow, creating conditions where deterrence must be continuously reestablished rather than achieving stability. Traditional military deterrence could achieve relatively stable equilibrium as capabilities evolved slowly and states understood mutual capabilities with reasonable clarity. However, cyber capabilities evolve rapidly, with new attack techniques, defensive measures, and counter-techniques emerging continuously. This dynamism means that deterrence calculations must be continually reassessed as capabilities change, creating inherent instability and uncertainty that weakens deterrent effects. The offense-dominant characteristics of cyberspace, where new attack techniques often prove more achievable than comprehensive defenses against them, create additional instability as attackers may believe they can succeed despite deterrent threats if they develop sufficiently novel techniques that bypass existing defenses.

## Conclusion

The broader implications of the Bangladesh Bank heist extend far beyond the immediate financial losses to illuminate fundamental transformations in international conflict, the economics of state behavior, and the adequacy of existing international frameworks for addressing twenty-first-century threats. The emergence of state-sponsored cybercrime as a viable funding model represents a strategic shift where nations facing economic pressure increasingly view cyber operations not just as intelligence tools but as revenue generation mechanisms that can help circumvent sanctions and generate hard currency despite international efforts to isolate them economically. The economics prove compelling for certain actors: relatively modest investment requirements, potential for substantial returns, scalability that enables multiple operations without proportional cost increases, and sanctions evasion capabilities that provide value beyond direct financial gains. This economic logic suggests that state-sponsored cybercrime will persist and likely increase as more nations recognize its potential and develop capabilities to pursue similar approaches.

North Korea's cyber operations funding model provides a template that other nations facing comparable circumstances may seek to emulate, having demonstrated that sophisticated cyber capabilities can generate hundreds of millions in revenue while serving multiple strategic purposes simultaneously. The organizational structures, personnel pipelines, overseas deployment models, and money laundering infrastructure that North Korea has developed represent innovations in how states can employ cyber capabilities for financial gain despite operating under severe constraints. The sustainability and evolution of North Korea's program over more than a decade demonstrates that the model can persist despite increased international attention and defensive improvements, validating the approach and potentially encouraging emulation. The concerning trajectory involves more states developing similar capabilities, increased sophistication as competition drives innovation, and potential escalation as financial warfare becomes normalized component of international competition.

The new landscape of financial warfare that cyber operations have enabled represents a fundamental shift in how states can threaten each other's interests and pursue strategic objectives below traditional thresholds of military conflict. The asymmetric advantages that financial warfare provides to smaller states, the systemic risks that attacks against interconnected financial infrastructure create, and the gray zone between crime and warfare that cyber financial operations occupy all create strategic challenges that existing international security frameworks struggle to address. The blurring of boundaries between economic competition, criminal activity, and strategic conflict creates ambiguities that adversaries exploit while defenders struggle to categorize threats and calibrate appropriate responses. The interconnected nature of global financial systems means that attacks targeting individual institutions can cascade into broader disruptions, creating systemic risks that extend beyond bilateral conflicts to threaten international community interests.

The limitations of international law in addressing cyber financial warfare reflect both the inadequacy of frameworks designed for different eras and the profound challenges of achieving international consensus on appropriate rules for cyberspace. The sovereignty ambiguities, use of force thresholds, attribution difficulties, and state responsibility questions that characterize legal frameworks' application to cyber operations create substantial gaps where harmful activities occur without clear legal violation or where legal prohibitions exist but enforcement proves impossible. The slow evolution of new cyber norms and agreements demonstrates both recognition of existing frameworks' inadequacy and the difficulty of achieving consensus among states with divergent interests and perspectives. The continuing legal ambiguities create conditions where states can conduct aggressive cyber operations while arguing they haven't violated international law, exploiting gaps between traditional legal concepts and digital-age realities.

The failure of traditional deterrence to prevent state-sponsored cyber financial operations reveals fundamental mismatches between deterrence frameworks designed for conventional military threats and the characteristics of cyber operations. The attribution challenges that enable plausible deniability, the asymmetric response problems that limit proportional retaliation options, the favorable cost-benefit calculations that make cyber operations attractive across a broad spectrum of objectives, the sanctuary from physical risk that cyber operators enjoy, the collective action challenges that fragment international response, and the regime characteristics that limit reputational costs all combine to weaken deterrence effectiveness. The result is a strategic environment where states can conduct persistent cyber operations despite general awareness of their responsibility and despite threats of consequences, calculating correctly that the limitations of deterrence mean that expected costs of operations remain lower than potential benefits.

The trajectory of these implications suggests that financial warfare through cyber operations will be a persistent and potentially growing challenge for international security and financial system stability. The economic logic favoring state-sponsored cybercrime for certain actors, the demonstrated success of pioneering states like North Korea, the strategic advantages that financial warfare provides, the inadequacy of international legal frameworks, and the limitations of traditional deterrence all point toward an environment where cyber attacks against financial institutions continue and potentially escalate despite defensive improvements and international efforts at response. The Bangladesh Bank heist, viewed in this context, represents not an isolated incident but rather a harbinger of fundamental shifts in international conflict that challenge existing frameworks and require new approaches to defense, deterrence, international cooperation, and regulation that have yet to be fully developed or implemented.

The implications extend beyond cybersecurity to touch fundamental questions about international order, the effectiveness of sanctions as policy tools, the stability of the international financial system, and how the international community can collectively respond to threats that transcend traditional categories and challenge assumptions about sovereignty, attribution, and appropriate response. The recognition that determined state actors can systematically attack financial institutions from remote locations, generating substantial revenue while facing limited consequences, represents a strategic challenge that requires rethinking not just cybersecurity but broader approaches to international security, economic statecraft, and the architecture of international cooperation. The transformation that the Bangladesh Bank case illuminated is still unfolding, with the full implications likely to become apparent only over years as more states develop capabilities, as defensive measures evolve, and as international frameworks adapt—or fail to adapt—to address threats that operate in the gray zones between crime, espionage, and warfare.

The sobering conclusion from examining these broader implications is that the international community faces a security challenge that existing tools and frameworks are poorly equipped to address, requiring innovation in defensive capabilities, international cooperation, legal frameworks, and deterrence approaches that goes far beyond incremental improvements to encompass fundamental rethinking of how states protect critical infrastructure, impose costs on adversaries, and cooperate to address shared threats. The gap between the challenge and current response capabilities creates a window of vulnerability that sophisticated adversaries like North Korea have exploited successfully and that other states may increasingly seek to exploit as they recognize opportunities and develop capabilities. Closing this gap will require sustained political will, substantial resource investment, difficult international negotiations to establish new norms and frameworks, and acceptance that perfect security and complete deterrence remain unachievable goals even as we work toward substantially better outcomes than current conditions provide.

The Bangladesh Bank heist thus serves as both warning and catalyst—warning about vulnerabilities and threats that will persist and potentially worsen without fundamental changes in how the international community addresses cyber financial warfare, and catalyst for transformations in security practices, international cooperation, and strategic thinking that the incident helped precipitate but that remain incomplete years after the attack. The broader implications challenge comfortable assumptions about the effectiveness of existing security measures, the adequacy of international law, and the applicability of traditional deterrence to modern threats. They demand recognition that the digital transformation of finance and broader society has created new attack surfaces and vulnerabilities that adversaries will continue exploiting, and that defending against sophisticated state-sponsored threats requires capabilities, cooperation, and frameworks that exceed what most institutions and nations have yet achieved. The work of addressing these implications remains ongoing, with the Bangladesh Bank case providing essential lessons about the nature of modern threats and the profound challenges facing efforts to create stability, security, and accountability in an increasingly digital international system.

# Part Four: The New Reality

## Chapter 11: Other Targets, Other Victims

The Bangladesh Bank heist, while capturing international attention and catalyzing security transformations, represented neither the beginning nor the end of sophisticated cyber attacks targeting financial institutions worldwide. Rather, it stood as the most visible incident within a sustained campaign of financially motivated cyber operations that stretched years before and continued long after, targeting banks across multiple continents with varying degrees of success but consistent sophistication. Understanding the full scope of this threat requires examining the broader pattern of attacks that the Bangladesh case illuminated, recognizing that dozens of institutions faced similar intrusions even as only a few became public knowledge through successful theft or investigative exposure. This chapter explores the landscape of other victims and targets, examining attacks that preceded Bangladesh and established the templates that later operations refined, incidents that followed which demonstrated that defensive improvements had not eliminated the threat, and the evolution of financially motivated cyber operations into increasingly diverse forms including ransomware that transformed the threat landscape entirely. The story that emerges reveals not an isolated incident but rather a systematic assault on global financial infrastructure by sophisticated adversaries who continue adapting their techniques, expanding their targets, and demonstrating that the vulnerabilities exposed by Bangladesh Bank persist across the financial sector despite heightened awareness and substantial security investments.

## Similar Attacks Before and After Bangladesh

The investigation into the Bangladesh Bank heist gradually revealed a disturbing reality: the February 2016 attack represented one visible success within a much larger campaign of similar operations targeting financial institutions worldwide, with forensic analysis and intelligence assessments identifying dozens of additional intrusions that employed comparable techniques, tools, and infrastructure. Understanding this broader campaign requires examining the timeline of attacks, the commonalities that linked diverse incidents to what appeared to be coordinated operations by the same threat actors, and the implications of recognizing that Bangladesh Bank was not anomalous but rather typical of a systematic approach to compromising financial institutions. The pattern that emerged suggested sophisticated adversaries had developed repeatable methodologies for targeting banks, tested and refined their techniques across multiple operations, and achieved a concerning success rate that indicated fundamental vulnerabilities persisted across the global financial sector despite varying levels of individual institutional security.

The precursor attacks that established the technical foundations and operational approaches later used against Bangladesh Bank dated back to at least 2014, with forensic evidence linking malware samples and infrastructure from earlier incidents to the tools employed in the February 2016 heist. Security researchers analyzing the Bangladesh Bank compromise discovered code similarities and infrastructure overlaps with attacks against financial institutions in Southeast Asia, Latin America, and other regions that had occurred months or even years earlier. Some of these earlier incidents had been detected and contained before significant theft occurred, providing glimpses of attacker capabilities but not triggering the comprehensive international response that Bangladesh Bank's successful theft would later generate. Other early attacks succeeded in stealing funds but received minimal public attention, either because victims chose not to disclose breaches or because successful money laundering meant losses weren't immediately recognized. The retrospective analysis revealed that by the time Bangladesh Bank was compromised, the attackers had already refined their techniques through multiple operations, learning from both successes and failures to optimize their approach.

The Sony Pictures Entertainment breach of November 2014, while not primarily financially motivated, demonstrated important technical capabilities and malware characteristics that would later appear in financially motivated attacks including Bangladesh Bank. The Sony attack, attributed to North Korean actors apparently retaliating for a comedy film about North Korea's leader, employed destructive malware that shared code elements with tools later used in bank heists. The connection suggested that the same threat actor group was developing capabilities for both destructive attacks serving political or strategic objectives and financially motivated operations targeting banks. The dual use of tools and infrastructure indicated sophisticated adversaries who could adapt their considerable technical capabilities to different operational goals depending on priorities and opportunities. The Sony case also demonstrated the attackers' willingness to conduct highly visible operations despite certain attribution and international condemnation, providing context for understanding the boldness of subsequent financial attacks.

The timeline of attacks immediately surrounding Bangladesh Bank revealed intense operational tempo during 2015 and 2016, with multiple institutions compromised in the months before and after the February 2016 heist. Security firms tracking the threat actor group identified intrusions at Vietnamese banks, Ecuadorian financial institutions, banks in the Philippines and other Southeast Asian countries, and attempts against targets in multiple other regions. The concentration of activity during this period suggested either that the threat actors were accelerating operations to capitalize on identified vulnerabilities before defensive improvements closed opportunities, or that success at Bangladesh Bank encouraged additional aggressive operations before the international response could effectively constrain their activities. The operational tempo also indicated substantial resources and organizational capacity, as conducting multiple simultaneous or near-simultaneous operations against sophisticated targets required significant personnel, infrastructure, and coordination capabilities.

The attacks that followed Bangladesh Bank demonstrated that neither the massive international attention, comprehensive forensic investigation, nor enhanced security measures fully prevented continued operations by the same threat actors. Throughout 2016 and subsequent years, security researchers continued identifying compromises attributable to the same group, with attacks showing evolution in techniques but continuity in basic approaches. Some post-Bangladesh operations showed attackers adapting to specific countermeasures that had been implemented—modifying malware to evade updated detection signatures, changing infrastructure to avoid discovered indicators of compromise, or adjusting money laundering techniques to address gaps that Bangladesh Bank investigations had exposed. This adaptive capability demonstrated that the threat actors represented sophisticated, learning adversaries rather than opportunistic criminals conducting isolated attacks, and that defensive improvements would need to be continuous and comprehensive rather than one-time fixes to address an evolving threat.

The success rate across the broader campaign of attacks proved difficult to determine precisely due to incomplete public information, victim reluctance to disclose breaches, and the challenge of distinguishing detected but foiled attempts from successful compromises that remained undiscovered. However, the pattern suggested that while many intrusions were detected and contained before significant theft occurred, enough succeeded in stealing funds to make the overall campaign financially successful from the attackers' perspective. Even assuming generous failure rates where the majority of attempts were thwarted, the scale of successful thefts—with Bangladesh Bank alone losing over $81 million and other successful operations collectively stealing additional tens or hundreds of millions—indicated that the campaign generated substantial returns that justified continued operations. The economics remained favorable for attackers even with high failure rates, as the cost of additional attempts remained relatively low while occasional successes produced outsized gains.

The geographic distribution of targeted institutions revealed both opportunistic selection based on perceived vulnerabilities and strategic targeting of regions where money laundering infrastructure was available and where international cooperation on investigation and asset recovery faced challenges. Institutions in developing countries appeared disproportionately targeted, likely reflecting assessments that these banks might have less sophisticated security capabilities and that investigative and recovery efforts would face greater obstacles than operations targeting institutions in major financial centers. The targeting also appeared to favor institutions with connections to Asian financial systems where the threat actors had developed money laundering relationships and infrastructure. However, evidence suggested that institutions in developed markets were also probed or compromised, indicating that the threat actors didn't limit themselves to perceived soft targets but rather conducted broad reconnaissance and attempted compromise across the global financial sector regardless of geography or perceived security sophistication.

The interconnected nature of the global financial system meant that attacks against any institution created ripple effects and concerns throughout the sector, with banks worldwide recognizing that if sophisticated central banks and major commercial institutions could be compromised, no institution could assume immunity from similar threats. This collective recognition drove the industry-wide security enhancements examined in previous chapters, but it also created persistent anxiety and resource demands as institutions grappled with the reality that determined, sophisticated adversaries were actively targeting their sector with proven capabilities to bypass security measures. The psychological impact of recognizing ongoing, active threat campaigns arguably exceeded the direct financial losses, as the demonstrated vulnerability of even sophisticated institutions undermined confidence in the security of digital financial infrastructure.

## The Ecuador Central Bank Hack

The Banco Central del Ecuador became one of several central banks targeted in the same sustained campaign that compromised Bangladesh Bank, with forensic evidence revealing an intrusion that bore remarkable similarities to the Bangladesh attack in its technical characteristics, operational approach, and apparent objectives. The Ecuador incident, while receiving less international attention than Bangladesh Bank, provided crucial additional data points for understanding the scope and sophistication of the threat actor campaign. The targeting of another central bank demonstrated that the Bangladesh attack was not an isolated opportunistic strike but rather part of a systematic approach where attackers specifically sought access to central banks' foreign exchange reserves and international payment capabilities. Understanding the Ecuador case requires examining what is publicly known about the compromise, how it related to the broader attack campaign, and what its partial success or failure revealed about both attacker capabilities and defensive measures.

The timeline of the Ecuador intrusion suggested it occurred roughly contemporaneously with or slightly before the Bangladesh Bank attack, indicating that threat actors were conducting multiple major operations simultaneously rather than focusing sequentially on individual targets. This parallel operational approach required substantial organizational capacity and resources, as each central bank compromise demanded months of reconnaissance, infrastructure preparation, malware customization, and operational planning. The simultaneous targeting demonstrated confidence in developed capabilities and willingness to accept the operational security risks that multiple concurrent operations entailed. It also suggested strategic prioritization of central banks as particularly attractive targets, presumably due to their holdings of foreign exchange reserves, their connections to international payment systems, and the potential for large-value transactions that individual commercial banks might not routinely process.

The technical characteristics of the Ecuador compromise, based on limited public information and security researcher analysis, indicated use of malware and techniques consistent with those employed against Bangladesh Bank and other targets in the campaign. The similarities included targeting of SWIFT-connected systems, deployment of custom malware designed to manipulate financial messaging, and apparent objectives of initiating fraudulent international transfers. The technical overlaps, combined with infrastructure connections and tactical similarities, led security researchers and intelligence analysts to attribute the Ecuador attack to the same threat actor group responsible for Bangladesh Bank and numerous other financial institution compromises. The consistency of approach across multiple targets reflected operational procedures and tool development that indicated professional, organized operations rather than ad hoc attacks.

The outcome of the Ecuador intrusion appeared to be mixed, with the compromise successfully executed but the attempted theft apparently detected and blocked before substantial funds could be stolen or successfully laundered. The reasons for this relative success in preventing major losses—compared to Bangladesh Bank's experience—remain somewhat unclear from public information but may have involved earlier detection of the intrusion, more effective monitoring that identified fraudulent transactions before they fully cleared, better coordination with correspondent banks that held Ecuador's reserves, or simply fortunate timing where the attack was discovered before optimal execution timing. The partial success demonstrated that even sophisticated, proven attack techniques could be defeated when defensive measures worked effectively and when detection occurred early enough to enable intervention before losses became irreversible.

The response and investigation into the Ecuador incident followed patterns similar to Bangladesh Bank, with engagement of international cybersecurity firms to conduct forensic analysis, coordination with intelligence agencies and law enforcement in multiple countries, and efforts to trace any stolen funds and identify perpetrators. However, the Ecuador case received substantially less international attention and media coverage than Bangladesh Bank, likely due to the lower financial losses and perhaps due to different institutional decisions about public disclosure and transparency. The relative lack of public information about the Ecuador incident created challenges for the broader financial sector's understanding of threat patterns, as fewer details were available about specific attack techniques, indicators of compromise, and lessons learned. This information asymmetry highlighted ongoing tensions between institutional desires to limit public disclosure of security incidents and the collective security benefits of information sharing.

The similarities between Ecuador and Bangladesh Bank attacks raised important questions about how threat actors selected targets and whether common characteristics made certain institutions particularly vulnerable or attractive. Both victims were central banks in developing countries, holding substantial foreign exchange reserves, connected to international payment systems, and potentially assessed by attackers as having less sophisticated security capabilities than central banks in major financial centers. However, attributing targeting decisions purely to perceived security weaknesses might oversimplify, as the attackers also demonstrated willingness to target well-defended institutions and may have selected victims based on money laundering infrastructure availability, correspondent banking relationships, or other operational factors beyond pure assessment of security posture. Understanding targeting logic remained challenging without insight into attackers' internal decision-making processes and reconnaissance assessments.

The Ecuador case contributed to growing recognition within central banking communities worldwide that they faced active, sophisticated threats specifically targeting their institutions, driving enhanced cooperation on security information sharing, adoption of stricter security standards, and implementation of additional controls around international payment systems. Central banks, traditionally focused primarily on monetary policy, banking supervision, and financial stability from macroeconomic perspectives, increasingly recognized cybersecurity as a critical operational risk and potential threat to the financial stability they were charged with maintaining. The transformation of central bank security postures from primarily physical security and traditional operational risk management to comprehensive cybersecurity programs represented a significant shift driven partly by incidents like Ecuador and Bangladesh Bank that demonstrated the severity and sophistication of threats.

## Vietnamese Bank Attempts

Vietnam's banking sector faced multiple attempted and successful cyber intrusions during the same period that Bangladesh Bank and Ecuador were compromised, with several Vietnamese financial institutions detecting sophisticated attacks that bore technical and operational hallmarks of the same threat actor campaign. The Vietnamese incidents provided additional perspectives on the geographic scope of targeting, the varying success rates across different institutional security postures, and the importance of detection and response capabilities in preventing substantial losses even when initial compromise occurred. Understanding the Vietnamese bank attempts requires examining what became publicly known about specific incidents, how Vietnamese institutions and authorities responded, and what the pattern of attacks against multiple banks within a single country revealed about threat actor operations and target selection.

The Tien Phong Bank incident of late 2015 represented one of the first publicly disclosed attacks in Vietnam that demonstrated characteristics consistent with the broader campaign. The bank detected sophisticated malware on systems connected to SWIFT infrastructure, with forensic analysis revealing tools and techniques similar to those later used against Bangladesh Bank. The critical difference was timing and detection—Tien Phong Bank discovered the compromise before attackers could successfully execute fraudulent transactions, enabling the institution to contain the breach, remove malware, and implement enhanced security measures. The early detection appeared to result from a combination of security monitoring that identified anomalous system behavior and perhaps fortunate timing where attackers had not yet completed their operational preparations when defensive measures intervened. The incident provided an important counterexample to Bangladesh Bank, demonstrating that sophisticated attacks could be detected and thwarted when security capabilities functioned effectively.

Multiple other Vietnamese banks reported detecting intrusion attempts or suspicious activity during 2015 and 2016, with varying levels of public disclosure and detail about specific incidents. The concentration of activity against Vietnamese institutions suggested either that Vietnam's banking sector presented particularly attractive or vulnerable targets from the attackers' perspective, or that the threat actors conducted broad reconnaissance across Southeast Asian financial institutions and pursued opportunities wherever initial access could be established. Vietnamese banks varied substantially in their security sophistication, with larger institutions and those with international operations generally maintaining more robust security programs while smaller domestic banks faced resource and expertise constraints. This variation created a diverse threat landscape where attackers could potentially identify softer targets while also probing more sophisticated institutions.

The response from Vietnamese banking regulators and government authorities reflected growing recognition of sophisticated cyber threats targeting financial institutions and the need for coordinated defensive measures across the sector. The State Bank of Vietnam issued security guidance, enhanced oversight of bank cybersecurity practices, and facilitated information sharing among institutions about threat indicators and defensive measures. The regulatory response balanced the need for enhanced security with concerns about potential economic impacts if overly restrictive requirements impeded banking operations or if public disclosure of vulnerabilities undermined confidence in the financial system. This balancing act reflected challenges facing regulators worldwide as they sought to strengthen cybersecurity without creating unintended consequences for financial stability or economic activity.

The varying outcomes across different Vietnamese bank incidents illustrated the importance of security fundamentals in determining whether sophisticated attacks succeed or fail. Institutions with robust network monitoring, timely patching and update procedures, properly configured security tools, and trained security personnel proved better able to detect and respond to intrusions before significant damage occurred. Conversely, institutions with gaps in basic security hygiene—outdated systems, inadequate monitoring, delayed patching—presented softer targets where sophisticated attackers could operate with reduced risk of detection. The pattern suggested that while the threat actors possessed sophisticated capabilities, they remained constrained by effective implementation of security basics, and that institutions investing in comprehensive security programs achieved meaningful protection even against advanced threats.

The international cooperation dimensions of responding to Vietnamese bank incidents highlighted both progress and continuing challenges in coordinated defense against transnational cyber threats. Vietnamese authorities engaged with international partners including the FBI, security agencies in other affected countries, and private sector cybersecurity firms to investigate attacks, share threat intelligence, and coordinate defensive measures. However, the cooperation faced obstacles including language and cultural differences, varying legal frameworks for evidence sharing and law enforcement cooperation, and the limited resources that some participating institutions and agencies could devote to investigation and response. The mixed success of international cooperation in the Vietnamese context reflected broader patterns where such coordination proved essential for understanding and responding to sophisticated campaigns but where practical limitations prevented fully effective cooperation.

The lessons from Vietnamese bank incidents reinforced conclusions emerging from Bangladesh Bank and other cases about the nature of modern financial sector cyber threats and effective defensive approaches. The importance of early detection, the value of information sharing within the financial sector, the necessity of strong security fundamentals rather than relying solely on advanced tools, and the challenges of responding to sophisticated adversaries willing to conduct sustained campaigns all appeared as consistent themes. Vietnamese institutions that learned from early incidents and implemented comprehensive security improvements generally fared better against subsequent attempts, demonstrating that institutional learning and adaptation could improve defensive postures over time even as threats continued evolving.

## Corporate Targets and Ransomware Evolution

The evolution of financially motivated cyber operations beyond targeted theft from banks to encompass ransomware attacks against corporate targets represented a significant transformation in the threat landscape that occurred parallel to and partially in response to enhanced defensive measures protecting traditional financial institutions. Ransomware—malicious software that encrypts victims' data and demands payment for decryption—evolved from relatively unsophisticated attacks targeting individuals with modest ransom demands to highly sophisticated operations against corporations and institutions capable of paying millions of dollars to restore operations. Understanding this evolution requires examining how ransomware emerged as a distinct threat, how some ransomware operations demonstrated links to or knowledge transfer from state-sponsored actors, and how the ransomware epidemic transformed the financial cybercrime landscape in ways that created new challenges for defenders while potentially reducing but not eliminating direct attacks against financial institutions.

The ransomware threat existed long before the Bangladesh Bank heist, but the sophistication, scale, and financial impact of ransomware operations increased dramatically during 2016 and subsequent years as criminal actors recognized the profit potential of targeting organizations rather than individuals and demanding ransoms calibrated to victims' ability and desperation to pay. Early ransomware variants like CryptoLocker demonstrated the basic model—encrypt valuable data, demand payment in cryptocurrency for decryption keys—but targeted primarily individuals and demanded relatively modest ransoms of hundreds or thousands of dollars. The evolution toward targeting corporations and institutions with ransoms in the millions represented a fundamental shift in scale and sophistication, requiring more advanced attack capabilities to compromise enterprise networks, more sophisticated data encryption to resist recovery without payment, and more professional operations to negotiate ransoms and manage payment processes at scale.

The emergence of "big game hunting" ransomware that specifically targeted large organizations capable of paying substantial ransoms demonstrated remarkable operational sophistication that paralleled capabilities seen in state-sponsored attacks like those against Bangladesh Bank. Ransomware operators began conducting reconnaissance to identify valuable targets, spending weeks or months within compromised networks to understand critical systems and data, deploying customized malware tailored to specific environments, and timing attacks for maximum impact when victims would feel greatest pressure to pay quickly. The operational approach bore striking similarities to advanced persistent threat operations conducted by nation-state actors, leading to speculation about whether some ransomware groups included former state-sponsored operators applying their skills to criminal enterprises or whether knowledge transfer occurred through criminal ecosystem connections. The technical sophistication of advanced ransomware—including capabilities for lateral movement, privilege escalation, defense evasion, and data exfiltration—matched or exceeded tools used in many state-sponsored campaigns.

The financial services sector found itself targeted by sophisticated ransomware operations alongside other industries, creating a dual threat environment where institutions needed to defend against both traditional theft-focused attacks and ransomware that threatened operational disruption rather than direct financial loss. Several financial institutions publicly acknowledged ransomware incidents during the years following Bangladesh Bank, with attacks ranging from relatively contained incidents affecting individual branches or departments to more serious compromises that encrypted critical systems and forced temporary operational disruptions. The financial sector's general reluctance to disclose ransomware incidents except when legally required meant that the true extent of attacks remained unclear, but industry surveys and incident response firms reported that financial institutions represented frequent ransomware targets due to their resources to pay substantial ransoms and their need for rapid operational restoration.

The economics of ransomware proved extraordinarily favorable for criminal operators, creating profit potential that arguably exceeded traditional bank heists while involving lower operational complexity and possibly reduced legal risks compared to theft operations that crossed more obvious criminal thresholds. Successful ransomware operations could generate millions in ransom payments with operational costs limited primarily to malware development and initial network compromise, as the ransom demand and payment process required minimal infrastructure compared to money laundering operations needed to convert stolen funds into usable assets. The cryptocurrency payment mechanism that most ransomware operations employed provided pseudo-anonymous fund transfer capabilities that were harder to trace and seize than traditional banking transfers, though not impossible as law enforcement capabilities for tracking cryptocurrency improved. The overall risk-reward calculation made ransomware attractive for sophisticated criminal groups seeking financial returns with arguably less complexity than elaborate bank heists required.

The debate over ransom payment—whether victims should pay to recover data and restore operations or refuse payment to avoid funding criminals and potentially incentivizing future attacks—created difficult ethical and practical dilemmas for targeted organizations. Financial institutions facing ransomware attacks needed to balance multiple considerations: the operational impact and duration of continuing disruption, the feasibility of restoring systems from backups without paying ransoms, the potential for data exfiltration and future extortion if ransoms weren't paid, the reputational impacts of public disclosure of successful attacks, and the ethical implications of funding criminal enterprises that threatened the broader ecosystem. Different institutions reached different conclusions based on their specific circumstances, with some paying ransoms to enable rapid recovery while others refused payment and worked through lengthy restoration processes. The variation in responses reflected genuine uncertainty about optimal strategies in the absence of clear evidence about whether payment or refusal better served long-term individual and collective interests.

The ransomware-as-a-service model that emerged during this period further democratized sophisticated cyber attacks by allowing less technically skilled criminals to conduct operations using tools and infrastructure developed by specialized providers who took a percentage of ransom payments. This service model separated malware development from operations, creating specialization where technically sophisticated developers could focus on creating effective ransomware while operators with access to target networks or social engineering capabilities could deploy tools without needing deep technical expertise. The result was a proliferation of ransomware attacks as the barriers to entry decreased and the number of actors capable of conducting sophisticated operations increased. The service model also created challenges for defenders and law enforcement, as attributing attacks became more complex when multiple parties with different capabilities and motivations contributed to individual operations.

## The Escalating Threat Landscape

The years following the Bangladesh Bank heist witnessed a dramatic escalation in the sophistication, frequency, and diversity of cyber threats targeting financial institutions and corporations, creating a threat landscape fundamentally more dangerous and complex than what existed before 2016. Understanding this escalation requires examining multiple dimensions: the increasing sophistication of attack techniques as threat actors continuously innovated to bypass defensive improvements, the expanding number of sophisticated adversaries as more nation-states and criminal groups developed advanced capabilities, the diversification of attack types as financially motivated actors employed ransomware, theft, extortion, and hybrid approaches, and the systemic nature of risks as interconnected systems created cascading vulnerabilities. The escalating threat landscape represented not temporary surge in activity but rather fundamental transformation in the cyber threat environment that all organizations and particularly financial institutions would need to navigate for the foreseeable future.

The sophistication escalation manifested in multiple technical dimensions as attackers continuously adapted to defensive measures and incorporated cutting-edge technologies into their operations. Malware became more evasive, employing sophisticated techniques to avoid detection by antivirus and endpoint protection tools that might have caught earlier generations of tools. Artificial intelligence and machine learning techniques began appearing in attacks, automating reconnaissance, optimizing social engineering, and adapting real-time to defensive responses. Supply chain attacks targeting software vendors and service providers represented increasingly common attack vectors as perimeter defenses improved and attackers sought alternative paths to target environments. The use of legitimate tools and "living off the land" techniques accelerated as sophisticated attackers recognized that custom malware faced detection risks while abuse of legitimate administrative tools proved harder to identify. Each defensive improvement prompted offensive adaptation, creating an arms race dynamic where defensive investment bought temporary advantages but never achieved lasting security against determined adversaries.

The proliferation of sophisticated actors dramatically increased the threat density facing financial institutions, as what was once primarily a concern about state-sponsored adversaries evolved into a multi-faceted threat environment including nation-state actors, sophisticated criminal groups, ideologically motivated hacktivists, and financially motivated individuals employing advanced techniques. The diffusion of tools, techniques, and expertise through criminal ecosystems meant that capabilities once exclusive to nation-state actors became available to well-resourced criminal groups willing to pay for access or recruit personnel with state-sponsored operations experience. The emergence of cyber mercenary groups that conducted sophisticated attacks on behalf of paying clients blurred lines between state-sponsored and criminal operations, creating situations where victims couldn't easily determine whether attacks represented nation-state operations, criminal enterprises, or hybrid scenarios involving both. The expanding adversary base meant that institutions faced threats from multiple directions with varying motivations, capabilities, and risk tolerances, complicating threat modeling and defensive prioritization.

The convergence of different attack types into hybrid operations that combined theft, ransomware, data exfiltration, and extortion created multifaceted threats more challenging to address than single-purpose attacks. Sophisticated adversaries began conducting attacks where initial network compromise enabled multiple potential monetization paths—direct theft if opportunities existed, ransomware deployment if theft proved infeasible, data exfiltration for extortion purposes, or simply selling access to other criminals. This hedging approach meant that even when primary objectives were thwarted, attackers might achieve secondary objectives that generated revenue or strategic value. Victims found themselves negotiating multiple dimensions of attacks simultaneously—paying ransom to decrypt systems while separately addressing threats to release exfiltrated data, or discovering theft attempts during investigation of apparent ransomware attacks. The multi-threaded nature of hybrid operations increased both attacker success rates and victim recovery complexity.

The targeting expansion beyond traditional financial institutions to encompass the broader financial services ecosystem created an expanded attack surface as third-party service providers, fintech companies, cryptocurrency exchanges, payment processors, and other entities became targets either for their own value or as stepping stones to more valuable ultimate targets. Attackers recognized that the financial services ecosystem extended far beyond banks to include numerous organizations that handled financial data, facilitated transactions, or provided services to traditional financial institutions—many of which maintained less sophisticated security than major banks. The interdependence within the financial ecosystem meant that compromise of service providers or smaller institutions could enable pivot attacks against larger, better-defended targets. The expanded targeting created collective security challenges where the ecosystem's overall security depended on the weakest participants, requiring that security practices improve broadly rather than only at the largest and most visible institutions.

The geopolitical dimensions of the threat landscape escalated as cyber operations became increasingly integrated into nation-state competition, with financially motivated attacks representing only one component of broader strategic cyber campaigns. The same actors conducting financial theft also engaged in espionage, intellectual property theft, and strategic positioning for potential future conflicts. The multi-purpose nature of state-sponsored cyber operations meant that financial institutions might find themselves targeted not just for their monetary value but also for intelligence about financial systems, for strategic positioning within critical infrastructure, or for testing capabilities that might be employed for more destructive purposes during conflicts. The geopolitical framing transformed financial institution security from purely economic concern to national security issue requiring coordination between commercial entities and government security agencies.

The psychological and organizational impacts of the escalating threat landscape created sustained pressure on security teams, executives, and boards as institutions grappled with the reality of persistent, sophisticated threats that could never be fully eliminated. Security fatigue set in as organizations confronted endless streams of threats, vulnerabilities, and incidents requiring attention and response. The impossibility of achieving perfect security against determined adversaries forced acceptance that breaches would occur and that detection and response capabilities mattered as much as prevention. The sustained high alert status required to maintain adequate security against sophisticated threats proved difficult to maintain organizationally, with resources, attention, and urgency naturally declining after immediate crises passed but needing to remain elevated against ongoing threats. Managing the long-term sustainability of security programs in an environment of escalating threats and persistent high pressure represented a challenge extending beyond technology into organizational psychology and leadership.

The future trajectory of threat landscape evolution remained concerning as emerging technologies created new attack vectors while defensive capabilities struggled to keep pace with adversarial innovation. The proliferation of internet-connected devices, the migration of critical systems to cloud environments, the adoption of artificial intelligence in both attacks and defenses, and the potential emergence of quantum computing capabilities that could break current encryption all represented developments that would reshape the threat landscape in ways not entirely predictable but likely favorable to sophisticated attackers. The fundamental asymmetry between attackers needing to find only single vulnerabilities while defenders must address all weaknesses meant that technological evolution generally expanded attack surfaces faster than defensive capabilities could comprehensively secure them. The implication was that the threat landscape would likely continue escalating in sophistication and complexity, requiring that defensive efforts remain continuously improving simply to maintain current risk levels rather than achieving meaningful risk reduction.

# Conclusion

The landscape of cyber attacks targeting financial institutions that the Bangladesh Bank heist illuminated extended far beyond that single incident to encompass a sustained campaign of sophisticated operations targeting dozens of institutions across multiple continents with varying but concerning success rates. The similar attacks before Bangladesh established the technical foundations and operational approaches that the February 2016 heist refined and executed with devastating effectiveness, while subsequent attacks demonstrated that neither international attention nor enhanced security measures had eliminated the threat. The pattern revealed systematic targeting of financial institutions by sophisticated adversaries who had developed repeatable methodologies, maintained operational tempo across multiple simultaneous operations, and demonstrated adaptive capabilities that enabled continuous evolution of techniques in response to defensive improvements.

The Ecuador central bank hack and Vietnamese bank attempts provided crucial additional data points demonstrating that Bangladesh Bank represented typical rather than exceptional targeting, with central banks and commercial institutions across developing markets facing particular pressure from attacks that exploited both technical vulnerabilities and the challenges of mounting effective defenses with limited resources. The varying outcomes across different incidents—some detected early and contained, others resulting in substantial theft—illustrated that while the threats were sophisticated and persistent, effective security practices including robust monitoring, timely detection, and rapid response could prevent catastrophic losses even when initial compromise occurred. The lesson proved both encouraging and sobering: institutions could defend successfully against sophisticated threats, but doing so required sustained investment, organizational commitment, and comprehensive security programs that many institutions struggled to achieve.

The evolution toward ransomware and targeting of corporate victims alongside traditional financial institutions transformed the threat landscape into something far more diverse and complex than the focused bank heist campaigns that characterized earlier periods. The emergence of sophisticated ransomware operations demonstrated that financially motivated actors could adapt their approaches based on defensive improvements, opportunity assessment, and economic calculations about optimal monetization strategies. The ransomware epidemic created dual threat environments where financial institutions needed to defend against both theft-focused attacks and operational disruption through encryption and extortion, multiplying defensive requirements and creating new dilemmas about response strategies. The evolution also suggested that as defenses against traditional theft improved, sophisticated actors would continue finding alternative approaches rather than abandoning financially motivated cyber operations entirely.

The escalating threat landscape that emerged in the years following Bangladesh Bank represented fundamental transformation rather than temporary increase in activity, driven by sophistication improvements, actor proliferation, attack diversification, and the integration of cyber operations into broader geopolitical competition. The arms race dynamics between attackers and defenders showed no signs of achieving stability, with each side's improvements prompting responses from the other in cycles that continuously elevated both threat sophistication and defensive requirements. The future trajectory suggested continuing escalation as emerging technologies created new attack vectors and as more actors developed sophisticated capabilities, meaning that the threat environment facing financial institutions would likely grow more rather than less challenging over time.

The collective picture revealed by examining other targets and victims demonstrated that Bangladesh Bank, far from being an isolated incident, represented one visible manifestation of systematic threats facing global financial infrastructure from sophisticated adversaries conducting sustained campaigns with strategic patience, substantial resources, and concerning success rates. The implications extended beyond individual institutional security to raise questions about collective defense of financial systems, the adequacy of current security investments and practices across the sector, and whether existing approaches to cybersecurity could achieve acceptable risk levels against threats that continued evolving and escalating. The answer appeared to be that substantial improvements were necessary but not yet sufficient, requiring ongoing transformation of financial sector security practices to address a new reality where sophisticated cyber threats represented persistent rather than occasional challenges to the integrity and stability of global financial systems.

# Chapter 12: The Arms Race

The response to the Bangladesh Bank heist and the broader pattern of sophisticated cyber attacks targeting financial institutions catalyzed what can only be described as an arms race—an accelerating competition between increasingly sophisticated attacks and ever-more-elaborate defenses, where each side's innovations prompt responses from the other in cycles of escalation that show no signs of reaching equilibrium. This chapter examines the defensive side of this arms race, exploring how financial institutions have transformed their security architectures, embraced emerging technologies like artificial intelligence and blockchain, and created an entire ecosystem of specialized security vendors and services attempting to stay ahead of or at least keep pace with evolving threats. The transformation represents one of the most dramatic shifts in banking technology investment priorities in modern history, with cybersecurity evolving from a supporting function to a strategic imperative commanding billions in investment and fundamentally reshaping how financial institutions architect systems, assess risks, and conduct operations. Understanding this arms race requires examining not just the technologies and practices being deployed but also the economic forces driving security investment, the organizational transformations required to implement sophisticated security programs, and the sobering reality that despite remarkable progress, the defensive side remains perpetually challenged by adversaries who continue finding new vulnerabilities to exploit and new techniques to bypass even advanced security measures.

## Modern Banking Security Measures

The security architecture of contemporary financial institutions bears little resemblance to what existed before the Bangladesh Bank heist exposed fundamental vulnerabilities in how banks protected their most critical systems. The transformation encompasses technical controls, organizational structures, operational procedures, and cultural shifts that collectively represent a comprehensive rethinking of banking security for the digital age. Understanding modern banking security measures requires examining multiple layers of defense that institutions now deploy, recognizing that no single technology or approach provides adequate protection but rather that comprehensive security demands integration of diverse capabilities working in concert to prevent, detect, and respond to sophisticated threats. The measures implemented since 2016 reflect hard-won lessons from Bangladesh Bank and countless other incidents about what actually works in defending against determined, sophisticated adversaries rather than theoretical best practices that prove inadequate when tested by real-world attacks.

The network segmentation and zero trust architectures that now characterize modern banking security represent fundamental departures from previous approaches that relied on perimeter defenses and assumed internal network traffic could be trusted. The Bangladesh Bank case demonstrated catastrophically that once attackers breached perimeters, flat network architectures allowed them to move freely and access critical systems including SWIFT infrastructure. Modern approaches implement micro-segmentation that divides networks into small zones with explicit access controls between segments, ensuring that compromise of one area doesn't automatically grant access to others. Zero trust principles that verify every access request regardless of network location or previous authentication extend this segmentation philosophy to assume that no user, device, or network segment can be inherently trusted. These architectural changes prove disruptive to implement, requiring network redesigns and often impacting operational workflows, but they dramatically reduce attackers' ability to move laterally through environments even after achieving initial compromise.

The endpoint detection and response capabilities that have become standard in banking environments represent significant evolution beyond traditional antivirus software that relied primarily on signature-based detection of known malware. Modern endpoint protection employs behavioral analysis that identifies suspicious activities based on what processes and users are doing rather than just what code they're running, enabling detection of novel malware variants and legitimate tool abuse that signature-based approaches would miss. The response capabilities enable security teams to remotely isolate compromised endpoints, capture forensic data, and remediate infections without requiring physical access to affected systems—critical capabilities for containing breaches rapidly before significant damage occurs. The integration of endpoint detection with broader security operations provides visibility into device-level activity that feeds threat hunting and incident response, creating comprehensive understanding of what's happening across institutional computing environments.

The security operations centers that financial institutions have built or contracted through managed service providers represent centralized capabilities for monitoring, detecting, and responding to threats across the entire organizational technology environment. These operations centers maintain 24/7/365 staffing with trained analysts reviewing security alerts, hunting for threats that automated tools might miss, coordinating incident response when breaches are detected, and continuously improving detection capabilities based on threat intelligence and lessons learned from incidents. The centers integrate data from diverse security tools—firewalls, intrusion detection systems, endpoint protection, application security tools, network monitoring, and numerous others—providing holistic visibility that enables detection of subtle patterns that might be invisible when examining any single data source. The investment in security operations centers represents one of the largest components of enhanced security spending, with institutions either building internal capabilities requiring substantial personnel costs or engaging managed security service providers that charge ongoing fees for continuous monitoring and response.

The multi-factor authentication and privileged access management that now protect access to critical banking systems address the credential compromise and insider threat vectors that the Bangladesh Bank attack exploited. Simple username-password authentication proved inadequate when sophisticated attackers could steal or guess credentials, phish them from users, or compromise systems where they were stored. Modern authentication requires multiple factors—something you know (password), something you have (security token or mobile device), and increasingly something you are (biometrics)—making credential compromise alone insufficient for gaining access. Privileged access management provides additional controls around administrative accounts that can access critical systems, implementing principles like just-in-time elevation where users receive elevated privileges only when needed for specific tasks, session recording for accountability, and additional verification for the most sensitive operations. These access controls create substantial friction in operational workflows but dramatically reduce the attack surface and the damage that compromised credentials can enable.

The comprehensive logging, monitoring, and audit capabilities that modern banking security demands generate enormous volumes of data about every significant activity within technology environments, creating trails that enable both real-time threat detection and after-the-fact forensic investigation. The Bangladesh

Bank case revealed inadequate logging that allowed attackers to operate with minimal trace and complicated investigation into exactly what they had done and how. Modern approaches capture detailed logs from every system, aggregate them in centralized platforms with massive storage and analysis capabilities, retain them for extended periods enabling historical analysis, and analyze them continuously for indicators of compromise or suspicious patterns. The technical infrastructure required to capture, store, and analyze logs at scale represents substantial investment, with large institutions processing terabytes of log data daily and smaller institutions facing challenges determining what logs to collect and how to analyze them effectively without overwhelming available resources.

The vulnerability management and patch management procedures that now operate with increased urgency and comprehensiveness address the reality that unpatched systems provided entry points for numerous sophisticated attacks including potentially Bangladesh Bank. Modern vulnerability management involves continuous scanning of all systems to identify security weaknesses, risk-based prioritization that focuses remediation on the most critical vulnerabilities first, and tracking to ensure that identified vulnerabilities are actually addressed rather than languishing indefinitely. Patch management procedures that once allowed weeks or months between vendor security patch releases and institutional deployment now target much faster timeframes, with critical patches sometimes deployed within days or hours of availability. The acceleration proves challenging operationally, as rapid patching increases risks of operational disruptions if patches cause unexpected problems, but the balance has shifted toward accepting some operational risk to reduce security risk from known, patchable vulnerabilities.

The integration of threat intelligence from commercial providers, government agencies, information sharing organizations, and institutional internal sources provides contemporary security programs with external context about threats, attack techniques, and indicators of compromise that enable proactive defense rather than purely reactive response. Threat intelligence feeds inform security tool configurations, guide threat hunting activities, provide context for investigating alerts, and support strategic planning about where to focus defensive investments. The challenge involves processing and prioritizing intelligence from multiple sources with varying quality and relevance, distinguishing genuine threats requiring immediate action from general information, and operationalizing intelligence so that it actually improves defensive capabilities rather than simply accumulating unused. Financial institutions increasingly employ dedicated threat intelligence teams that contextualize external intelligence for their specific environments and generate internal intelligence from their own security operations.

## AI and Machine Learning in Fraud Detection

The application of artificial intelligence and machine learning to fraud detection and cybersecurity represents one of the most significant technological transformations in banking security, promising capabilities that could fundamentally shift the balance in favor of defenders by enabling detection of subtle patterns that traditional rule-based systems would miss and allowing security measures to adapt continuously as threats evolve. The enthusiasm surrounding AI and machine learning in financial security is matched only by the complexity of actually implementing these technologies effectively and the reality that while they offer genuine advantages, they are neither silver bullets that solve all security challenges nor fully mature technologies without significant limitations and failure modes. Understanding the role of AI and machine learning in modern banking security requires examining both their legitimate contributions to fraud detection and threat identification and the more sobering realities about implementation challenges, algorithmic limitations, and the arms race dynamic where adversaries increasingly employ their own AI capabilities to evade detection.

The behavioral anomaly detection that machine learning enables represents perhaps its most valuable contribution to fraud detection, allowing systems to establish baseline patterns of normal activity for accounts, users, transactions, and systems, then identifying deviations that might indicate fraud or compromise even when the specific patterns haven't been previously observed. Traditional rule-based fraud detection relies on explicit criteria—transactions above certain amounts, transfers to high-risk countries, unusual login locations—that sophisticated attackers learn to work around. Machine learning approaches can identify subtle combinations of factors that collectively appear anomalous even when no individual factor triggers rule-based alerts. The models continuously learn from new data, refining their understanding of normal behavior and adjusting anomaly detection thresholds as patterns evolve. This adaptive capability proves particularly valuable against sophisticated adversaries who continuously modify their techniques to evade static detection rules.

The transaction monitoring applications of machine learning have revolutionized how financial institutions identify potentially fraudulent payments, money laundering patterns, and suspicious account activity across enormous volumes of daily transactions. Machine learning models can process and analyze millions of transactions in real-time, identifying patterns and relationships that human analysts could never detect manually and that traditional rule-based systems would miss due to their complexity. The models consider hundreds of variables simultaneously—transaction amounts, recipient patterns, timing, geographic factors, historical account behavior, relationships with other accounts, and numerous others—generating risk scores that prioritize which transactions require human review. The reduction in false positive rates compared to traditional approaches proves particularly valuable, as overwhelming analysts with alerts for legitimate transactions that happen to match simple rules reduces their ability to identify genuine fraud hidden among the noise.

The natural language processing capabilities that advanced AI systems possess enable analysis of text-based data—emails, chat messages, document contents—for indicators of social engineering attempts, policy violations, or insider threat activity. These systems can identify phishing emails by analyzing message content, sender characteristics, and embedded links or attachments for signs of malicious intent, providing an additional layer of defense before humans even see suspicious messages. Natural language analysis can flag potentially problematic communications between employees and external parties that might indicate social engineering or bribery attempts. The technology can also analyze internal communications for signs of disgruntled employees who might pose insider threats, though this application raises significant privacy concerns and ethical questions about surveillance of employee communications.

The challenges of implementing machine learning effectively in banking environments prove substantial, involving technical complexities, data quality requirements, model validation difficulties, and operational integration challenges that limit the technology's practical impact compared to its theoretical promise. Machine learning models require enormous quantities of high-quality training data to learn patterns effectively, but financial institutions often struggle with data that is incomplete, inconsistent across systems, or reflects historical biases that models perpetuate rather than correct. The "black box" problem where complex models make decisions that humans cannot easily understand or explain creates regulatory and operational challenges, particularly when models deny transactions or flag accounts and institutions need to explain the rationale to customers or regulators. Model validation and ongoing monitoring to ensure that performance doesn't degrade over time require specialized expertise that many institutions lack, and the consequences of model failures—missed fraud or excessive false positives—can be severe enough that conservative implementation approaches limit adoption of more aggressive machine learning techniques.

The adversarial machine learning dimension where attackers deliberately attempt to poison training data, evade detection models, or exploit model weaknesses creates an evolving challenge that mirrors the broader cybersecurity arms race. Sophisticated adversaries understand that financial institutions employ machine learning for fraud detection and deliberately craft their attacks to evade these systems—conducting reconnaissance to understand normal patterns and mimicking them closely, introducing noise into training data if they can access it, and probing detection systems to identify their boundaries and blind spots. The adversarial dynamic means that machine learning models require continuous updating and refinement as attackers adapt, and that the advantage machine learning provides may be temporary rather than permanent as adversaries develop their own countermeasures. Some threat actors employ their own machine learning capabilities to optimize their attacks, creating a AI-versus-AI dynamic where both sides employ algorithmic approaches in competition.

The integration of explainable AI techniques represents an important development addressing the black box problem by creating models that can provide human-understandable reasoning for their decisions alongside the decisions themselves. Explainable AI enables institutions to comply with regulatory requirements for transparency in decision-making, allows fraud analysts to understand why particular transactions were flagged so they can make informed judgments about investigating or dismissing alerts, and facilitates model improvement by identifying when models flag transactions for inappropriate reasons. The tradeoff often involves some reduction in pure predictive accuracy compared to complex black box models, as explainability constraints limit model complexity, but many institutions accept this tradeoff to gain transparency benefits.

The future trajectory of AI in banking security points toward increasingly sophisticated applications including autonomous response capabilities where systems not only detect threats but also take defensive actions without human intervention, advanced threat hunting using AI to proactively search for hidden threats, and predictive security that attempts to identify vulnerabilities before attackers exploit them. However, the same trajectory raises concerns about over-reliance on AI systems that might be manipulated or that might fail in unexpected ways during critical incidents, about the escalating sophistication required to maintain effective AI security as adversaries employ their own AI capabilities, and about the ethical and social implications of algorithmic decision-making in financial contexts. The balance between embracing AI's genuine capabilities and maintaining appropriate human oversight and accountability remains an evolving challenge.

## Blockchain and Distributed Security Models

The exploration of blockchain and distributed ledger technologies as potential foundations for more secure financial systems represents one of the more speculative but potentially transformative responses to the vulnerabilities that attacks like Bangladesh Bank exposed. The fundamental characteristics of blockchain technology—distributed consensus, immutability of recorded transactions, cryptographic verification, and elimination of single points of trust or failure—address some of the architectural vulnerabilities that enabled the Bangladesh Bank heist, suggesting that fundamentally different approaches to financial infrastructure might provide security advantages that incremental improvements to existing systems cannot achieve. However, the enthusiasm for blockchain as a security panacea must be tempered by sober assessment of the technology's actual maturity, the substantial challenges of implementing blockchain in contexts requiring traditional banking performance and regulatory compliance, and the reality that blockchain introduces its own vulnerabilities and limitations. Understanding blockchain's potential role in future financial security requires examining both its genuine contributions to addressing specific security challenges and the more nuanced reality about where blockchain proves genuinely advantageous versus where traditional approaches remain superior.

The distributed consensus mechanisms that form blockchain's foundation eliminate single points of failure and create tamper-evident records that address some fundamental vulnerabilities in traditional financial infrastructure. The Bangladesh Bank attack succeeded partly because centralized systems could be compromised by attackers who then had unilateral ability to generate fraudulent transactions that appeared authentic. Blockchain approaches require distributed validation where multiple parties must agree on transaction legitimacy before transactions are recorded, making it substantially harder for attackers to inject fraudulent transactions even if they compromise some participants. The immutability of blockchain records means that once transactions are recorded, they cannot be quietly altered or deleted without detection, addressing the evidence manipulation that Bangladesh Bank attackers attempted. These characteristics suggest that blockchain-based payment systems might resist certain types of fraud more effectively than centralized alternatives.

The cryptocurrency context where blockchain technology originally emerged provides working examples of financial systems operating without traditional centralized intermediaries, demonstrating both the potential and limitations of blockchain approaches at scale. Bitcoin, Ethereum, and other cryptocurrencies have processed billions in value transfers using blockchain technology, proving that distributed consensus can work for financial applications. However, cryptocurrency systems also demonstrate blockchain's limitations: transaction processing speeds far below what traditional payment networks handle, energy consumption concerns for proof-of-work consensus, volatility and lack of stability mechanisms, and persistent security challenges including exchange hacks, wallet compromises, and smart contract vulnerabilities. The cryptocurrency experience suggests that while blockchain offers certain security advantages, it isn't a comprehensive solution to all financial security challenges and introduces new complexities and risks alongside its benefits.

The exploration of blockchain for interbank payment and settlement represents perhaps the most serious investigation of how distributed ledger technology might transform traditional financial infrastructure in ways that improve security and efficiency. Several major banks and central banks have explored or piloted blockchain-based systems for cross-border payments, securities settlement, or other wholesale financial operations where blockchain's characteristics might provide advantages over existing infrastructure. The potential benefits include faster settlement times, reduced counterparty risk through distributed verification, lower operational costs by eliminating intermediaries, and enhanced transparency through shared ledgers that all participants can audit. However, practical implementation faces substantial challenges including scalability limitations, privacy concerns when transaction details are visible across distributed networks, regulatory uncertainty about how existing financial regulations apply to blockchain systems, and the massive coordination required to transition existing infrastructure to fundamentally different technological foundations.

The smart contract capabilities that advanced blockchain platforms provide enable programmable money and automated transaction processing based on predefined conditions, potentially reducing fraud by encoding business logic directly into the transaction infrastructure. Smart contracts could automatically verify that transaction prerequisites are met before allowing execution, implement multi-party approval workflows that require consensus before large transfers proceed, or enforce compliance with regulatory requirements through code rather than relying on manual procedures. However, smart contract security remains a significant concern, with numerous high-profile incidents where vulnerabilities in smart contract code enabled theft or manipulation of funds. The immutability that makes blockchain tamper-resistant also means that bugs in smart contracts cannot be easily fixed once deployed, creating situations where security flaws may be permanent and exploitable.

The private and permissioned blockchain variants that financial institutions favor for practical applications represent significant departures from public blockchain models, sacrificing some decentralization and openness for improved performance, privacy, and regulatory compliance. Private blockchains restrict participation to authorized entities rather than allowing anyone to join the network, enabling faster transaction processing and greater control over who can view transaction data. Permissioned models implement governance structures where known entities maintain the network rather than purely algorithmic consensus among anonymous participants. These modifications address some practical barriers to blockchain adoption in regulated financial contexts but also reduce some of the security benefits that public blockchain's radical decentralization provides, creating systems that represent hybrid approaches between traditional centralized infrastructure and pure blockchain models.

The realistic assessment of blockchain's near-term impact on banking security suggests that the technology will likely remain niche rather than revolutionary for the foreseeable future, providing genuine value in specific use cases while failing to transform core banking infrastructure in ways that fundamentally alter security architectures. Blockchain may prove valuable for specific applications like trade finance, cross-border payments, or securities settlement where its characteristics address particular pain points, while remaining impractical for core banking functions requiring higher performance, greater flexibility, or tighter regulatory oversight than current blockchain technology can provide. The hype that surrounded blockchain during its peak enthusiasm period has given way to more measured assessment of where the technology genuinely adds value versus where it introduces complexity without commensurate benefits.

The future evolution of blockchain technology may address current limitations through advances in consensus mechanisms, scaling solutions, privacy techniques, and integration with traditional financial infrastructure. Second-generation blockchain platforms address some first-generation limitations, regulatory frameworks are slowly developing to provide greater legal certainty, and financial institutions are gaining experience with what works and what doesn't in blockchain implementations. However, the fundamental question of whether blockchain represents genuinely transformative technology for financial security or merely incremental improvement in specific contexts remains open, with the answer likely depending on continued technological development and practical experience with large-scale implementations.

## The Security Industry Boom

The escalation of cyber threats targeting financial institutions and other sectors catalyzed explosive growth in the cybersecurity industry, transforming it from a niche specialty into one of the fastest-growing sectors of the global economy with market valuations in the hundreds of billions and demand for products, services, and personnel far outstripping supply. Understanding this boom requires examining multiple dimensions: the proliferation of specialized security vendors offering increasingly sophisticated tools and services, the emergence of cybersecurity as a strategic priority commanding substantial portions of IT budgets, the transformation of professional services consulting where cybersecurity capabilities became essential offerings, and the human capital challenges as demand for skilled security professionals dramatically exceeded available supply. The security industry boom represents both response to genuine needs and, critics might argue, opportunistic exploitation of security anxiety where vendors market solutions to every conceivable threat regardless of whether those solutions actually address priority risks or simply add to already-overwhelming technology sprawl.

The venture capital investment that flooded into cybersecurity startups during and after 2016 reflected investor recognition that the market for security solutions would grow dramatically as institutions responded to escalating threats. Hundreds of cybersecurity startups received funding to develop novel approaches to threat detection, endpoint protection, identity management, cloud security, application security, and numerous other specialties within the broad cybersecurity domain. Some of these startups developed genuinely innovative technologies that addressed gaps in existing security tools, while others offered incremental improvements or marketing differentiation rather than fundamental innovations. The proliferation of vendors created an increasingly fragmented marketplace where enterprises struggled to evaluate which solutions actually addressed their needs versus which simply added another point product to already complex security architectures. The consolidation through acquisitions by larger security vendors or technology platforms represented an inevitable market response to the unsustainable proliferation of specialized point solutions.

The managed security service provider model experienced dramatic growth as financial institutions and other organizations recognized they couldn't build sufficient internal capabilities to address sophisticated threats and instead outsourced security operations to specialized firms. MSSPs offered to assume responsibility for security monitoring, threat detection, incident response, and various operational security functions, leveraging economies of scale and specialized expertise to provide capabilities that individual institutions might struggle to develop internally. The model proved particularly attractive to smaller institutions that lacked resources for building comprehensive internal security programs, though even large institutions increasingly engaged MSSPs to supplement internal capabilities. The MSSP industry matured from providing primarily network monitoring to offering comprehensive managed security portfolios including endpoint protection, threat intelligence, security orchestration, and incident response services. However, questions about MSSP effectiveness, the risk of over-dependence on external parties for critical security functions, and the challenge of ensuring MSSP personnel understood specific client environments well enough to provide truly effective monitoring created ongoing debates about optimal balancing between internal and outsourced security capabilities.

The consolidation of security tools into integrated platforms represented market response to the overwhelming complexity of managing dozens of separate point solutions, with major vendors acquiring or developing comprehensive security suites that promised to address multiple needs through integrated platforms rather than requiring separate tools for every function. Security operations platforms that integrated threat intelligence, security orchestration, case management, and workflow automation aimed to provide comprehensive environments for security teams rather than forcing them to work across numerous separate tools. Extended detection and response platforms that unified endpoint, network, cloud, and application security data into single interfaces addressed the challenge of correlating indicators across diverse security tools. The platform consolidation created its own tensions, as comprehensive platforms from single vendors risked creating strategic dependencies and potential single points of failure, while best-of-breed approaches that selected optimal tools for each function created integration and management complexity.

The professional services explosion around cybersecurity reflected both genuine needs for expertise to implement and operate complex security programs and the consulting industry's recognition of cybersecurity as a lucrative growth area. Major consulting firms developed or acquired cybersecurity practices offering strategy consulting, security assessment, incident response, compliance services, and managed security operations. Specialized boutique firms focused on incident response, penetration testing, security assessment, or other specific domains where deep expertise commanded premium rates. The challenge for organizations purchasing security consulting involved determining whether recommendations reflected genuine expertise and client interests versus consultants' incentives to sell additional services or particular vendor solutions with which they had partnerships. The variable quality across security consultants—ranging from deeply experienced practitioners providing genuine value to less experienced personnel learning on client engagements—created buyer challenges in identifying truly capable providers.

The cybersecurity workforce shortage that accompanied industry growth created intense competition for talented security professionals, driving dramatic salary increases and creating situations where demand for skilled personnel exceeded supply by factors that some estimates placed at three-to-one or higher. Financial institutions found themselves competing not just with each other but also with technology companies, consulting firms, government agencies, and security vendors for the same limited pool of experienced security personnel. The shortage proved particularly acute for specialized roles requiring deep technical expertise—malware analysts, threat hunters, security architects, incident responders—where the combination of necessary technical skills and practical experience produced very limited candidate pools. The competition for talent drove institutions to offer increasingly generous compensation, develop internal training programs to grow talent, and implement retention strategies to prevent competitors from poaching their security staff. The talent shortage also accelerated adoption of automation, managed services, and other approaches that could supplement human capabilities with technology or external resources.

The certification and training industry that emerged to address workforce shortages attempted to systematize security knowledge and provide credentials that could identify qualified practitioners, though with mixed success in actually ensuring that certified individuals possessed practical capabilities beyond test-taking ability. Numerous certification programs offered credentials in various security domains—CISSP for security management, CISM for information security managers, CEH for ethical hacking, and dozens of vendor-specific and domain-specific certifications. Training providers offered courses ranging from introductory security awareness to advanced technical training in penetration testing, malware analysis, or security architecture. However, the relationship between certifications and actual capability remained imperfect, with experienced practitioners sometimes lacking formal credentials while certified individuals might lack practical experience. Organizations struggled to use certifications effectively in hiring and professional development, recognizing them as potentially useful signals but insufficient indicators of whether candidates could actually perform security roles effectively.

The future trajectory of the security industry points toward continued growth as threats persist and expand but also toward maturation and possible correction as unrealistic expectations about security solutions' capabilities encounter practical realities. The market will likely see continued consolidation as the unsustainable proliferation of specialized vendors gives way to more integrated platforms and as weaker companies fail or are acquired. The emphasis may shift from acquiring more security tools to actually effectively deploying and operating the substantial capabilities institutions have already invested in but often underutilize. The workforce shortage may gradually ease as more individuals enter security careers and as automation and managed services supplement human capabilities, though the most specialized roles will likely remain highly competitive. The overall market for security products and services will almost certainly continue growing given persistent and evolving threats, but the growth may become more selective as buyers become more sophisticated about what actually provides value versus what simply adds cost and complexity.

## Future Vulnerabilities

Despite remarkable progress in banking security capabilities and substantial investment in defensive technologies, the future threat landscape promises to create new categories of vulnerabilities that will challenge even significantly improved security postures. Understanding these future vulnerabilities requires examining emerging technologies and trends that will reshape banking and financial services, recognizing that each innovation creating new capabilities also introduces new attack surfaces and risks. The sobering reality is that security improvements, while essential and valuable, cannot eliminate vulnerability but rather represent continuous adaptation to evolving threats—an endless arms race where defenders must anticipate and prepare for threats that don't yet exist while addressing current challenges. The future vulnerabilities discussed here represent not speculation about exotic scenarios but rather logical extensions of observable trends in technology evolution and threat actor capabilities that will almost certainly create security challenges in coming years.

The quantum computing threat represents perhaps the most fundamental long-term vulnerability facing current security architecture, as quantum computers capable of breaking widely used encryption algorithms would undermine the cryptographic foundations upon which nearly all digital security depends. Current public key cryptography that secures internet communications, authenticates financial transactions, and protects sensitive data relies on mathematical problems that classical computers cannot solve efficiently but that sufficiently powerful quantum computers could crack. The timeline for quantum computers reaching this capability remains uncertain—estimates range from a decade to potentially several decades—but the threat is real enough that organizations are beginning preparations for post-quantum cryptography. The transition to quantum-resistant algorithms represents an enormous undertaking requiring replacement of cryptographic systems throughout global information infrastructure, and the extended timeline means that data encrypted today could potentially be collected and stored by adversaries who decrypt it years from now when quantum capabilities become available. Financial institutions face particularly acute quantum threats as authentication, transaction signing, and data protection all depend on cryptography that quantum computing could break.

The artificial intelligence capabilities that are revolutionizing defensive security will simultaneously enhance attackers' capabilities, creating an AI-versus-AI arms race where both sides employ machine learning and automation to optimize their operations. Attackers will use AI to automate reconnaissance at scale, craft more effective social engineering by analyzing vast amounts of personal data to create targeted phishing, generate polymorphic malware that continuously modifies itself to evade detection, and adapt attack techniques in real-time based on defensive responses. The democratization of AI capabilities through cloud services and open-source tools means that sophisticated AI-enabled attacks won't remain exclusive to nation-state actors but will become available to increasingly wide range of threat actors. The speed at which AI-enabled attacks can operate—conducting reconnaissance, identifying vulnerabilities, launching exploits, and adapting to defenses faster than humans can respond—will compress response timelines and potentially overwhelm human-dependent defensive procedures. The challenge for defenders involves not just deploying their own AI capabilities but ensuring that their AI systems can effectively counter adversarial AI without creating brittle dependencies on algorithmic decision-making that sophisticated adversaries learn to manipulate.

The Internet of Things proliferation creates exponentially expanding attack surfaces as billions of connected devices—from smart office equipment to building automation systems to employee wearables—join networks and potentially provide entry points for attackers or collection points for reconnaissance. Many IoT devices are designed with minimal security, lack update mechanisms for patching vulnerabilities, use default credentials that are never changed, and operate on networks where they receive inadequate security monitoring. The diversity of IoT device types, manufacturers, and operating systems creates nightmare scenarios for security teams attempting to inventory what's on their networks, understand what vulnerabilities might exist, and implement appropriate security controls. Financial institutions face particular challenges as IoT devices proliferate in branch offices, back-office operations, and increasingly in financial products themselves as connected devices incorporate payment capabilities. The future where billions of inadequately secured devices operate on and adjacent to financial networks creates threat scenarios that current security architectures struggle to address comprehensively.

The cloud migration that financial institutions increasingly pursue for operational efficiency and technology modernization creates new security architectures where traditional perimeter-based security models prove inadequate and where shared responsibility between institutions and cloud providers creates potential gaps if not carefully managed. Cloud environments operate on fundamentally different models than traditional data centers, with greater dynamism, shared infrastructure among multiple tenants, and reliance on provider security capabilities that institutions must trust but cannot fully control or verify. The misconfigurations that plague cloud security—improperly configured storage buckets exposing sensitive data, overly permissive access controls, inadequate network segmentation—represent vulnerabilities distinct from traditional on-premises security challenges. The rapid pace of cloud evolution means that new services and capabilities emerge faster than security best practices can be fully established and disseminated. Financial institutions navigating cloud adoption must develop new security competencies, implement cloud-specific security tools, and carefully manage the shared responsibility model where they remain ultimately accountable for security even when relying on cloud provider capabilities.

The supply chain vulnerabilities that have become increasingly prominent create scenarios where attackers compromise not target institutions directly but rather software vendors, hardware manufacturers, or service providers whose compromised products then infect target environments. The SolarWinds supply chain attack that came to light in 2020 demonstrated how compromising a widely-used software product's update mechanism could enable access to thousands of organizations including financial institutions, government agencies, and major corporations. The complexity of modern software supply chains—where applications incorporate numerous third-party components, dependencies, and libraries—creates vast attack surfaces where compromise of any component could affect downstream users. Hardware supply chain vulnerabilities where malicious components are inserted during manufacturing or shipping represent even more insidious threats as they potentially compromise systems at foundational levels that software security tools cannot address. Financial institutions must somehow secure supply chains involving thousands of vendors and millions of software components, a task that exceeds current capabilities even as the threat continues growing.

The insider threat evolution represents continuing vulnerability as the line between external attackers and malicious insiders blurs through compromised employees, sophisticated social engineering that creates unwitting insider accomplices, and the potential for radicalization or recruitment of personnel who have privileged access to systems and data. The increasing sophistication of adversaries in cultivating insider relationships—through social media, professional networking, romance scams, or financial coercion—creates threats that technical security controls struggle to address. The remote work trend that distributes employees across uncontrolled environments and reduces informal oversight that office environments provide potentially increases insider threat risks.

The challenge involves implementing monitoring and controls sufficient to detect malicious insider activity without creating invasive surveillance that damages employee trust, morale, and privacy. Future threats will likely involve increasingly sophisticated approaches to compromising or manipulating insiders, requiring that institutions balance security monitoring against employee relations and ethical considerations.

The regulatory compliance complexity that continues expanding creates vulnerabilities where the burden of meeting numerous overlapping requirements diverts security resources from risk-based priorities to checkbox compliance, potentially leaving genuinely important vulnerabilities unaddressed while ensuring superficial compliance with regulations. The proliferation of data protection regulations, cybersecurity requirements, and industry standards creates situations where institutions spend enormous resources on compliance activities that may or may not materially improve security against actual threats. The tension between demonstrable compliance and actual security effectiveness represents an ongoing challenge, particularly when regulations emphasize documentation and process over measurable security outcomes. Future regulatory expansion seems likely as governments respond to continuing incidents with new requirements, creating additional compliance burden that may or may not align with institutions' actual risk profiles and threat landscapes.

## Conclusion

The arms race between financial institution defenders and sophisticated attackers has intensified dramatically since the Bangladesh Bank heist, with both sides investing substantial resources in improving their capabilities in cycles of innovation and counter-innovation that show no signs of reaching equilibrium. The defensive side has made remarkable progress in implementing comprehensive security measures that address many vulnerabilities Bangladesh Bank exposed—network segmentation that limits lateral movement, endpoint detection that identifies sophisticated malware, security operations that provide continuous monitoring and rapid response, multi-factor authentication that reduces credential compromise risks, and numerous other controls that collectively represent dramatically improved security postures compared to pre-2016 conditions. These improvements have demonstrably increased the difficulty of conducting successful attacks, with numerous intrusions detected and contained before they could achieve objectives that earlier might have succeeded.

The application of artificial intelligence and machine learning to fraud detection and threat identification represents one of the most promising defensive innovations, enabling identification of subtle patterns that traditional approaches would miss and adaptive security that continuously evolves as threats change. However, the promise must be tempered by recognition of implementation challenges, algorithmic limitations, and the emerging adversarial AI landscape where attackers employ their own machine learning capabilities to evade detection. The AI arms race appears likely to continue indefinitely with neither side achieving decisive advantages, though the application of AI to both offensive and defensive operations will transform the speed and sophistication of cyber conflicts in ways that strain human ability to maintain meaningful oversight and decision-making authority.

The exploration of blockchain and distributed security models provides valuable lessons about technological silver bullets and the reality that fundamentally different architectural approaches offer certain advantages while introducing new challenges and limitations. Blockchain may prove valuable in specific applications but is unlikely to transform core banking infrastructure in near future, with practical implementations representing hybrid approaches that sacrifice some blockchain purity for necessary performance, privacy, and regulatory compliance. The experience with blockchain reflects broader patterns where new technologies are initially hyped as revolutionary solutions to security challenges but eventually find more modest but still valuable roles in specific contexts rather than wholesale replacement of existing approaches.

The security industry boom that followed escalating threats created an ecosystem of vendors, service providers, consultants, and training organizations attempting to address legitimate security needs but also adding complexity through tool proliferation and creating challenges in distinguishing genuinely valuable capabilities from marketing hype. The industry maturation likely involves consolidation as unsustainable vendor proliferation gives way to more integrated platforms, and the workforce shortage gradually eases as more individuals enter security careers. However, the fundamental demand for security products, services, and personnel will almost certainly continue growing given persistent threats and expanding attack surfaces as technology continues evolving.

The future vulnerabilities that loom on the horizon—quantum computing threats to current cryptography, AI-enabled attacks of unprecedented sophistication, IoT attack surface expansion, cloud security challenges, supply chain compromises, and evolving insider threats—suggest that despite remarkable defensive progress, the security challenge will remain perpetually demanding. Each new technology and capability introduced to improve banking operations also creates new vulnerabilities and attack vectors that adversaries will attempt to exploit. The arms race appears destined to continue indefinitely, with neither side achieving lasting decisive advantages but rather engaging in continuous competition where today's defensive innovations become tomorrow's challenges to overcome as attackers adapt and evolve.

The sobering conclusion is that perfect security remains impossible and that the goal must be continuous improvement that makes attacks sufficiently difficult that fewer adversaries possess necessary capabilities and resources to succeed, that detected breaches can be contained before catastrophic damage occurs, and that the cost-benefit calculation for attackers shifts unfavorably through improved defenses and enhanced consequences for successful attacks. The Bangladesh Bank heist catalyzed remarkable transformation in banking security, but that transformation represents beginning rather than completion of the journey toward adequate security in the face of sophisticated, persistent, and evolving threats. The arms race will continue, requiring that financial institutions maintain sustained investment in security capabilities, organizational commitment to security as strategic priority, and willingness to continuously adapt as new vulnerabilities emerge and new defensive approaches become necessary.

The ultimate measure of success in this arms race will not be elimination of all successful attacks—an impossible standard—but rather the substantial reduction in successful sophisticated attacks, the limitation of damage when breaches do occur through rapid detection and response, and the creation of security architectures resilient enough to maintain operations and protect critical assets despite ongoing threat activity. The progress since Bangladesh Bank, while substantial and commendable, represents only one phase in perpetual competition between attackers and defenders. The institutions that will fare best in this continuing conflict will be those that recognize security as never-ending journey rather than achievable destination, that balance investment in emerging technologies with mastery of fundamental security practices, that cultivate organizational cultures where security is everyone's responsibility rather than delegated to specialists, and that maintain realistic expectations about what security can achieve while remaining committed to continuous improvement in the face of persistent adversity.

The arms race metaphor, while apt in many ways, also risks creating fatalistic mindset that accepts continuing escalation as inevitable without recognizing that defenders possess certain inherent advantages that can be leveraged more effectively. Defenders operate on familiar terrain—their own networks and systems—while attackers must conduct reconnaissance to understand unfamiliar environments. Defenders benefit from accumulated experience and institutional knowledge about their specific systems and threats, while attackers must constantly adapt to different target environments. Defenders can implement comprehensive security architectures where multiple layers of defense create cumulative protection, while attackers must successfully navigate all layers to achieve objectives. The challenge involves actualizing these inherent defensive advantages through comprehensive security programs, sustained investment, organizational commitment, and continuous adaptation—challenging requirements but nonetheless achievable for institutions willing to prioritize security appropriately and maintain discipline in implementation.

# Chapter 13: Recovery and Resilience

The immediate aftermath of the Bangladesh Bank heist left the institution reeling from both the direct financial losses and the devastating blow to its credibility as the nation's central bank and guardian of monetary stability. The path from crisis to recovery proved far more complex and protracted than simply recouping stolen funds or implementing technical security improvements, requiring fundamental organizational transformation, painful personnel changes, prolonged legal battles, and sustained efforts to rebuild trust among international partners, domestic stakeholders, and the Bangladeshi public. This chapter examines Bangladesh Bank's arduous journey from catastrophic breach victim to a reformed institution that, while forever marked by the incident, emerged with substantially strengthened capabilities and renewed commitment to its responsibilities. The recovery journey illuminated universal truths about institutional resilience in the face of crisis—that rebuilding trust requires transparency rather than obfuscation, that meaningful reform demands accountability including at senior levels, that some damage proves irreparable regardless of subsequent efforts, and that true resilience emerges not from denying vulnerabilities but from acknowledging them honestly while demonstrating commitment to comprehensive improvement. Understanding Bangladesh Bank's recovery provides lessons applicable far beyond this specific case to any organization attempting to rebuild after catastrophic security failures.

## Bangladesh Bank's Recovery Journey

The initial weeks and months following the February 2016 heist represented a period of profound institutional crisis as Bangladesh Bank confronted the reality of what had occurred while simultaneously attempting to contain ongoing damage, investigate the breach comprehensively, and maintain operational continuity in the face of internal chaos and external scrutiny. The recovery journey began not with clear roadmaps or established playbooks but rather with urgent damage control efforts that unfolded amid confusion about the attack's full scope, recriminations about who bore responsibility, and intense pressure from government officials, international partners, and media demanding answers and accountability. Understanding the early recovery phase requires recognizing the fog of crisis that surrounded the institution during these critical months when every decision occurred under extraordinary pressure with incomplete information and when mistakes made during crisis response could compound the original damage.

The immediate operational priorities centered on securing systems that had been compromised, restoring confidence that the bank could safely conduct international transactions, and coordinating with law enforcement and foreign partners on investigation and fund recovery efforts. Bangladesh Bank needed to demonstrate to the Federal Reserve Bank of New York and other correspondent banks that it had regained control of its systems and could prevent additional fraudulent transactions—a challenge when the institution's own understanding of how the compromise occurred remained incomplete and when enhanced security measures needed to be implemented while maintaining critical banking operations. The parallel demands of cooperating with multiple investigations while conducting internal assessments, managing public communications while protecting sensitive information about ongoing investigations, and implementing security improvements while ensuring they didn't disrupt operations created overwhelming complexity during a period when the institution's capabilities were already strained by the crisis.

The psychological and cultural toll on Bangladesh Bank personnel proved as significant as technical and operational challenges, with the breach creating an atmosphere of suspicion, demoralization, and fear that complicated recovery efforts. Staff members questioned whether they were under investigation, worried about their career prospects at an institution suffering massive reputational damage, and struggled with the shame of being associated with one of history's largest banking security failures. The forensic investigations that examined how the breach occurred required intrusive examinations of personnel activities, creating tensions between investigative necessity and employee privacy and dignity. Some staff members departed voluntarily, seeking opportunities at institutions not tainted by scandal, while others were removed as accountability measures unfolded. The institutional knowledge loss from departing experienced personnel complicated recovery even as removing individuals was necessary for demonstrating accountability and potentially addressing insider threat issues.

The relationship management with international partners represented another critical dimension of early recovery, as Bangladesh Bank needed to maintain or restore connections that the breach had severely strained. The Federal Reserve Bank of New York, while cooperative during investigation and fund recovery efforts, necessarily reassessed its relationship with Bangladesh Bank and implemented additional scrutiny and controls around the account relationship. SWIFT, dealing with its own reputational concerns from the breach, required that Bangladesh Bank implement comprehensive security enhancements before fully restoring normal services. Other central banks and financial institutions that had previously engaged with Bangladesh Bank on routine matters approached the relationship more cautiously, implementing additional verification procedures or simply reducing engagement rather than accepting the perceived risks of dealing with a compromised institution. Rebuilding these international relationships required patient demonstration that Bangladesh Bank had genuinely addressed the vulnerabilities that enabled the breach rather than simply implementing cosmetic changes.

The political dimensions of recovery proved particularly challenging in Bangladesh's context, where the heist became entangled in broader political dynamics and where government officials faced their own pressure to demonstrate decisive action in response to the crisis. The government's response included high-level investigations, parliamentary inquiries, and public statements that sometimes helped recovery efforts by demonstrating seriousness of purpose but other times complicated matters by creating additional reporting requirements, constraining management flexibility, or making the incident more politically charged than purely technical and operational responses might have preferred. The balance between appropriate government oversight and allowing institutional management sufficient autonomy to implement necessary reforms proved difficult to maintain, with the political attention ensuring accountability but sometimes creating pressures for rapid visible action over thoughtful long-term reform.

The financial pressures from the theft itself, while substantial, proved manageable for Bangladesh Bank given its role as central bank with access to resources that a commercial bank would not possess. However, the incident created indirect financial costs through legal expenses for fund recovery efforts, consulting fees for security assessments and implementations, technology investments in enhanced security infrastructure, and increased operational costs from additional staffing and procedures. The overall financial impact extended well beyond the direct loss of funds to encompass years of elevated expenses related to recovery, reform, and reputation restoration. For a developing country institution where resources are always constrained and where the stolen funds represented money that could have supported economic development or monetary policy operations, these indirect costs added to the burden of an already catastrophic incident.

The timeline of recovery proved far longer than initial hopes suggested, with meaningful progress measured in years rather than months as comprehensive reform required sustained effort across multiple dimensions simultaneously. Early optimism that Bangladesh Bank could quickly implement technical fixes and restore normal operations gave way to recognition that genuine recovery required fundamental organizational transformation that would take years to fully accomplish. The extended timeline tested institutional patience and commitment, as maintaining reform momentum proved challenging when immediate crisis had passed and when competing priorities reemerged. The institutions that successfully navigate long-term recovery from catastrophic incidents are those that maintain discipline and commitment to reform even after immediate pressure subsides—a test that Bangladesh Bank continued facing years after the initial breach.

## Personnel Changes and Accountability

The question of accountability—who bore responsibility for the security failures that enabled the heist and what consequences they would face—became central to Bangladesh Bank's recovery journey and to broader questions about institutional governance and consequences for security failures. The accountability measures ultimately implemented ranged from removal of senior leadership to disciplinary actions against mid-level personnel to changes in organizational structures and reporting relationships designed to prevent similar failures. Understanding these personnel changes requires examining both the specific individuals and roles affected and the broader organizational culture implications of how accountability was implemented. The balance between identifying and removing individuals whose actions or inactions contributed to the breach versus creating scapegoats for systemic failures proved difficult to navigate, with risks both of insufficient accountability that would leave problems unaddressed and excessive punishment that might demoralize remaining staff or make the institution an unattractive employer.

The governor of Bangladesh Bank at the time of the heist became the most visible target of accountability measures, facing intense pressure to resign and ultimately departing amid controversy about whether the removal served justice or simply provided a politically convenient scapegoat. The governor's responsibility for the institution's overall security posture was clear at a conceptual level—the ultimate accountability for organizational success or failure rests with senior leadership—but the direct causal connection between specific governor decisions or actions and the technical security failures that enabled the breach was more complex. The removal sent strong signals about accountability at the highest levels and may have been necessary for beginning the institution's reputation recovery regardless of detailed analysis of personal culpability. However, leadership changes alone could not address the systemic vulnerabilities and organizational culture issues that contributed to the breach, requiring that accountability extend beyond symbolic removal of visible figures to encompass substantive organizational reforms.

The senior IT and security personnel whose direct responsibilities included the systems that were compromised faced detailed scrutiny about their actions, decisions, and potential negligence that might have enabled or facilitated the attack. Some individuals were removed from their positions amid allegations of inadequate security practices, failure to implement necessary controls, or potentially negligent management of critical systems.

The investigations into individual responsibility proved complex, as determining whether specific actions or inactions constituted culpable negligence versus merely reflected inadequate institutional resources, unclear responsibilities, or genuine limitations in expertise required difficult judgments. The risk of creating scapegoats who individually bore blame for systemic institutional failures needed to be balanced against the legitimate need to identify and remove individuals whose performance fell below acceptable standards or who had failed to fulfill their responsibilities.

The question of whether insider involvement facilitated the breach remained subject to investigation and speculation but never resulted in definitive public conclusions about specific personnel complicity. The sophistication of the attack and the attackers' apparent knowledge of internal systems raised inevitable questions about whether external attackers received assistance from insiders with access to sensitive information about systems, procedures, and security measures. However, proving such complicity to evidentiary standards sufficient for criminal charges proved challenging, and the alternative explanation—that sophisticated external attackers conducted thorough reconnaissance and developed their knowledge without insider assistance—remained plausible. The lingering uncertainty about potential insider involvement created an atmosphere of suspicion that complicated recovery and made personnel management more difficult even as definitive evidence remained elusive.

The restructuring of IT and security organizations within Bangladesh Bank represented organizational accountability beyond individual personnel changes, acknowledging that reporting structures, resource allocation, and institutional positioning of security functions had contributed to vulnerabilities. The reforms elevated security to higher organizational priority with more direct reporting to senior leadership, consolidated fragmented security responsibilities that had been distributed across multiple organizational units, and provided security functions with enhanced authority and resources to implement necessary controls. These structural changes addressed some of the systemic organizational issues that had limited security effectiveness even when individual personnel might have possessed adequate technical knowledge but lacked authority, resources, or organizational support to implement comprehensive security measures.

The implementation of enhanced hiring and vetting procedures for personnel with access to critical systems represented accountability in the form of acknowledging that previous personnel management practices had been inadequate. Bangladesh Bank strengthened background checks, implemented more rigorous technical assessments in hiring processes, established clearer criteria for positions requiring access to sensitive systems, and created enhanced monitoring and supervision of personnel with critical access. These procedural changes acknowledged that institutional vulnerabilities had extended beyond technology to encompass human resource practices that hadn't adequately ensured that personnel with critical responsibilities possessed necessary qualifications and trustworthiness.

The cultural changes around accountability and transparency represented perhaps the most significant but also most difficult aspects of personnel and organizational reform. Creating an institutional culture where security concerns are voiced and addressed rather than ignored, where acknowledging vulnerabilities is viewed as responsible rather than career-limiting, and where learning from failures takes priority over assigning blame requires sustained leadership commitment and cultural transformation that extends far beyond specific personnel changes. Bangladesh Bank's success in achieving these cultural shifts would ultimately determine whether the institutional reforms proved genuine and sustainable or merely represented temporary responses to crisis that faded as immediate pressure subsided. The challenge of maintaining accountability culture over time while avoiding the opposite extreme of blame-heavy environments where risk-taking and honest mistake acknowledgment become impossible represented an ongoing balancing act requiring thoughtful leadership.

## Some Funds Recovered: The Philippine Legal Battles

The efforts to recover stolen funds through Philippine legal proceedings represented one of the more successful aspects of Bangladesh Bank's post-heist recovery, though success remained partial with only a fraction of the stolen eighty-one million dollars ultimately returned through these channels. The Philippine legal battles illuminated both the possibilities and limitations of international asset recovery, demonstrating that determined pursuit through legal channels could achieve meaningful results while also revealing how much stolen money successfully laundered through sophisticated operations remains permanently beyond recovery. Understanding the Philippine recovery efforts requires examining the legal proceedings initiated, the cooperation and complications in working through Philippine judicial systems, the competing claims on frozen assets, and the ultimate disposition of funds that were successfully seized and returned versus those that disappeared permanently into the money laundering pipeline.

The initial asset freeze efforts in the Philippines, occurring in the weeks immediately following the heist's discovery, succeeded in securing some portion of funds before they could be completely dispersed beyond recovery. Philippine authorities, responding to urgent requests from Bangladesh Bank and international law enforcement partners, moved to freeze accounts at RCBC and other institutions where stolen funds had been traced. The speed of this initial response proved crucial, as delays of even days could have allowed additional funds to flow through the laundering operation and become irrecoverable. However, the frozen amounts represented only a portion of the total stolen funds that had flowed through the Philippines, with substantial amounts having already been withdrawn as cash or converted to other forms before freezing orders could be implemented. The partial success of the initial freeze set the pattern for the overall Philippine recovery efforts—meaningful progress but far from complete recovery.

The legal proceedings to actually return frozen funds to Bangladesh Bank rather than simply holding them indefinitely proved complex and protracted, involving multiple Philippine courts, numerous parties claiming interests in the funds, and legal arguments about jurisdiction, due process, and the application of both Philippine and international law. Bangladesh Bank needed to prove through Philippine legal processes that specific frozen assets represented proceeds of crime traceable to the theft—a burden that required comprehensive documentation of transaction flows, authentication of evidence from Bangladesh, and navigation of Philippine legal procedures that differed from those Bangladesh Bank personnel were familiar with. The proceedings extended over years as various parties contested the freeze and sought release of funds, requiring Bangladesh Bank to maintain sustained legal presence in the Philippines through local counsel and to accept the Philippine judicial system's pace rather than the urgency that the victim institution felt.

The contested claims from individuals and entities in the Philippines who asserted interests in frozen funds created additional complications, as some claimed they had received funds in good faith without knowledge that the money represented proceeds of crime and should therefore be allowed to retain proceeds. Philippine law, like legal systems worldwide, provides some protections for good faith purchasers or recipients who acquired assets without knowledge of criminal origins, creating situations where even clearly traceable stolen funds might not be fully recoverable if current holders could demonstrate innocent acquisition. The burden of proof around knowledge and good faith created opportunities for parties who had received stolen funds to argue they should be allowed to keep them, requiring Bangladesh Bank to demonstrate that recipients knew or should have known about the money's criminal origins. These legal battles over competing claims consumed years and substantial legal fees while portions of stolen funds remained frozen pending judicial resolution.

The role of RCBC in the Philippine legal proceedings proved particularly contentious, with questions about the bank's liability for facilitating money laundering, its responsibility to compensate Bangladesh Bank, and whether the bank should face penalties beyond regulatory sanctions for the security and compliance failures that had allowed massive funds to flow through accounts it maintained. Bangladesh Bank sought compensation from RCBC beyond just return of frozen funds, arguing that the Philippine bank's negligence in allowing money laundering created liability. RCBC defended itself by arguing it had been victimized by sophisticated criminals and that its obligations to Bangladesh Bank were limited. The legal questions about RCBC's liability under Philippine law and whether Bangladesh Bank could pursue recovery from RCBC as well as from accounts holding traced stolen funds added complexity to already intricate proceedings.

The settlements and judicial decisions that ultimately determined disposition of frozen funds resulted in partial recovery for Bangladesh Bank, with approximately fifteen to twenty million dollars eventually returned through various legal proceedings and settlements. This recovery, while representing only about twenty percent of the total stolen amount, nonetheless provided meaningful partial restitution and demonstrated that international asset recovery, while difficult and incomplete, could achieve results when victims pursued recovery aggressively through available legal channels. The returned funds provided some vindication for Bangladesh Bank's sustained pursuit of recovery despite the challenges and uncertainties involved. However, the low recovery percentage also demonstrated the harsh reality that sophisticated money laundering operations achieve their intended purpose of making stolen funds irrecoverable even when authorities understand what happened and who was involved.

The lessons from Philippine recovery efforts for future asset recovery operations included the critical importance of speed in freezing assets before they can be fully laundered, the value of international cooperation and coordination between victim countries and jurisdictions where stolen funds are laundered, the need for victim institutions to commit to sustained multi-year legal efforts rather than expecting rapid resolution, and the realistic expectation that even relatively successful recovery efforts will return only fractions of stolen amounts rather than complete restitution. The Philippine proceedings also highlighted limitations of existing international frameworks for asset recovery, with the absence of streamlined procedures for returning seized proceeds of transnational crimes requiring that each case navigate complex jurisdictional issues and legal proceedings rather than following established efficient processes.

## Institutional Reforms Implemented

The comprehensive reforms that Bangladesh Bank implemented in response to the heist represented the most substantive and enduring aspect of institutional recovery, transforming technology infrastructure, operational procedures, organizational structures, and institutional culture in ways that extended far beyond addressing the specific vulnerabilities that enabled the February 2016 attack. Understanding the reform program requires examining reforms across multiple dimensions—technical security enhancements, procedural changes to transaction processing and verification, organizational restructuring to elevate security as institutional priority, governance improvements to provide better oversight, and cultural transformation to create sustained commitment to security. The challenge involved implementing reforms comprehensive enough to address systemic vulnerabilities while managing the disruption that major change inevitably creates and ensuring that reforms proved sustainable beyond the immediate crisis period when pressure for change was at its peak.

The technical security infrastructure overhaul represented the most visible reform dimension, with Bangladesh Bank implementing comprehensive improvements to systems, networks, and security tools that addressed both the specific vulnerabilities exploited in the heist and broader security gaps identified through post-breach assessments. The institution implemented robust network segmentation isolating SWIFT infrastructure from other systems, deployed advanced endpoint protection and detection capabilities, established comprehensive security monitoring through a security operations center model, implemented multi-factor authentication for system access, and deployed numerous additional security tools and technologies. The technology investments represented tens of millions of dollars and required multi-year implementation timelines to complete comprehensively, with the institution needing to balance security improvements against operational continuity and limitations in available resources. The technical reforms, while essential, represented only one component of comprehensive improvement as Bangladesh Bank learned that technology alone couldn't ensure security without accompanying procedural, organizational, and cultural changes.

The procedural reforms to transaction processing implemented multiple additional verification layers designed to prevent fraudulent transactions from executing even if authentication systems were compromised. Bangladesh Bank implemented enhanced multi-party authorization requirements for large transactions, out-of-band verification procedures requiring confirmation through channels separate from systems used to initiate transactions, real-time monitoring of all SWIFT activity with alerts for anomalous patterns, and more frequent reconciliation of accounts and transaction logs. These procedural changes created additional operational friction and slowed transaction processing compared to pre-breach practices, but the institution accepted this as necessary tradeoff for substantially enhanced security. The key insight was that authentication alone provided inadequate security—procedural controls that verified transactions made operational sense and matched expected patterns were necessary even when authentication appeared valid.

The organizational restructuring elevated security from a mid-level IT function to a senior leadership priority with direct reporting to top management and board oversight. Bangladesh Bank created a Chief Information Security Officer role with authority and resources to implement security measures across the institution, consolidated fragmented security responsibilities that had been distributed across multiple units, and established regular security reporting to senior leadership and the board. The organizational changes addressed the reality that security had been inadequately positioned and resourced prior to the breach, with security personnel lacking authority to implement necessary measures or escalate concerns effectively. The structural reforms acknowledged that effective security required it be treated as strategic institutional priority rather than merely a technical IT concern.

The governance and oversight enhancements implemented board-level cybersecurity committees, regular security briefings for senior leadership, formalized risk assessment procedures that explicitly incorporated cybersecurity risks, and enhanced audit and compliance functions with specific responsibilities for reviewing security controls. These governance improvements created accountability structures ensuring that security would receive sustained senior-level attention rather than being relegated to operational levels. The board and senior leadership commitment to security governance represented crucial cultural signal that security was genuinely institutional priority deserving of time, resources, and attention from the highest organizational levels. The sustainability of reforms would ultimately depend on whether this senior-level commitment persisted beyond the immediate crisis or gradually eroded as memory of the breach faded.

The personnel and training investments represented recognition that technology and procedures alone were insufficient without qualified people to operate security systems, make sound security decisions, and maintain security-conscious culture. Bangladesh Bank invested in recruiting experienced security professionals to fill newly created roles, provided enhanced security training to existing IT and security personnel to improve their capabilities, implemented security awareness training for all personnel to address human factors and social engineering risks, and established ongoing professional development programs to maintain staff capabilities as threats evolved. The personnel investments represented sustained costs that would continue indefinitely rather than one-time expenditures, requiring institutional commitment to funding security workforce adequately over the long term.

The partnerships and external support relationships that Bangladesh Bank developed post-breach provided access to expertise and capabilities that the institution could not economically develop entirely internally. The bank engaged managed security service providers for security operations center functions, maintained relationships with incident response firms that could be engaged rapidly if future breaches occurred, participated in financial services information sharing organizations to receive threat intelligence, and established relationships with government cybersecurity agencies for support and coordination. These external relationships acknowledged that no institution, particularly one with Bangladesh Bank's resource constraints, could maintain entirely self-sufficient security capabilities and that leveraging external expertise represented sound strategy for addressing capability gaps.

## Reputation Restoration Efforts

The challenge of restoring Bangladesh Bank's reputation after suffering one of history's most publicized banking security breaches proved at least as difficult as implementing technical and organizational reforms, requiring sustained efforts to rebuild trust with international partners, demonstrate to domestic stakeholders that the institution had addressed its vulnerabilities, and reshape public narrative from catastrophic failure toward institutional recovery and resilience. Reputation restoration could not be achieved through public relations alone but rather required that genuine reforms be implemented and demonstrated through sustained performance over time, with transparency about what had occurred and what had been done to prevent recurrence. Understanding Bangladesh Bank's reputation restoration efforts requires examining multiple stakeholder groups whose trust needed to be rebuilt, the communication strategies employed, the role of time in allowing demonstrated performance to gradually overcome immediate crisis perceptions, and the sobering reality that some reputational damage may prove permanent regardless of subsequent efforts.

The international financial community whose trust was essential for Bangladesh Bank to effectively perform its central banking functions represented perhaps the most critical audience for reputation restoration efforts. The institution needed to convince the Federal Reserve Bank of New York and other correspondent banks that it could safely maintain accounts and conduct international transactions, persuade SWIFT and other financial infrastructure providers that its systems met security requirements, and demonstrate to foreign central banks and financial regulators that it operated with appropriate security and controls. This restoration required more than public statements—it demanded detailed briefings about security improvements implemented, submission to enhanced scrutiny and verification of controls, and ultimately sustained performance demonstrating that the institution could conduct operations without security incidents. The gradual restoration of normal correspondent banking relationships as counterparties gained confidence in Bangladesh Bank's improved security represented crucial validation of recovery efforts.

The domestic stakeholders including the Bangladesh government, domestic banks supervised by Bangladesh Bank, and the Bangladeshi public required different reputation restoration approaches that acknowledged the impact on national pride and confidence in key institutions. The government, facing its own political pressures about the breach, needed reassurance that Bangladesh Bank had accountability processes, had implemented genuine reforms, and would not embarrass the nation through additional incidents. Domestic banks needed confidence that their supervisor and partner in monetary policy operated with appropriate competence and security. The broader public needed reassurance that the institution protecting their financial system could do so effectively. These domestic audiences required communication strategies that balanced transparency about failures and reforms with maintaining sufficient confidence in the institution to preserve financial system stability.

The transparency challenges in reputation restoration involved determining how much detail to disclose about the breach, the vulnerabilities that enabled it, and the reforms implemented in response. Complete transparency risked exposing details that could inform future attackers or that might embarrass individuals and the institution, while excessive secrecy could fuel speculation and prevent stakeholders from evaluating whether reforms were adequate. Bangladesh Bank needed to provide sufficient transparency to demonstrate genuine reform commitment while protecting sensitive security details and respecting privacy of individuals involved. The balance proved difficult to manage, with different stakeholders often demanding different levels of disclosure than the institution preferred to provide. The general trend favored greater transparency than Bangladesh Bank might have initially preferred, as experience demonstrated that attempting to minimize or obscure the breach proved counterproductive for reputation restoration.

The participation in international forums and conferences where Bangladesh Bank personnel presented their experience, lessons learned, and recovery journey represented important reputation restoration opportunities. By openly discussing what had occurred and how the institution had responded, Bangladesh Bank demonstrated willingness to contribute to collective learning rather than simply hiding from the embarrassment. The presentations and publications about the incident and recovery helped reshape narrative from catastrophic failure that reflected poorly on the institution to valuable case study that provided lessons for the entire financial sector. The transformation of the breach from purely negative to also educational and contributory to collective security represented subtle but meaningful reputational improvement that acknowledged past failures while emphasizing present contributions.

The time dimension of reputation restoration proved significant, as meaningful change in perceptions required sustained demonstration of improved performance over periods measured in years rather than months. No amount of immediate communication or rapid reforms could instantly restore trust that had been shattered by such a public, catastrophic security failure. Instead, reputation gradually rebuilt as years passed without additional major incidents, as international audits and assessments verified security improvements, and as Bangladesh Bank's sustained competent performance in its core functions reminded stakeholders of the institution's overall capabilities beyond the single catastrophic failure. The patience required for reputation restoration tested institutional commitment, as the sustained effort without immediate visible results could prompt pressure to move on from recovery efforts before genuine reputation restoration had been achieved.

The realistic assessment of reputation restoration recognized that some damage might prove permanent, with the Bangladesh Bank heist likely remaining the institution's most internationally visible characteristic for the foreseeable future. When international audiences thought of Bangladesh Bank, the 2016 breach would likely be the first association for many years if not indefinitely. This reality required accepting that perfect reputation restoration to pre-breach status might be impossible and that the more achievable goal involved demonstrating sufficient recovery and reform that the breach became one part of the institution's history rather than its defining characteristic. The transformation from "the bank that got hacked" to "the bank that suffered a major breach but implemented comprehensive reforms and emerged stronger" represented the realistic aspiration for long-term reputation recovery.

# Conclusion

Bangladesh Bank's recovery journey from the catastrophic February 2016 heist represented one of the most comprehensive institutional transformations in modern banking history, encompassing technical infrastructure improvements, organizational restructuring, personnel changes, procedural reforms, and cultural evolution that collectively addressed the systemic vulnerabilities the breach exposed. The recovery process proved far more complex and extended than simple implementation of technical security fixes, requiring Bangladesh Bank to simultaneously manage immediate crisis response, conduct comprehensive investigations, pursue asset recovery through complex international legal proceedings, implement sweeping reforms across multiple dimensions, and restore reputation with stakeholders whose trust had been severely damaged. The years-long journey tested institutional resilience and commitment, requiring sustained effort even as immediate crisis pressure subsided and competing priorities reemerged.

The personnel changes and accountability measures implemented demonstrated that genuine recovery required acknowledging failures at all organizational levels including senior leadership, though the balance between appropriate accountability and scapegoating remained delicate and subject to ongoing debate. The removal of some personnel, elevation of security functions within organizational structures, and enhanced hiring and vetting procedures for positions with critical access addressed some of the human and organizational factors that had contributed to vulnerabilities. However, the more fundamental challenge of creating sustainable culture where security is genuinely prioritized and where personnel at all levels understand and fulfill their security responsibilities remained an ongoing effort extending beyond specific personnel changes.

The partial recovery of funds through Philippine legal proceedings provided some financial restitution and demonstrated that international asset recovery, while difficult and incomplete, could achieve meaningful results when pursued aggressively over multiple years. The approximately twenty percent recovery rate, while better than complete loss, also provided sobering confirmation that sophisticated money laundering operations achieve their intended purpose of making stolen funds largely irrecoverable even when authorities understand generally what happened and where money went. The Philippine legal battles illuminated both the possibilities for international cooperation on asset recovery and the limitations of current legal frameworks for efficiently addressing transnational financial crimes.

The comprehensive institutional reforms implemented addressed not just the specific vulnerabilities that enabled the 2016 breach but broader security gaps identified through post-incident assessments and industry best practices. The combination of technical security infrastructure improvements, procedural enhancements to transaction processing, organizational restructuring that elevated security priorities, governance reforms that ensured senior leadership oversight, and personnel investments in security capabilities represented a holistic approach to security transformation rather than narrow focus on fixing specific exploited vulnerabilities. The sustainability of these reforms will ultimately depend on whether Bangladesh Bank maintains commitment to security investment and attention even as memory of the breach fades and as budget pressures or competing priorities create temptations to reduce security investments.

The reputation restoration efforts demonstrated that rebuilding trust after catastrophic security failures requires transparency about what occurred and what has been done in response, sustained demonstration of improved capabilities over extended periods, and acceptance that some reputational damage may prove permanent regardless of subsequent efforts. Bangladesh Bank's gradual success in restoring working relationships with international partners, demonstrating to domestic stakeholders that it had addressed its vulnerabilities, and contributing to collective learning through sharing its experience represented meaningful progress while acknowledging that the institution will likely remain internationally known primarily for the breach for many years. The transformation from pure victim to contributor to industry learning represented subtle but meaningful reputational evolution that acknowledged failure while emphasizing reform and resilience.

The ultimate measure of Bangladesh Bank's recovery will be sustained performance over coming years and decades—whether the reforms implemented prove durable, whether the cultural transformation toward genuine security priority maintains momentum, whether the institution successfully defends against future sophisticated attacks, and whether it effectively performs its critical functions as Bangladesh's central bank despite the scars from the 2016 breach. The early signs suggest genuine institutional transformation rather than merely cosmetic changes, but the true test will come over time as initial crisis-driven reform momentum either sustains through institutional commitment or gradually erodes through complacency. Bangladesh Bank's journey from catastrophic breach to reformed institution provides valuable lessons about institutional resilience, the possibilities and limitations of recovery after major security failures, and the reality that building genuinely secure organizations requires sustained comprehensive efforts across technical, organizational, procedural, and cultural dimensions simultaneously.

# Chapter 14: The Human Cost

Behind every technical analysis of the Bangladesh Bank heist, beyond the forensic examination of malware and money laundering techniques, and underneath the policy discussions about international cybersecurity frameworks lies a profoundly human story of lives disrupted, careers destroyed, families devastated, and trust shattered. The tendency to analyze sophisticated cyber attacks through purely technical or strategic lenses often obscures the human toll—the individuals whose professional reputations were irreparably damaged, the families whose financial security evaporated, the employees caught between impossible circumstances and accountability demands, and the broader communities whose confidence in fundamental institutions eroded. This chapter examines the human cost of the Bangladesh Bank heist across multiple dimensions and geographies, exploring how a sophisticated cyber operation translated into deeply personal tragedies for individuals who found themselves, through circumstance or implication, connected to one of history's most audacious financial crimes. Understanding these human dimensions provides essential context often missing from technical post-mortems, reminding us that cyber attacks are not bloodless abstract events but rather concrete incidents with devastating consequences for real people whose lives intersected with digital crime in ways they never anticipated and could not have prepared for.

## Careers Destroyed

The professional devastation that followed the Bangladesh Bank heist extended far beyond the immediate perpetrators to encompass dozens of individuals whose careers were irreparably damaged through association with the incident, whether through direct responsibility for security failures, proximity to compromised systems, or simply the misfortune of holding leadership positions when catastrophe struck. The career destruction took multiple forms—terminations for cause, forced resignations under political pressure, reputational damage that made individuals unemployable in their fields, and the psychological toll of being associated with massive institutional failure that overshadowed any previous professional accomplishments. Understanding the career impacts requires examining specific cases while also recognizing broader patterns about how organizations assign blame after catastrophic failures and how professional reputations, once damaged by high-profile incidents, prove extraordinarily difficult to restore regardless of individual culpability or subsequent efforts at rehabilitation.

The governor of Bangladesh Bank, Atiur Rahman, whose resignation came within weeks of the heist's public disclosure, experienced perhaps the most visible career destruction as the senior-most official held accountable for institutional failures. Rahman had served with distinction for years, earning recognition for financial inclusion initiatives and monetary policy management, but these accomplishments became irrelevant overshadowed by the catastrophic security breach that occurred under his leadership. The resignation, occurring amid intense political and media pressure, transformed Rahman from respected central banker to cautionary tale about accountability for security failures. The question of whether Rahman bore genuine personal responsibility for specific decisions that enabled the breach versus simply occupying the ultimate leadership position when institutional vulnerabilities were exploited proved complex and contested, but the outcome remained the same—a distinguished career ending in forced departure and permanent association with one of banking's greatest security failures.

The senior IT and security personnel at Bangladesh Bank whose direct responsibilities included the compromised systems faced terminations and professional reputations so damaged that continued employment in banking technology became nearly impossible. These individuals, who had worked to secure systems with whatever resources and authority their positions provided, found themselves blamed for failures that reflected broader institutional resource constraints, organizational prioritization decisions, and sophisticated adversaries who specifically targeted their defenses. The challenge of distinguishing between individuals who were genuinely negligent versus those who were simply inadequately resourced or supported by their institution proved difficult, with accountability measures often conflating systemic institutional failures with individual performance shortcomings. For those terminated or forced to resign, the professional stigma of association with the breach followed them regardless of the complexity of their actual culpability, making alternative employment difficult to secure as potential employers viewed them as too risky or too publicly associated with failure.

The RCBC branch manager in the Philippines, Maia Deguito, whose role in facilitating accounts that received stolen funds led to her termination and criminal charges, experienced career destruction compounded by legal jeopardy that transformed her from banking professional to defendant in money laundering cases. Deguito's situation illustrated the complex questions about individual culpability in sophisticated financial crimes—was she a willing participant in money laundering who deserved criminal prosecution, an unwitting tool manipulated by sophisticated criminals, or something between these extremes where inadequate diligence or questionable judgment fell short of criminal intent? Regardless of eventual legal outcomes, Deguito's career in banking ended permanently, her reputation destroyed by association with the largest bank heist in history, and her financial resources depleted by legal defense costs. The case demonstrated how individuals at operational levels who facilitate transactions without fully understanding their criminal nature can find their lives devastated by crimes they may not have known they were enabling.

The broader RCBC personnel whose careers suffered from association with the institution's role in money laundering experienced secondary career impacts even when they bore no direct responsibility for the specific accounts or transactions involved. The reputational damage to RCBC as an institution affected promotion prospects, career trajectories, and marketability of employees across the organization, with the taint of scandal making RCBC experience less valuable on resumes than employment at institutions without such high-profile failures. Some employees departed voluntarily, seeking to distance themselves from an institution whose reputation had been severely damaged, while others found their career advancement stalled as the bank struggled with regulatory sanctions and internal turmoil. The ripple effects of career impact extended far beyond those with direct involvement to affect hundreds or thousands of professionals whose misfortune was simply working for an institution that became entangled in sophisticated financial crime.

The cybersecurity professionals and consultants who had provided services to Bangladesh Bank before the breach faced uncomfortable questions about whether their assessments, recommendations, or implementations had been adequate, with some experiencing reputational damage from association with such a visible security failure. The challenge for these professionals involved the fundamental difficulty of proving that security measures they recommended or implemented were adequate for the time but that institutional decisions not to fully fund or implement those measures, or that sophisticated adversaries developed novel techniques that bypassed defenses, explained the breach. The tendency to judge security measures by their outcomes—if a breach occurred, security must have been inadequate—created unfair assessments that failed to account for the sophisticated of attacks and the reality that perfect security proves impossible against determined adversaries. However, the market for security services operates partly on reputation and perception, making association with high-profile breaches professionally damaging regardless of the complexity of actual responsibility.

The psychological and financial toll on individuals whose careers were destroyed extended beyond immediate job loss to encompass lasting damage to professional identity, financial security, and family stability. For senior professionals whose careers spanned decades, sudden termination in circumstances that made them effectively unemployable in their fields represented not just economic hardship but profound loss of identity and purpose. The legal expenses for those facing investigations or charges depleted savings and created financial distress beyond the income loss from termination. Families experienced instability and stress as breadwinners faced uncertain employment prospects and social stigma from association with scandal. The long-term impacts—diminished retirement security, derailed career trajectories, psychological trauma—persisted for years or decades beyond the immediate incident. These human costs rarely appear in technical post-mortems but represent the lived reality for individuals whose lives intersected catastrophically with sophisticated cybercrime.

## Political Ramifications in Bangladesh

The Bangladesh Bank heist catalyzed intense political controversy within Bangladesh as the government, opposition parties, media, and public grappled with questions about accountability, institutional competence, and the embarrassing international attention that the incident focused on the nation's financial system. The political dimensions transformed what might have been purely an institutional banking crisis into a broader national scandal with implications for government credibility, inter-party recriminations, and Bangladesh's international reputation. Understanding the political ramifications requires examining how different political actors used the incident to advance their agendas, how the government managed damage control and accountability measures, and how the incident influenced broader political dynamics in ways that extended far beyond banking and cybersecurity to touch fundamental questions about governance, competence, and national pride.

The immediate political crisis centered on questions about government oversight of Bangladesh Bank and whether adequate supervision, resources, and attention had been provided to the institution responsible for safeguarding the nation's foreign exchange reserves. Opposition parties seized on the heist as evidence of government incompetence, demanding investigations into how such a catastrophic security failure could occur and whether government officials bore indirect responsibility through inadequate oversight or resource allocation. The government, meanwhile, sought to contain political damage by demonstrating decisive action—removing the central bank governor, initiating investigations, pursuing fund recovery, and implementing reforms—while attempting to characterize the breach as sophisticated external attack rather than systemic governance failure. The political contestation over narratives about responsibility and appropriate response transformed the incident from technical security failure into political liability for the government in power.

The parliamentary investigations and inquiries that followed the breach became forums for political theater as much as serious investigation, with opposition members using hearings to embarrass government officials and government supporters using them to demonstrate accountability and reform commitment. The public proceedings provided transparency about what had occurred but also created incentives for political posturing that sometimes obscured rather than illuminated the complex technical and organizational factors that had enabled the breach. Witnesses called before parliamentary committees faced questioning that often reflected political agendas more than genuine inquiry into security failures, with the proceedings generating headlines and political ammunition rather than necessarily contributing to comprehensive understanding or meaningful reform. The political nature of oversight sometimes complicated rather than supported Bangladesh Bank's recovery efforts, as institutional leaders navigated between genuine accountability demands and politically motivated attacks.

The international embarrassment that the heist created for Bangladesh represented significant political cost beyond domestic accountability questions, as the incident focused global attention on the nation's financial security in ways that damaged its international reputation and potentially affected foreign investment and international financial relationships. For a developing nation seeking to attract foreign investment, establish itself as reliable international partner, and build modern financial sector, the revelation that its central bank had suffered one of history's largest cyber heists created perception problems that extended far beyond the specific incident. The government faced pressure to demonstrate that Bangladesh's financial system was secure and well-regulated despite the breach, requiring substantial diplomacy and relationship management with international partners whose confidence had been shaken. The political leadership needed to balance transparency about failures with maintaining sufficient confidence to prevent broader damage to Bangladesh's international standing and economic prospects.

The nationalism and defensive reactions that emerged in some quarters of Bangladesh's political discourse reflected wounded national pride and resistance to international criticism that some viewed as patronizing or excessive given that sophisticated cyber attacks affected institutions worldwide. Some political voices emphasized that Bangladesh Bank had been victimized by sophisticated state-sponsored attackers rather than having failed through simple incompetence, and that international criticism sometimes reflected double standards given that major institutions in developed countries had also suffered significant breaches. The defensive nationalism, while perhaps emotionally understandable, sometimes complicated international cooperation on investigation and asset recovery by framing the incident in terms of national dignity rather than as shared international challenge requiring collaborative response. The political dynamics around nationalism versus accountability for failures created tensions that Bangladesh's leadership needed to navigate carefully.

The regulatory and legislative responses that emerged from the political process included enhanced cybersecurity requirements for financial institutions, increased oversight of Bangladesh Bank by government agencies, and potential legislative changes to address gaps that the incident exposed. Some of these policy responses represented genuine improvements that would strengthen Bangladesh's financial sector security, while others reflected political imperatives to be seen as taking action regardless of whether specific measures actually addressed priority risks. The challenge for effective policy-making involved distinguishing between measures that would materially improve security and those that primarily served political purposes of demonstrating responsiveness to crisis. The most effective reforms often required sustained technical effort outside the public spotlight rather than dramatic legislative action that generated positive political attention but limited practical security improvement.

The long-term political impacts included lasting sensitivity around Bangladesh Bank and cybersecurity within Bangladesh's political discourse, with the incident remaining available for opposition parties to reference when criticizing government competence and with successive governments facing pressure to demonstrate they had adequately addressed financial sector security. The incident influenced how political actors thought about technology governance, institutional oversight, and Bangladesh's position in the international financial system. The political memory of the heist would likely persist for years or decades, serving as cautionary tale and reference point for debates about institutional competence, government oversight, and national security in the digital age. Whether this lasting political impact would translate into sustained attention to cybersecurity and institutional security practices or would fade as more immediate political concerns captured attention remained to be seen.

## Lives Disrupted in the Philippines

The individuals in the Philippines whose involvement in receiving and laundering stolen funds ranged from willing participation to possible unwitting manipulation experienced life disruptions extending from criminal investigations and prosecutions to social stigma and destroyed livelihoods. The Philippine dimension of the human cost illustrated how sophisticated money laundering operations exploit individuals, some of whom may not fully understand they are participating in major international crimes, and how the consequences of that participation—whether knowing or unknowing—can devastate lives. Understanding these disruptions requires examining specific cases while recognizing patterns about how financial crimes that seem abstract when discussed in terms of digital transfers and international accounts translate into concrete human consequences for individuals who served as operational components of the laundering infrastructure.

The individuals who opened accounts at RCBC that received stolen funds and who subsequently withdrew cash or facilitated transfers to casinos faced criminal charges for money laundering that exposed them to imprisonment, financial penalties, and permanent criminal records. Some of these individuals claimed they were merely following instructions from business associates or employers and didn't understand they were participating in laundering proceeds of major theft, while prosecutors argued that the scale and suspicious nature of transactions should have been obvious red flags that participants willfully ignored. The legal proceedings to determine culpability and appropriate punishment proved complex as courts weighed evidence about knowledge and intent, with defendants' futures hanging on legal determinations about what they knew and when. For those convicted, the consequences included incarceration that separated them from families, criminal records that made legitimate employment nearly impossible after release, and social stigma that affected their families as well as themselves personally.

The casino personnel who processed the massive chip purchases and cashouts that converted electronic transfers into physical money faced questions about their knowledge of money laundering and their responsibilities to report suspicious activity. Some casino employees claimed the transactions, while large, weren't obviously illegal given that casinos regularly hosted high-rolling gamblers conducting substantial transactions, and that they lacked training or authority to question transactions from apparent VIP customers. However, prosecutors and regulators argued that the scale, speed, and patterns of activity should have triggered enhanced due diligence that casino personnel either failed to perform or deliberately ignored. The careers of implicated casino employees ended regardless of eventual legal outcomes, as the industry could not afford to employ individuals publicly associated with major money laundering cases. The financial hardship from lost employment combined with legal defense costs created severe economic distress for individuals and families dependent on those incomes.

The families of individuals implicated in the money laundering scheme experienced social stigma, economic hardship from lost incomes and legal expenses, and emotional trauma from seeing loved ones face criminal charges and potential imprisonment. Children whose parents were arrested or charged faced playground taunts and social isolation as classmates learned about their parents' legal troubles. Spouses struggled with sudden single parenting responsibilities when partners were detained and with the psychological strain of supporting partners through legal proceedings while managing family finances depleted by legal costs. The extended families experienced reputation damage by association in communities where family name and social standing mattered significantly. The ripple effects of one family member's implication in international financial crime extended throughout family networks in ways that persisted long after any legal proceedings concluded.

The broader Filipino community members who had no involvement in the money laundering but who suffered from intensified scrutiny and stereotyping that followed the incident experienced secondary impacts that, while less severe than direct legal jeopardy, nonetheless represented real costs. The international attention on Philippine casinos and financial institutions as venues for money laundering affected the reputation of legitimate businesses and professionals who operated with integrity but who found themselves tainted by association. Filipino financial services professionals faced increased suspicion in international contexts, with some reporting that their nationality became subject of additional questions in job interviews or business dealings as international partners became more cautious about Philippine connections. The national pride damage from the Philippines' prominent role in the money laundering operation created psychological costs for a population sensitive to international perceptions and eager to see their nation recognized for positive rather than negative reasons.

The whistleblowers and cooperating witnesses who provided information to investigators about money laundering operations faced their own challenges including security concerns about potential retaliation, social isolation from communities or social networks where they were viewed as betrayers, and uncertain futures given that cooperation often required severing connections to previous lives. The decision to cooperate with investigators, while potentially legally beneficial, created practical and social difficulties as individuals navigated between legal pressures to provide information and social or security risks from doing so. The inadequate witness protection resources in the Philippines meant that cooperating individuals sometimes faced ongoing risks without the robust support systems that more developed witness protection programs in other jurisdictions might provide. The challenge of rebuilding lives after serving as witnesses in high-profile cases with limited institutional support for that transition created ongoing struggles.

The long-term impacts on Philippine individuals implicated in or affected by the money laundering extended years beyond the immediate incident and legal proceedings, with criminal records limiting employment options, social stigma affecting relationships and opportunities, and psychological trauma from the stress of criminal proceedings or imprisonment affecting mental health and life satisfaction. For those who served prison sentences, reintegration into society with criminal records and gaps in employment history proved extraordinarily difficult in an economy where legitimate employment opportunities were already competitive. The lasting impacts represented permanent life alterations stemming from involvement—whether willing or unwitting—in a sophisticated international financial crime that most participants probably didn't fully understand when they made the decisions that would come to devastate their lives.

## The Victims of Money Laundering

While Bangladesh Bank stands as the most obvious victim of the theft, the broader category of money laundering victims encompasses individuals and institutions whose legitimate funds or activities were exploited to facilitate the laundering operation, who suffered reputational damage from association with the scheme, or who experienced indirect consequences from the money laundering success. Understanding the full scope of victimization requires looking beyond the direct theft to examine how money laundering operations create cascading impacts affecting numerous parties who may not even realize their connection to international financial crimes. The complexity of victimization in sophisticated financial crimes demonstrates how determining who suffered harm and how extends far beyond simple identification of who lost money, encompassing reputational, economic, and social impacts that ripple through communities and institutions.

The legitimate businesses whose accounts, services, or facilities were exploited in the money laundering operation found themselves involuntarily connected to major international crime with resulting reputational damage, regulatory scrutiny, and potential legal liability. The Shalika Foundation in Sri Lanka, whose name appeared in the fraudulent transfer instruction that contained the fateful "fundation" typo, had no involvement in the money laundering attempt but nonetheless found its name associated with international headlines about massive financial crimes. The foundation faced questions from donors, partners, and the public about its involvement, requiring it to expend resources explaining that it had been victimized by identity theft rather than being a participant. The reputational damage, while ultimately manageable through transparency about the foundation's non-involvement, nonetheless represented real cost in terms of time, attention, and potential impacts on relationships with supporters concerned about the organization's governance and security.

The casino establishments in the Philippines that processed fraudulent transactions experienced multifaceted victimization including reputational damage that affected their businesses, regulatory sanctions that imposed operational and financial burdens, and potential legal liability depending on determinations about their knowledge and complicity. While some casinos may have had employees who knowingly facilitated money laundering, the institutions themselves claimed to be victims of criminal exploitation rather than willing participants. Regardless of the complex questions about institutional versus individual responsibility, the casinos faced years of regulatory scrutiny, legal proceedings, enhanced compliance requirements that increased operational costs, and reputation damage that potentially affected their ability to attract legitimate customers concerned about the establishments' governance and security. The costs of being implicated—even if ultimately determined to have been victimized rather than complicit—exceeded what simple monetary accounting could capture.

The legitimate high-rollers and casino patrons whose gambling activities provided cover for money laundering operations experienced unwanted scrutiny as investigators attempted to distinguish genuine gambling from money laundering transactions disguised as gambling. These individuals, who had no connection to the Bangladesh Bank theft and were conducting legal gambling activities, found themselves subject to additional questioning, account freezes pending investigation, and scrutiny that invaded their privacy and disrupted their activities. The challenge of distinguishing innocent parties whose transactions happened to overlap with money laundering from potential accomplices or knowing participants created inevitable situations where investigation cast nets widely enough to ensnare uninvolved individuals. The innocent parties caught up in investigations experienced disruption, legal expenses if they needed to hire attorneys to protect their interests, and potential reputation damage if their names became publicly associated with money laundering investigations.

The remittance service users whose legitimate transactions for sending money to support families were subjected to enhanced scrutiny and delays following the Bangladesh Bank incident experienced disruption to essential financial services. As authorities and financial institutions implemented enhanced monitoring of remittance channels that had been exploited for money laundering, legitimate users faced additional verification requirements, transaction delays, and in some cases denial of service if their transaction patterns triggered overly aggressive fraud detection rules. For individuals dependent on remittance services to support families across borders, these disruptions represented more than inconvenience—they affected the ability to fulfill family obligations and created hardship for dependents waiting for funds. The tension between preventing money laundering and maintaining accessible legitimate financial services created situations where tightened controls imposed costs on innocent users.

The RCBC shareholders who owned stakes in an institution whose value plummeted following the money laundering scandal experienced financial losses from their investment declining and from reduced dividend prospects as the bank faced regulatory fines and invested heavily in remediation. While shareholders of public companies accept investment risk, the scale of loss resulting from money laundering that exploited their investment represented a form of victimization distinct from normal market volatility. The challenge of holding institutions accountable for enabling money laundering while recognizing that penalties ultimately affect shareholders who may have had no involvement in or knowledge of security and compliance failures created tension in determining appropriate institutional accountability that didn't disproportionately harm innocent investors.

The broader communities whose confidence in financial institutions eroded following revelations about money laundering vulnerabilities experienced a collective victimization through reduced trust in systems they depended upon for economic activity. When major financial institutions prove vulnerable to exploitation by sophisticated criminals, and when the sophistication required to distinguish legitimate from fraudulent transactions exceeds what normal users can exercise, the result is erosion of the trust that makes modern financial systems function. While this diffuse collective harm is difficult to quantify, it nonetheless represents real cost as individuals and businesses become more cautious, transaction costs increase due to enhanced verification requirements, and the psychological security of trusting that financial institutions will protect customers from fraud diminishes. The restoration of this trust requires sustained demonstration of improved security across the financial sector.

## Trust Eroded in Global Banking

The Bangladesh Bank heist's most pervasive and lasting human cost may prove to be the erosion of trust in the global banking system's security and reliability—a diffuse but profound impact affecting millions of individuals and thousands of institutions whose confidence in fundamental financial infrastructure was shaken by revelations about the system's vulnerability to sophisticated cyber attacks. Understanding this trust erosion requires examining how trust functions in modern banking, why the Bangladesh Bank case specifically damaged that trust, and how the incident continues affecting relationships between financial institutions, between institutions and customers, and among all parties who depend on the assumption that sophisticated security protects the digital financial infrastructure on which global commerce depends. The challenge of measuring and restoring trust makes this dimension of human cost difficult to quantify but no less real for individuals and institutions navigating financial systems they now view with increased skepticism and anxiety.

The fundamental nature of banking depends on trust more than almost any other institutional relationship, as customers entrust financial institutions with their money, life savings, and business operations based on confidence that banks will safeguard deposits, process transactions accurately, and protect customers from fraud and theft. The Bangladesh Bank heist demonstrated that even central banks with presumed sophisticated security could suffer catastrophic breaches where tens of millions of dollars vanished through compromised payment systems. For individuals whose understanding of banking technology remained limited, the revelation that such massive theft could occur raised uncomfortable questions about whether their own funds were truly secure and whether the systems processing their transactions could be trusted. The psychological impact of this revealed vulnerability, while not as immediate or visible as direct financial loss, nonetheless represented real cost as individuals experienced increased anxiety about financial security.

The institutional trust between correspondent banks that facilitate international transactions suffered as the Bangladesh Bank case demonstrated that properly authenticated payment instructions might nonetheless represent fraudulent transactions from compromised institutions. Correspondent banks that had previously processed payment instructions with confidence in SWIFT authentication and sender bank reputation now faced uncomfortable recognition that authentication alone provided inadequate assurance of transaction legitimacy. The enhanced verification procedures, additional scrutiny, and more cautious approach to correspondent banking relationships that followed the incident created friction in international financial transactions as institutions balanced risk management against operational efficiency. The relationships built on trust and streamlined processes became more defensive and procedurally complex as banks implemented additional safeguards against exploitation through trusted channels.

The erosion of confidence in SWIFT as secure infrastructure for financial messaging represented particularly significant trust damage, as SWIFT had been considered the gold standard for secure international financial communications for decades. While the Bangladesh Bank breach involved compromise of member institution systems rather than the SWIFT network itself, the incident nonetheless undermined confidence in SWIFT infrastructure and raised questions about whether the security architecture remained adequate for modern threat environments. The organization's comprehensive response through the Customer Security Program aimed to restore confidence, but the psychological impact of demonstrated vulnerability persisted beyond what technical improvements could fully address. Financial institutions implementing required security enhancements did so under the shadow of knowing that a trusted system had been exploited for massive theft.

The generational dimension of trust erosion created particular challenges for financial institutions attempting to maintain confidence among younger customers who had grown up digital natives comfortable with technology but also more aware of cybersecurity risks than previous generations. The Bangladesh Bank case and broader pattern of financial institution breaches fed into existing generational skepticism about traditional financial institutions, potentially accelerating adoption of alternative financial technologies while paradoxically also raising questions about the security of fintech alternatives. The institutions attempting to build or maintain relationships with younger customers faced the challenge of acknowledging real security risks while maintaining sufficient confidence to keep customers engaged with the financial system rather than seeking to store wealth in forms that avoided digital financial infrastructure entirely.

The international dimension of trust erosion particularly affected institutions in developing markets as the Bangladesh Bank case reinforced existing suspicions that financial institutions in less developed economies lacked security sophistication of peers in major financial centers. The incident potentially exacerbated international financial relationships where institutions in developed markets viewed emerging market partners with increased caution and skepticism. This dynamic created concerning implications for financial inclusion and economic development, as the trust deficit potentially increased costs and reduced access for institutions and businesses in markets whose development depended partly on integration into global financial systems. The challenge of overcoming the trust gap created by high-profile incidents while building the security capabilities to deserve that trust represented ongoing struggle for many developing market institutions.

The restoration of trust eroded by the Bangladesh Bank heist required more than just technical security improvements or successful prosecution of perpetrators, instead demanding sustained demonstration over years that financial institutions had genuinely addressed vulnerabilities and could maintain security against evolving sophisticated threats. Trust builds slowly through consistent positive experiences but can erode quickly through single dramatic failures, creating an asymmetry where the effort required to restore confidence exceeded what was necessary to maintain it before breach. The financial institutions worldwide that benefited from continued customer and partner trust despite the Bangladesh Bank case's demonstration of systemic vulnerabilities faced ongoing responsibility to justify that trust through comprehensive security programs, transparent communication about risks, and demonstrated competence in protecting the assets and transactions entrusted to them.

The philosophical dimension of trust in an increasingly digital financial system raised deeper questions about whether the levels of trust that traditional banking relationships involved could be sustained in environments of demonstrated vulnerability to sophisticated cyber attacks. If determined nation-state attackers could breach even sophisticated financial institutions, and if perfect security proved impossible regardless of investment and effort, what level of risk should individuals and institutions accept as the price of participating in digital financial systems? The uncomfortable answer seemed to be that some level of cyber risk had become inherent in modern financial systems, requiring not zero-risk expectations but rather realistic understanding of threats combined with confidence that institutions were managing those risks appropriately. The adjustment of expectations from perfect security to adequate security represented a significant shift in the psychological contract between financial institutions and those who entrusted them with money and transactions.

## Conclusion

The human cost of the Bangladesh Bank heist extended far beyond the eighty-one million dollars stolen to encompass destroyed careers, disrupted lives, eroded trust, and countless individual tragedies that rarely appear in technical post-mortems but that represent the lived reality of sophisticated cyber crime's impact. The careers destroyed included not just the immediate perpetrators but numerous professionals whose association with the incident—whether through direct responsibility, organizational proximity, or simply bad timing of holding leadership positions when catastrophe struck—resulted in professional reputations so damaged that recovery proved impossible. The individual human stories behind the accountability measures and personnel changes represented personal tragedies that technical analyses of security failures often overlook but that nonetheless constitute real costs measured in shattered life plans and devastated families.

The political ramifications in Bangladesh demonstrated how institutional failures become political crises that extend far beyond the organizations directly involved to affect government credibility, inter-party dynamics, and national reputation. The political contestation over responsibility and appropriate response sometimes helped drive accountability and reform but other times complicated recovery through politicization that obscured technical realities and created incentives for blame-shifting rather than genuine institutional improvement. The lasting sensitivity around Bangladesh Bank within the nation's political discourse ensured that the incident would remain available for political exploitation years after the immediate crisis passed, affecting how political actors approached questions of institutional oversight and technological governance.

The disrupted lives in the Philippines illustrated how money laundering operations exploit individuals who become operational components of financial crime infrastructure, with consequences ranging from imprisonment for those convicted to social stigma and economic hardship affecting even those whose involvement may have been unwitting. The complexity of determining culpability when individuals claim they didn't understand they were participating in major international crime highlighted the often-blurry lines between willing criminal participation and exploitation by sophisticated operations that obscure their true nature from operational participants. The lasting impacts on Philippine individuals and families demonstrated how the human costs of international financial crime extend far beyond the immediate victims to affect numerous parties whose lives intersected with sophisticated criminal operations.

The victims of money laundering extended beyond Bangladesh Bank to encompass legitimate businesses whose identities were exploited, institutions that processed fraudulent transactions and suffered reputational and regulatory consequences, and innocent parties whose legitimate activities were disrupted by enhanced scrutiny following the incident. The concept of victimization in complex financial crimes proves far more expansive than simple identification of who lost money, encompassing reputational, economic, and operational impacts affecting numerous parties who may not have even realized their connection to international financial crimes until investigations and regulatory actions brought those connections to light.

The eroded trust in global banking represented perhaps the most diffuse but potentially most significant human cost, as millions of individuals and thousands of institutions whose daily lives and operations depend on financial infrastructure found their confidence shaken by revelations about the system's vulnerability to sophisticated attacks. The challenge of restoring trust after dramatic demonstrations of vulnerability exceeded what technical security improvements alone could achieve, requiring sustained performance over years demonstrating that financial institutions had genuinely addressed weaknesses and could maintain security against evolving threats. The adjustment from expectations of perfect security to realistic understanding of manageable risk represented significant psychological shift in how individuals and institutions related to financial systems they depended upon but could no longer assume were invulnerable.

The human cost dimension of the Bangladesh Bank heist provides essential context often missing from technical and policy analyses, reminding us that sophisticated cyber attacks are not abstract events in digital space but rather concrete incidents with devastating consequences for real people. The destroyed careers, disrupted lives, eroded trust, and individual tragedies represented in these human stories constitute costs that balance sheets and technical post-mortems rarely capture but that nonetheless represent real harm that any comprehensive understanding of the incident must acknowledge. The challenge moving forward involves learning from these human costs to inform policies and practices that better protect not just systems and money but the people whose lives and livelihoods depend on the security and integrity of the institutions we charge with safeguarding our financial infrastructure.

# Conclusion: Eight Years Later

Eight years have passed since the February 2016 morning when Bangladesh Bank discovered that sophisticated attackers had stolen eighty-one million dollars through compromised SWIFT systems, triggering one of the most consequential cybersecurity incidents in financial services history. The passage of nearly a decade provides sufficient distance to assess what lasting changes the heist catalyzed, what fundamental vulnerabilities persist despite remarkable defensive progress, and whether the financial sector has genuinely transformed in ways that would prevent or at least substantially impede similar attacks. The perspective of time reveals a complex reality where dramatic improvements in specific areas coexist with persistent vulnerabilities in others, where some lessons have been thoroughly learned and implemented while others remain more aspirational than actual, and where the threat landscape has evolved in ways that both validate and challenge the defensive strategies developed in response to Bangladesh Bank. This conclusion examines the current state of global banking security through the lens of that pivotal incident, assessing honestly what has changed and what hasn't, exploring why certain reforms succeeded while others stalled, and confronting the uncomfortable question of whether the financial sector is genuinely prepared for the next billion-dollar heist that sophisticated adversaries are almost certainly already planning.

## What Changed and What Didn't

The eight years since the Bangladesh Bank heist have witnessed transformative changes in how financial institutions approach cybersecurity, implementing comprehensive improvements that have genuinely elevated defensive capabilities across multiple dimensions. The most visible and consequential change involves the elevation of cybersecurity from a mid-level IT concern to a board-level strategic priority, with financial institutions worldwide recognizing that cyber threats represent existential risks rather than merely operational challenges. The governance transformation means that cybersecurity now receives regular senior leadership and board attention, commands substantially larger budgets than pre-2016, and influences strategic decision-making about technology investments, operational procedures, and risk management. This elevation of organizational priority has enabled security professionals to implement measures that might have been rejected as too expensive or operationally disruptive in earlier eras, creating conditions where comprehensive security programs can receive the authority, resources, and attention necessary for effectiveness.

The technical security architecture improvements that financial institutions have implemented represent another area of genuine transformation, with modern banking security bearing little resemblance to what existed before Bangladesh Bank exposed fundamental vulnerabilities. Network segmentation that isolates critical systems like SWIFT infrastructure from less-trusted networks has become standard practice rather than aspirational goal, dramatically reducing the attack surface that adversaries can reach after initial compromise. Endpoint detection and response capabilities that identify sophisticated malware through behavioral analysis rather than just signature matching have replaced or supplemented traditional antivirus, enabling detection of novel threats that earlier generations of security tools would miss. Security operations centers providing 24/7/365 monitoring and threat hunting have become common at larger institutions and increasingly accessible to smaller ones through managed service providers. Multi-factor authentication protecting access to critical systems has evolved from optional enhancement to mandatory requirement in most regulated financial institutions. These technical improvements, while not eliminating all vulnerability, have demonstrably increased the difficulty of conducting successful attacks against well-defended institutions.

The SWIFT-specific security enhancements implemented through the Customer Security Program represent targeted improvements directly addressing the vulnerabilities that the Bangladesh Bank attack exploited. The mandatory security controls that SWIFT requires all member institutions to implement, the attestation framework that creates accountability for security postures, the enhanced information sharing about threats and indicators of compromise, and the architectural improvements to SWIFT software itself have collectively strengthened the security of international financial messaging infrastructure. While sophisticated adversaries continue probing for weaknesses, the specific attack path that Bangladesh Bank attackers used has been substantially hardened through these targeted improvements. The SWIFT ecosystem's collective security has improved measurably, though the distributed nature of the network means that vulnerabilities at less-sophisticated member institutions continue creating systemic risks.

However, alongside these genuine improvements, numerous fundamental challenges persist largely unchanged despite eight years of effort and investment. The human vulnerability to social engineering and phishing remains as exploitable as ever, with sophisticated adversaries continuously refining their techniques to bypass improved security awareness training and technical email filtering. The insider threat challenge has arguably intensified as remote work has distributed employees across uncontrolled environments where monitoring and oversight prove more difficult than in traditional office settings. Legacy system vulnerabilities persist at many institutions where the economic and operational barriers to wholesale technology modernization continue outweighing security imperatives despite general recognition of the risks. The third-party and supply chain security challenges have grown more complex as financial institutions have increased their dependence on vendors and service providers while struggling to implement comprehensive vendor risk management at scale.

The attribution and accountability challenges that limit deterrence of state-sponsored cyber attacks remain fundamentally unchanged despite marginal improvements in forensic capabilities and international cooperation. North Korea and other nation-states conducting financially motivated cyber operations continue these activities despite attribution, international condemnation, and sanctions, demonstrating that current international frameworks prove inadequate for imposing costs sufficient to modify behavior. The fundamental asymmetry between attackers needing to succeed only occasionally to achieve objectives and defenders needing to succeed continuously to prevent compromise persists as a structural advantage that no amount of defensive improvement can fully overcome. The arms race dynamic where each side's innovations prompt responses from the other shows no signs of reaching stability, suggesting that the security challenge will remain perpetually demanding rather than converging toward manageable equilibrium.

The uneven implementation of security improvements across different types of institutions and geographic regions creates persistent vulnerabilities in the global financial system despite dramatic progress at leading institutions. Large banks in major financial centers have generally implemented comprehensive security programs incorporating best practices and substantial technology investments, but smaller regional banks, institutions in developing markets, and specialized financial services firms often lag significantly behind. The financial sector's interconnected nature means that compromise of any participant creates potential pathways to others, making the ecosystem's overall security dependent on its weakest links. The gap between security leaders and laggards has arguably widened rather than narrowed over eight years, as the resources and expertise required for sophisticated security programs have increased faster than many institutions' capabilities have developed.

The cultural transformation toward genuine security consciousness that comprehensive security requires has proven more difficult to achieve and sustain than technical or procedural changes. While many institutions have improved security culture through training, awareness programs, and leadership emphasis, creating environments where every employee understands their role in security and where security considerations influence daily decisions across the organization remains aspirational rather than achieved for many. The tendency for security attention to decline as memory of specific incidents fades creates cycles where crisis drives improvement but subsequent complacency allows backsliding. The challenge of maintaining security culture and vigilance over extended periods without the motivating urgency of immediate crisis represents one of the more difficult aspects of sustaining security improvements.

## Current State of Global Banking Security

Assessing the current state of global banking security eight years after Bangladesh Bank requires acknowledging substantial progress while recognizing persistent vulnerabilities and emerging challenges that continue to threaten even significantly improved defensive postures. The financial sector as a whole has achieved a higher baseline of security capability than existed in 2016, with mandatory requirements, regulatory pressure, industry standards, and shared threat intelligence collectively raising the floor for what constitutes minimally acceptable security. However, this elevated baseline coexists with sophisticated threats that have evolved at least as rapidly as defenses, creating a situation where improved security has not eliminated risk but rather shifted it—making opportunistic attacks more difficult while determined, well-resourced adversaries continue finding ways to succeed against high-value targets.

The regulatory landscape has evolved significantly to emphasize cybersecurity more explicitly and to create clearer requirements and accountability mechanisms. Financial regulators in major jurisdictions have implemented or strengthened cybersecurity requirements for supervised institutions, mandating specific controls, regular assessments, incident reporting, and board-level oversight. The regulatory evolution has been uneven across jurisdictions, with more developed financial centers generally implementing more comprehensive requirements while some emerging markets continue with lighter-touch regulation that creates regulatory arbitrage opportunities for institutions seeking to minimize compliance burdens. The regulatory pressure has been instrumental in driving security improvements, but it has also created compliance-focused approaches where institutions sometimes prioritize demonstrable adherence to specific requirements over comprehensive risk-based security that addresses actual threat landscapes.

The threat intelligence sharing and collaboration among financial institutions has improved substantially through formal mechanisms like Financial Services Information Sharing and Analysis Centers and through informal networks of security professionals who share indicators of compromise, attack techniques, and defensive strategies. This collective defense approach enables institutions to benefit from each other's experiences and to respond more rapidly to threats that have targeted peers. However, the information sharing remains imperfect due to continuing concerns about reputational damage from publicly acknowledging breaches, legal liability from information disclosure, and competitive sensitivities about sharing information that might reveal institutional vulnerabilities or strategic approaches. The balance between collective security benefits of information sharing and individual institutional interests in limiting disclosure continues to constrain how much cooperation actually occurs despite general recognition of its value.

The technology solutions available to financial institutions for implementing security programs have matured and expanded dramatically, with comprehensive security tool markets offering solutions for every conceivable security need and with managed security service providers enabling even smaller institutions to access sophisticated capabilities. The challenge has shifted from availability of security technology to effective selection, implementation, and operation of appropriate tools from overwhelming options. Many institutions struggle with technology sprawl where they have deployed numerous security tools that don't integrate effectively, creating operational complexity and gaps where threats slip through tools that don't share information or coordinate responses. The consolidation toward integrated security platforms represents market response to this sprawl, but effective platform selection and implementation remain challenging for institutions lacking deep security expertise.

The workforce challenge has evolved from acute crisis-level shortages to more manageable but still concerning gaps between demand for security talent and available supply. The cybersecurity profession has grown substantially as more individuals enter the field through academic programs, career transitions, and certification paths, partially easing the talent crisis that followed Bangladesh Bank. However, specialized expertise in areas like threat hunting, malware analysis, incident response, and security architecture remains scarce and expensive, with institutions competing intensely for limited numbers of truly experienced practitioners. The maturation of managed security services has provided alternative to building complete internal capabilities, enabling institutions to access expertise through service providers rather than hiring it directly. The talent situation, while improved from its worst crisis conditions, continues requiring that institutions invest substantially in competitive compensation, professional development, and retention strategies.

The cloud adoption that has accelerated in financial services creates new security architectures that differ fundamentally from traditional on-premises infrastructure, requiring different skills, tools, and approaches. Many institutions have migrated substantial portions of their infrastructure to public cloud providers or hybrid models combining cloud and on-premises systems. This migration creates new security challenges around cloud-specific vulnerabilities, shared responsibility models where security is split between institutions and cloud providers, and the need for cloud security expertise that many institutions are still developing. However, cloud adoption also provides opportunities for improved security through cloud providers' substantial security investments, scalable infrastructure that can absorb attack volumes that might overwhelm on-premises systems, and cloud-native security services that provide capabilities difficult to implement in traditional environments. The net security impact of cloud adoption remains debated, with the answer likely depending on how effectively institutions implement cloud security rather than on inherent characteristics of cloud versus on-premises deployment.

The emerging threats from artificial intelligence, quantum computing, Internet of Things proliferation, and continued sophistication of nation-state adversaries ensure that the threat landscape will continue evolving in ways that challenge even improved security postures. Financial institutions are investing in defensive AI capabilities while simultaneously preparing for threats from adversarial AI that could attack at machine speed and scale.

The quantum computing threat to current cryptography remains years away from practical realization but requires preparation now through post-quantum cryptographic transitions that will take years to complete. The IoT attack surface continues expanding as connected devices proliferate throughout banking operations. The assessment of current security state must therefore acknowledge not just present capabilities but also whether institutions are preparing adequately for foreseeable future threats.

## North Korea's Continued Operations

Perhaps the most sobering aspect of assessing the eight years since Bangladesh Bank involves recognizing that North Korea, the nation-state actor attributed with the heist, has not only continued conducting financially motivated cyber operations but has arguably intensified and diversified them despite international attribution, condemnation, and sanctions. The persistence of North Korean cyber operations demonstrates both the limitations of current deterrence and accountability frameworks and the strategic success, from North Korea's perspective, of the cyber operations model pioneered and refined through attacks like Bangladesh Bank. Understanding North Korea's continued operations provides crucial context for assessing whether defensive improvements have actually reduced the threat or merely forced adversaries to adapt their techniques while maintaining operational effectiveness.

The post-Bangladesh Bank evolution of North Korean cyber operations has included continued targeting of financial institutions worldwide, with numerous attempted and successful breaches attributed to the same general threat actor group in the years following 2016. While specific technical details remain largely classified in intelligence assessments, public reporting from cybersecurity firms and occasional government attributions indicate that North Korean actors have maintained sustained campaigns against banks, payment processors, and cryptocurrency exchanges. The operational tempo suggests that North Korea views cyber operations as successful strategic approach worthy of continued investment rather than as failed experiment to be abandoned. The adaptations observable in subsequent attacks indicate organizational learning where techniques that succeeded are refined while those that failed or were detected are modified, demonstrating sophisticated threat actor evolution.

The cryptocurrency focus that has characterized much of North Korea's recent financially motivated cyber activity reflects strategic adaptation to defensive improvements in traditional banking that made bank heists like Bangladesh Bank more difficult. Cryptocurrency exchanges often possess weaker security than traditional banks, hold enormous aggregated value in digital assets, and facilitate transactions that are more difficult to trace and reverse than traditional banking transfers. North Korea has been attributed with thefts from numerous cryptocurrency exchanges totaling hundreds of millions of dollars, demonstrating that when defenses in one area improved, sophisticated adversaries shifted focus to alternative targets offering better risk-reward profiles. The cryptocurrency targeting also provides sanctions evasion capabilities beyond simple theft, enabling North Korea to conduct transactions and move money through channels outside traditional banking systems where sanctions enforcement proves more effective.

The diversification beyond pure financial theft to include ransomware operations represents another evolution in North Korean cyber operations, with the WannaCry ransomware attack of 2017 attributed to North Korean actors demonstrating willingness to conduct globally disruptive attacks for financial gain. The attribution of WannaCry to North Korea suggested that the same capabilities and infrastructure used for targeted attacks like Bangladesh Bank could be repurposed for widespread indiscriminate attacks that generated revenue through mass extortion. The shift demonstrated that North Korean cyber strategy encompasses multiple approaches simultaneously rather than committing exclusively to targeted operations, and that the line between financially motivated attacks and strategically motivated disruption can blur when single operations serve multiple objectives.

The geopolitical context surrounding North Korean cyber operations has remained relatively unchanged despite their continued activity, with the international community maintaining sanctions and diplomatic pressure but achieving minimal success in modifying North Korean behavior through these mechanisms. The fundamental challenge remains that North Korea, already facing comprehensive sanctions and diplomatic isolation, has limited additional costs to fear from international responses to cyber operations. The sanctions already imposed approach maximum sustainable levels, diplomatic isolation is already nearly complete, and the prospects for meaningful accountability through international legal proceedings or collective military response remain remote. This creates a permissive environment where North Korea can continue cyber operations with reasonable confidence that the costs will remain manageable regardless of international awareness and attribution.

The technical sophistication of North Korean cyber capabilities has continued advancing, with the passage of time allowing for personnel development, tool refinement, infrastructure improvement, and operational experience that collectively enhance effectiveness. While North Korean cyber operations still exhibit characteristics suggesting resource constraints and operational security lapses compared to the most sophisticated nation-state actors, they demonstrate continuously improving capabilities that have proven sufficient for achieving strategic objectives. The investment in cyber operations appears to be sustained and possibly increasing, reflecting North Korean leadership assessment that cyber provides asymmetric advantages that justify continued resource allocation despite the country's severe economic constraints.

The revenue generation success of North Korean cyber operations, while difficult to estimate precisely from publicly available information, appears to have been substantial enough to validate the strategic approach and incentivize continued operations. Various estimates suggest North Korea has stolen hundreds of millions to potentially over a billion dollars through cyber operations in the years since Bangladesh Bank, generating significant hard currency that helps sustain the regime despite international sanctions intended to limit its access to foreign exchange. This financial success from cyber operations makes them strategically rational from North Korea's perspective regardless of international condemnation, creating conditions where continued operations can be expected unless the cost-benefit calculation shifts dramatically through either improved defenses that make operations less successful or enhanced consequences that make success less valuable.

## Lessons Still Being Learned

While the Bangladesh Bank heist immediately provided obvious lessons about specific technical vulnerabilities and procedural gaps, the passage of eight years has revealed deeper, more complex lessons that the financial sector continues to absorb, implement, and refine. Some lessons that seemed clear in the immediate aftermath have proven more nuanced or difficult to implement than initially apparent, while others that weren't immediately obvious have emerged from sustained analysis of the incident's causes, consequences, and the broader pattern of similar attacks. Understanding these evolving lessons requires examining not just what the incident taught but how those teachings have been internalized, operationalized, and sometimes modified through practical experience attempting to implement them in complex real-world environments.

The lesson about defense in depth that emphasizes layered security controls rather than relying on any single defensive mechanism has been widely acknowledged but incompletely implemented, with many institutions still exhibiting security architectures where compromise of one layer creates catastrophic exposure rather than triggering additional defensive responses. The theoretical understanding that multiple independent security layers create cumulative protection has not always translated into actual architectures where each layer operates independently and effectively. The challenge involves not just deploying multiple security tools but ensuring they work together to create genuine defense in depth rather than security theater where apparent comprehensive coverage masks gaps and single points of failure. The continuing refinement of defense in depth principles eight years after Bangladesh Bank suggests that implementing genuinely layered security proves more difficult than conceptually understanding its importance.

The lesson about the critical importance of security basics—timely patching, proper network segmentation, comprehensive logging, adequate access controls, and other fundamental security hygiene—has been repeatedly reinforced but continues to require emphasis as institutions discover that exotic security technologies cannot compensate for failures in fundamental practices. The tendency to focus on advanced threats and sophisticated security solutions while neglecting basics that sophisticated adversaries readily exploit represents a persistent pattern that incidents like Bangladesh Bank should theoretically have corrected but that continues appearing in post-mortems of subsequent breaches. The ongoing need to emphasize security fundamentals suggests that the lesson, while learned intellectually, has not been fully internalized into sustained operational practice across institutions.

The lesson about the necessity of rapid detection and response capabilities that can identify and contain breaches before catastrophic damage occurs has driven substantial investment in security operations centers and incident response programs. However, the practical reality of operating effective detection and response capabilities has proven more challenging than simply deploying technology and hiring analysts. The integration of detection tools, the tuning of alerting rules to balance sensitivity against false positive rates, the development of analyst expertise in distinguishing genuine threats from benign anomalies, and the organizational coordination required for effective incident response all represent ongoing challenges. The recognition that detection and response require continuous operation, refinement, and investment rather than one-time implementation represents an evolution in understanding about what the lesson actually requires.

The lesson about the inadequacy of purely compliance-driven security approaches that emphasize meeting regulatory checkboxes over comprehensive risk-based security has become clearer through eight years of observation about what actually works versus what simply demonstrates compliance. Institutions that implemented security measures primarily to satisfy regulatory requirements without genuine commitment to understanding and addressing their actual threat landscapes have often achieved compliance without achieving adequate security. The recognition that compliance represents a minimum baseline rather than a sufficient security program, and that risk-based approaches tailored to specific institutional contexts often prove more effective than one-size-fits-all compliance frameworks, represents an evolution toward more sophisticated security thinking. However, the regulatory pressure and institutional inertia favoring compliance-focused approaches creates ongoing tension between this lesson and operational reality.

The lesson about the critical importance of security culture where every employee understands their role in institutional defense and where security considerations influence decisions at all organizational levels has proven to be simultaneously the most important and most difficult to fully implement. Creating genuine security culture requires sustained leadership commitment, continuous communication and training, alignment of incentives to reward security-conscious behavior, and organizational patience to allow cultural change to develop gradually rather than expecting rapid transformation. The institutions that have successfully developed strong security cultures demonstrate measurably better security outcomes, but achieving that cultural transformation proves elusive for many organizations where security competes with numerous other priorities and where short-term operational pressures can override long-term security investments. The ongoing challenge of security culture development eight years after Bangladesh Bank suggests that this lesson requires generational organizational change rather than quick implementation.

The lesson about the necessity of international cooperation for addressing transnational cyber threats has driven enhanced information sharing and collaborative threat response, but practical cooperation continues to face obstacles from divergent national interests, varying legal frameworks, and resource constraints that limit what even willing partners can accomplish together. The recognition that no single country's law enforcement or regulatory authorities can effectively address threats that operate globally has led to enhanced formal cooperation mechanisms and informal networks, but the gap between the ideal of seamless international cooperation and the reality of bureaucratic, political, and practical barriers remains substantial. The evolution toward more effective international cooperation represents ongoing process rather than accomplished goal eight years after Bangladesh Bank demonstrated its necessity.

## The Next Billion-Dollar Heist: Are We Prepared?

The uncomfortable question that haunts financial security professionals eight years after Bangladesh Bank involves whether the sector has genuinely achieved sufficient defensive improvement to prevent or at least detect and contain similar attacks before they can achieve comparable success. The assessment requires honest evaluation of defensive capabilities against realistic assumptions about adversary sophistication, recognizing that the most concerning threats come not from average criminal actors but from well-resourced, patient, sophisticated nation-state or criminal organizations willing to invest substantial time and effort in operations targeting high-value institutions. The sobering answer appears to be that while defensive improvements have been substantial and while conducting successful billion-dollar heists has become more difficult, such attacks remain plausible against institutions that have not implemented comprehensive security programs or against attackers who identify novel techniques that bypass current defensive measures.

The vulnerabilities that would enable another massive heist exist across multiple dimensions despite eight years of improvement, with the most concerning involving the persistent gaps in security implementation at some financial institutions, the continued exploitability of human vulnerabilities through sophisticated social engineering, and the possibility that determined adversaries might identify attack vectors that current defensive approaches don't adequately address. Institutions that have implemented comprehensive security programs following industry best practices, that maintain robust security operations and incident response capabilities, and that have developed genuine security cultures are substantially more difficult targets than Bangladesh Bank was in 2016. However, the global financial sector includes thousands of institutions with widely varying security capabilities, and the system's interconnected nature means that compromise of less-sophisticated institutions creates potential pathways to more valuable targets through correspondent banking relationships and other connections.

The scenario of another major heist most likely involves adversaries who have studied defenses implemented in response to Bangladesh Bank and who have developed techniques specifically designed to bypass those improvements. The attackers would likely invest months or years in reconnaissance and preparation, identify institutions whose security postures contain exploitable gaps despite general sector improvements, employ sophisticated social engineering targeting individuals whose roles provide access to critical systems, implement malware designed to evade current detection tools, and carefully plan their operational timing and money laundering infrastructure to maximize chances of success. The hypothetical attack would likely differ substantially in technical details from Bangladesh Bank while sharing fundamental characteristics of patience, sophistication, and exploitation of the gap between best possible security and actual implemented controls.

The defensive capabilities that give hope that future attacks might be prevented or contained include the substantially improved security architectures at leading financial institutions, the enhanced information sharing that enables rapid dissemination of threat intelligence about novel attack techniques, the security operations capabilities that provide continuous monitoring and threat hunting, and the organizational priority that elevates security issues to senior leadership attention more rapidly than occurred in earlier eras. An attack similar to Bangladesh Bank would likely face detection at multiple points that might not have existed in 2016, and the probability of early detection before significant theft occurs has increased meaningfully. However, probability is not certainty, and sophisticated adversaries specifically design operations to minimize detection while maximizing their window of opportunity during the critical hours when fraudulent transactions clear through international systems.

The money laundering phase represents another dimension where defensive improvements have occurred but where determined adversaries with sophisticated infrastructure might still succeed in converting stolen electronic funds into forms beyond recovery. The enhanced scrutiny of international transfers, the improved anti-money laundering controls at banks and cryptocurrency exchanges, and the better coordination between victim countries and jurisdictions where stolen funds are laundered collectively make money laundering more difficult than it was in 2016. However, the fundamental challenge remains that once funds successfully clear through initial international transfers, the window for freezing them before they enter laundering operations becomes extremely narrow, and sophisticated laundering networks can move money through multiple conversions and jurisdictions faster than legal and regulatory responses can coordinate across international boundaries.

The preparation for preventing or mitigating future attacks requires continued investment in security capabilities, ongoing adaptation to evolving threats, sustained information sharing about attack techniques and indicators of compromise, regular testing of detection and response capabilities through exercises and simulations, and organizational commitment to maintaining security priority even when immediate threats aren't visible. The institutions best prepared for future attacks will be those that avoid complacency following their own security improvements, that maintain realistic understanding of sophisticated adversaries' capabilities, that continuously test and refine their defensive and responsive capabilities, and that view security as never-ending journey rather than destination that can be reached and maintained without continued effort. The sector's overall preparation depends on whether this sustained commitment characterizes the majority of institutions or merely the leading practitioners.

The realistic assessment involves acknowledging that another billion-dollar heist remains plausible despite substantial improvements since Bangladesh Bank, but that such attacks have become more difficult, require more sophisticated adversaries, face higher probability of detection and containment, and represent lower probability events than they were eight years ago. The progress represents meaningful improvement even if it falls short of elimination of risk, and the ongoing adaptation of defenses to evolving threats provides reason for continued advancement. However, the persistence of North Korean and other sophisticated actors conducting financially motivated cyber operations, the identification of successful attacks even against improved defenses, and the fundamental asymmetries favoring attackers over defenders all suggest that declaring the sector fully prepared would be premature and potentially dangerous.

## Final Thoughts on Digital Trust and Vulnerability

The Bangladesh Bank heist and its aftermath ultimately reveal profound truths about the nature of trust, security, and vulnerability in our increasingly digital world—truths that extend far beyond banking to encompass the fundamental challenge of maintaining security and reliability in complex technological systems that society depends upon but that remain inherently vulnerable to sophisticated exploitation. The eight years since that February morning in 2016 have demonstrated both humanity's remarkable capacity for adaptation and improvement in response to demonstrated threats and the sobering reality that perfect security remains impossible, that determined adversaries continuously find new vulnerabilities to exploit, and that the trade-offs between security, functionality, and usability create persistent tensions that resist definitive resolution. Understanding what Bangladesh Bank ultimately teaches requires stepping back from technical details and specific lessons to examine deeper questions about how we should think about trust in digital systems, what level of vulnerability we must accept as inevitable, and how we can build resilience when perfect security proves unattainable.

The nature of digital trust fundamentally differs from trust in physical systems in ways that the Bangladesh Bank case illuminated starkly. When money existed primarily as physical currency or ledger entries maintained in isolated institutional systems, theft required physical access to vaults or ledgers and left clear evidence of forced entry or manipulation. The digitalization of finance created systems of extraordinary efficiency and convenience that enabled global commerce and financial inclusion on unprecedented scales, but that also created new forms of vulnerability where sophisticated actors on the other side of the world could steal tens of millions of dollars without ever physically entering a building or confronting security guards. The trust that banking depends upon transformed from faith in physical security and human reliability to trust in digital authentication, network security, and software integrity—forms of trust that rest on technical foundations that most people, including many institutional leaders, do not fully understand and cannot personally verify.

The Bangladesh Bank case demonstrated that even institutions specifically charged with financial security and stability—central banks with presumed sophisticated security—remain vulnerable to sophisticated attacks that exploit the complexity of modern digital systems and the impossibility of eliminating all vulnerability in systems involving millions of lines of code, complex network architectures, numerous human operators, and integration with external systems beyond institutional control. This revelation forced uncomfortable recognition that the trust we place in digital financial infrastructure rests not on certainty of perfect security but rather on probabilistic confidence that security proves adequate against most threats most of the time, combined with resilience mechanisms that can detect and respond to the inevitable occasional failures. The psychological adjustment from assuming invulnerability to accepting managed vulnerability represents a significant shift in how we conceptualize security in the digital age.

The vulnerability inherent in complex digital systems stems not primarily from lack of understanding about security principles or inadequate technology solutions but rather from the fundamental characteristics of software systems, human organizations, and the economic and operational trade-offs that constrain what security measures prove practical to implement. Software of the scale and complexity required for modern financial systems inevitably contains flaws that create security vulnerabilities, and while software development practices can reduce vulnerability density, eliminating all exploitable flaws remains impossible given current capabilities. Human operators remain vulnerable to social engineering and mistakes regardless of training and awareness, as the psychological characteristics that make people susceptible to manipulation are fundamental aspects of human cognition rather than correctable defects. Organizations must balance security against functionality, usability, and cost, creating situations where economically or operationally optimal decisions sometimes accept security risks rather than implementing perfect but prohibitively expensive or disruptive controls.

The resilience approach that recognizes the impossibility of perfect prevention and that emphasizes rapid detection, effective response, and recovery capabilities represents perhaps the most important evolution in security thinking that Bangladesh Bank helped catalyze. The traditional security paradigm that focused almost exclusively on prevention—keeping attackers out through perimeter defenses and access controls—proved inadequate against sophisticated adversaries who could eventually overcome prevention measures through sufficient time, effort, and resources. The resilience paradigm acknowledges that breaches will occur and focuses on ensuring that organizations can detect compromise rapidly, respond effectively to contain damage, and recover operational capabilities quickly. This shift from prevention-only to prevention-plus-detection-response-recovery represents philosophical evolution toward more realistic security thinking that accepts vulnerability while working to ensure that inevitable breaches remain contained and recoverable rather than catastrophic.

The collective security challenge that Bangladesh Bank illuminated involves recognizing that in interconnected systems like global finance, individual institutional security proves necessary but insufficient—the system's overall security depends on the security of all participants, with vulnerabilities at any institution creating potential risks to others through the connections that enable normal business operations. This collective security reality creates challenging questions about responsibility, appropriate levels of coordination and cooperation, and how to address the reality that some institutions have far greater resources and sophistication than others yet the system depends on all maintaining adequate security. The SWIFT Customer Security Program represents one approach to collective security that establishes minimum standards for all participants, but questions remain about whether such baseline requirements prove sufficient and how to address the ongoing challenge of resource disparities that mean adequate security for well-resourced institutions may prove unaffordable for smaller or less-developed participants.

The forward-looking perspective requires acknowledging that the security challenge will intensify rather than diminish as emerging technologies create new vulnerabilities, as adversaries continue developing their capabilities, and as society's dependence on digital systems increases. The artificial intelligence capabilities that promise to enhance defensive capabilities will simultaneously provide adversaries with new tools for automating attacks and adapting to defenses. The quantum computing that threatens current cryptographic systems will eventually require wholesale transitions to post-quantum algorithms—a transformation of extraordinary scope and complexity. The expanding Internet of Things attack surface and the continued migration to cloud architectures create new categories of vulnerability that require new defensive approaches. The trajectory suggests that cybersecurity will remain a perpetual challenge demanding continuous adaptation rather than converging toward stable solutions that can be implemented and maintained without constant evolution.

The ultimate lesson that Bangladesh Bank provides involves accepting that living in a digital world requires embracing a degree of vulnerability while working continuously to minimize it, developing resilience to manage inevitable failures, and maintaining realistic expectations about what security can achieve rather than assuming perfect protection. The trust that digital systems require from users must be earned through demonstrated competence in managing risks, transparency about vulnerabilities and incidents when they occur, and honest communication about what security can and cannot guarantee. The institutions and technologies that will thrive in this environment are those that acknowledge vulnerability honestly while demonstrating commitment to comprehensive security programs, that invest in resilience to manage inevitable breaches, and that maintain continuous adaptation as threats evolve. Eight years after Bangladesh Bank, we understand more clearly both how far we have come in improving security and how far we still must go in addressing threats that continue evolving alongside our defenses.

## Closing Reflection

The Bangladesh Bank heist will be remembered not primarily for the money stolen or even for the technical sophistication of the attack, but rather as a watershed moment that transformed how the financial sector understands and addresses cybersecurity in an age where digital systems underpin global commerce yet remain inherently vulnerable to sophisticated exploitation. The incident revealed uncomfortable truths about vulnerabilities that existed throughout the financial sector, catalyzed remarkable improvements in security practices and capabilities, and ultimately served as a painful but valuable teacher about the realities of trust, security, and resilience in our digital age. Eight years later, the financial sector has genuinely transformed in response to the lessons that catastrophic failure taught, yet the persistence of sophisticated threats and the continued evolution of attack techniques remind us that security remains a journey rather than a destination, requiring sustained commitment and continuous adaptation rather than one-time fixes that can be implemented and forgotten.

The human stories behind the technical narrative—the destroyed careers, disrupted lives, political controversies, and eroded trust—remind us that cyber attacks are not abstract digital events but concrete incidents with profound human consequences for individuals and communities whose lives intersect with international financial crime. These human costs demand that we approach cybersecurity not merely as technical challenge or business problem but as fundamental responsibility to protect the people and institutions that depend on the integrity of the systems we build and operate. The progress achieved since 2016 represents countless professionals' dedicated efforts to learn from failure, implement comprehensive improvements, and build more secure financial infrastructure. That progress deserves recognition even as we acknowledge that the work continues and that new challenges will inevitably emerge requiring continued adaptation.

The question of whether we are prepared for the next billion-dollar heist admits no simple answer, as preparation exists on a spectrum rather than as binary state of readiness versus vulnerability. The financial sector is substantially better prepared than in 2016, with improved technical security, enhanced detection and response capabilities, better information sharing, and elevated organizational priority for cybersecurity. Yet determined sophisticated adversaries continue operating, continue evolving their capabilities, and continue finding success against some targets despite general improvements in sector-wide security. The realistic assessment involves acknowledging both genuine progress and persistent vulnerability, both reason for confidence in improved defenses and humility about the limits of what security can achieve against the most sophisticated threats.

As we look forward, the Bangladesh Bank heist stands as both warning and inspiration—warning about the consequences of inadequate security in an age of sophisticated cyber threats, and inspiration about what the financial sector can accomplish when crisis drives comprehensive reform and sustained commitment to improvement. The legacy of that February 2016 morning lives on not in the money that was stolen and never fully recovered, but in the transformed security postures of financial institutions worldwide, the enhanced international cooperation on cyber threats, the elevated awareness about digital vulnerability, and the ongoing commitment to building more resilient financial systems that can withstand the sophisticated attacks that will inevitably continue. The ultimate test of whether we have truly learned from Bangladesh Bank will not be measured in the immediate years following the incident, but rather in whether the reforms, improvements, and commitment to security prove sustainable over decades as memory of the specific incident fades but the threats that it illuminated continue to evolve and intensify.

The digital age demands a new understanding of security that acknowledges vulnerability while refusing to accept defeat, that recognizes the impossibility of perfect protection while remaining committed to comprehensive defense, and that balances the enormous benefits of interconnected digital systems against the inherent risks that connectivity creates. The Bangladesh Bank heist taught us that trust in digital financial infrastructure cannot rest on assumptions of invulnerability but must be earned through demonstrated competence in risk management, through transparency when failures occur, and through resilience that enables recovery from inevitable breaches. The financial institutions that will thrive in coming decades are those that internalize these lessons, that maintain security as enduring strategic priority rather than temporary crisis response, and that view the perpetual challenge of cybersecurity not as burden to be minimized but as fundamental responsibility to stakeholders whose trust they depend upon.

The story of the Bangladesh Bank heist ultimately transcends its specific details to become a parable about the human condition in the digital age—about our remarkable capacity to create systems of extraordinary power and utility, about our persistent vulnerability to those who would exploit our creations for criminal purposes, about our ability to learn from catastrophic failures and implement genuine improvements, and about the eternal tension between our aspirations for perfect security and the reality that perfection remains forever beyond reach. Eight years later, we are wiser, better defended, and more realistic about both capabilities and limitations. Yet we remain vulnerable, not through ignorance or negligence, but through the fundamental characteristics of the complex digital systems we depend upon and through the persistence of sophisticated adversaries who continue probing for weaknesses.

The final truth that Bangladesh Bank teaches is that cybersecurity is not a problem to be solved but rather a condition to be managed—a perpetual challenge that will evolve alongside technology and human society for as long as we continue building digital systems that create value and opportunity alongside vulnerability and risk. The question is not whether we can achieve perfect security, for we cannot, but whether we can maintain the commitment, resources, discipline, and adaptation necessary to manage digital risks adequately even when that management requires sustained effort without guaranteed success. Eight years after Bangladesh Bank, the answer to that question remains being written by security professionals, institutional leaders, policymakers, and ultimately by all of us whose lives depend on the integrity of digital systems we may not understand but must nonetheless trust. The legacy of the heist will be determined not by what happened on that February morning in 2016, but by how we continue responding to the challenges it revealed in all the years that follow.

# Epilogue: A Timeline of Events

The Bangladesh Bank heist unfolded across months of patient preparation, hours of intense operational execution, and years of investigation, recovery efforts, and institutional reform. Understanding the full scope of this complex international incident requires organizing its many components chronologically, tracing how reconnaissance evolved into compromise, how compromise erupted into theft, how theft triggered investigation, and how investigation catalyzed transformation. This epilogue provides a comprehensive chronological framework that positions key events in temporal context, tracks the fates of principal actors whose lives intersected with this historic crime, accounts for the disposition of stolen funds through the complex web of recovery efforts and permanent losses, and summarizes the ongoing investigations that continue even years after the initial breach. The timeline reveals patterns invisible when examining events in isolation—the methodical patience of attackers during reconnaissance, the compressed urgency of the theft execution, the chaotic early response period, and the extended aftermath where consequences continued unfolding long after the immediate crisis had passed.

## Detailed Chronological Breakdown

The chronology of the Bangladesh Bank heist extends far beyond the dramatic February 2016 weekend when fraudulent transactions flooded through compromised systems, reaching back months into 2015 when initial reconnaissance and compromise likely began and forward years into ongoing legal proceedings, security reforms, and continued investigations. Reconstructing this timeline requires synthesizing information from forensic analyses, investigative reports, legal proceedings, and public disclosures that emerged gradually over years, creating a narrative that connects scattered pieces into coherent progression from first intrusion to lasting legacy. The timeline demonstrates that what appeared to the world as a sudden dramatic incident actually represented the culmination of extensive preparation and the beginning of protracted consequences that continue reverberating through the global financial sector.

The reconnaissance and initial compromise phase likely began in mid-to-late 2015, though the precise timeline remains subject to some uncertainty given the sophistication of the attackers' operational security and the challenges of forensic timeline reconstruction when evidence has been partially destroyed or obscured. Forensic analysis of Bangladesh Bank's systems revealed malware artifacts and attacker infrastructure suggesting presence in the network extending back months before the February 2016 theft. During this extended reconnaissance period, the attackers conducted detailed mapping of Bangladesh Bank's systems and networks, identified the SWIFT infrastructure as their ultimate target, studied legitimate transaction patterns to understand what normal activity looked like, tested their access to ensure persistence, and developed the custom malware that would enable both transaction manipulation and evidence destruction. The patience demonstrated during this phase—where attackers maintained access for months while conducting reconnaissance rather than immediately attempting theft—reflected sophisticated operational discipline characteristic of advanced persistent threat operations.

The specific compromise vector through which attackers initially gained access to Bangladesh Bank's network remains somewhat unclear from publicly available information, though the most likely scenarios involve either phishing attacks that compromised employee credentials or exploitation of internet-facing systems with known vulnerabilities. Regardless of the specific entry vector, by late 2015 or early January 2016, the attackers had established persistent presence within Bangladesh Bank's networks with the ability to access systems, install additional malware, and position themselves for the eventual theft operation. The attackers demonstrated careful operational security during this period, maintaining low profiles that avoided triggering security alerts while progressively deepening their access toward the SWIFT infrastructure that represented their ultimate objective. The successful maintenance of covert access for months without detection reflected both attacker sophistication and the inadequate security monitoring that characterized Bangladesh Bank's defensive posture during this period.

The transition from reconnaissance to active operational preparation accelerated in January and early February 2016 as attackers finalized their malware, tested their ability to manipulate SWIFT systems, and established the money laundering infrastructure that would receive stolen funds. The attackers deployed customized malware specifically designed to manipulate Bangladesh Bank's SWIFT Alliance Access software, enabling them to generate fraudulent payment messages while simultaneously hiding those messages from the database queries that bank staff used to monitor transactions. The sophistication of this SWIFT-specific malware indicated substantial effort in either reverse-engineering the commercial software or obtaining detailed information about its operation through other means. Simultaneously, the money laundering infrastructure was established in the Philippines and potentially other countries, with accounts opened at RCBC and relationships developed with casinos and individuals who would facilitate the rapid conversion of electronic transfers into difficult-to-trace cash and other assets.

The operational execution phase began on the evening of Thursday, February 4, 2016, as attackers initiated the flood of thirty-five fraudulent SWIFT messages directing transfers from Bangladesh Bank's accounts at the Federal Reserve Bank of New

York to accounts in the Philippines, Sri Lanka, and potentially other locations. The timing—Thursday evening in Dhaka, corresponding to early morning hours in New York—was carefully calculated to exploit the approaching weekend when reduced staffing and delayed investigation would provide maximum opportunity for fraudulent transactions to clear before detection and response could interdict them. The messages directed transfers totaling nearly one billion dollars, though most were blocked through a combination of the fortuitous "fundation" typo that triggered scrutiny at Deutsche Bank, patterns that raised red flags at the Federal Reserve, and possibly other detection mechanisms that prevented the majority of the attempted theft from succeeding. The eighty-one million dollars that did successfully clear to accounts in the Philippines represented only a fraction of the attackers' ambitions but nonetheless constituted one of the largest successful cyber heists in history.

The discovery phase began on Friday morning, February 5, 2016, as Bangladesh Bank staff arriving for work began their routine review of overnight transactions and gradually recognized the catastrophic reality of what had occurred. The initial confusion—with staff uncertain whether they were seeing technical glitches, data errors, or actual fraud—created crucial delays before the full scope of the breach was understood and appropriate response measures were initiated. By late Friday, Bangladesh Bank had notified the Federal Reserve Bank of New York, initiated internal investigation efforts, and begun the chaotic process of attempting to freeze assets in the Philippines before they could be fully laundered beyond recovery. The weekend that followed proved critical, with attackers' money laundering operations in the Philippines moving rapidly to convert electronic transfers into casino chips, cash, and other forms while Bangladesh Bank struggled to coordinate effective response across time zones, jurisdictions, and with incomplete information about where all the money had gone.

The immediate aftermath period from mid-February through March 2016 was characterized by frantic activity on multiple fronts—forensic investigation to understand how the breach occurred, coordination with Philippine authorities to freeze and recover stolen funds, engagement with law enforcement in multiple countries, damage control communications with international partners and media, and initial accountability measures including the governor's resignation. FireEye's Mandiant division was engaged to conduct comprehensive forensic analysis of compromised systems, discovering the sophisticated malware and beginning the process of understanding the attack's technical characteristics. Philippine authorities moved to freeze accounts at RCBC where stolen funds had been traced, though by this time substantial amounts had already been withdrawn and laundered through casinos. The public disclosure of the breach generated international headlines and triggered the beginning of what would become comprehensive transformation in global banking security practices.

The investigation and attribution phase extending through the remainder of 2016 and into 2017 involved detailed forensic analysis, intelligence community assessments, and international cooperation to understand not just how the attack occurred but who was responsible. The technical similarities between malware used against Bangladesh Bank and tools from previous incidents attributed to North Korean threat actors, combined with infrastructure overlaps and operational patterns, led security researchers and intelligence agencies to assess with increasing confidence that the same North Korean-affiliated threat actor group had conducted the Bangladesh Bank operation. The public attribution evolved gradually from private intelligence assessments to public statements by security firms and eventually government officials, building a case through accumulating evidence rather than immediate definitive attribution. The investigation also revealed the broader pattern of similar attacks targeting multiple financial institutions, demonstrating that Bangladesh Bank represented one visible incident within a sustained campaign.

The recovery and reform period extending from 2016 through subsequent years involved the long, complex legal proceedings in Philippine courts to secure return of frozen funds, the comprehensive security enhancements implemented at Bangladesh Bank and throughout the global financial sector, and the regulatory and policy responses that formalized many improvements as mandatory requirements rather than voluntary best practices. The Philippine legal proceedings proved protracted, with competing claims on frozen assets, questions about RCBC's liability, and the complex jurisdictional and procedural issues that characterize international asset recovery creating delays measured in years rather than months. Bangladesh Bank eventually recovered approximately fifteen to twenty million dollars through various channels, representing partial success but leaving the majority of the stolen eighty-one million permanently beyond recovery. The security transformation catalyzed by the incident included SWIFT's Customer Security Program, enhanced regulatory requirements in multiple jurisdictions, and the widespread adoption of improved security practices throughout the financial sector.

The long-term legacy period continuing to the present involves the ongoing evolution of cyber threats and defenses, the continued operations of North Korean and other sophisticated actors conducting financially motivated cyber operations, and the gradual institutional memory development about the incident as it transitions from recent crisis to historical case study. The security improvements implemented in direct response to Bangladesh Bank have measurably elevated defensive capabilities across the financial sector, though new vulnerabilities and evolving attack techniques ensure that the security challenge remains dynamic rather than resolved. The incident has become required study in cybersecurity education, regularly referenced in industry conferences and security training, and established as a defining case study about sophisticated cyber attacks targeting financial infrastructure. The timeline's endpoint remains open, with the story continuing to unfold through ongoing security evolution, occasional revelations about aspects of the original incident, and the persistent threat environment that ensures Bangladesh Bank's lessons remain relevant rather than merely historical.

## Key Players and Their Fates

The human actors whose lives intersected with the Bangladesh Bank heist experienced dramatically divergent outcomes ranging from destroyed careers and criminal prosecution to continuing successful operations and ongoing investigations where ultimate accountability remains uncertain. Understanding these individual fates provides essential human context to what could otherwise remain an abstract technical incident, demonstrating how sophisticated international cyber crime creates cascading consequences affecting numerous individuals across multiple countries and organizational levels. The fates of key players also illuminate broader patterns about accountability, justice, and the challenges of imposing meaningful consequences on the actual perpetrators of sophisticated cyber attacks who often remain beyond the practical reach of prosecution despite clear evidence of their responsibility.

Atiur Rahman, who served as Governor of Bangladesh Bank at the time of the heist, experienced the most immediate and visible career destruction among institutional leaders, resigning in March 2016 under intense political and media pressure despite having established a generally respected record during his tenure. Rahman's departure occurred within weeks of the breach's public disclosure as political leaders sought to demonstrate accountability and as criticism mounted about whether adequate oversight and resources had been provided to the institution during his leadership. The forced resignation effectively ended Rahman's career in central banking despite his previous accomplishments and his arguable distance from the technical security failures that enabled the breach. His post-resignation activities have reportedly included academic work and involvement in development organizations, but the stigma of association with the Bangladesh Bank heist has permanently overshadowed his previous contributions to financial inclusion and monetary policy. The trajectory of Rahman's career illustrates the harsh reality that senior institutional leaders bear accountability for catastrophic failures regardless of the complex chain of causation that might have distributed responsibility across multiple organizational levels.

The senior IT and security personnel at Bangladesh Bank whose direct responsibilities included the compromised systems faced terminations and professional reputations so severely damaged that continued employment in banking technology became essentially impossible. These individuals, whose names have generally been kept from public disclosure, found their careers ending not through retirement or voluntary moves to new opportunities but through forced departures connected to massive security failures. The challenge these former Bangladesh Bank personnel face in rebuilding careers involves the permanent association with one of history's largest banking security breaches—a stigma that makes potential employers view them as unacceptable risks regardless of whether they bore personal culpability or were simply inadequately resourced or supported by their institution. Some have reportedly left the technology sector entirely, while others have struggled to find positions at small institutions willing to accept candidates whose previous employers view as toxic associations. The long-term economic and psychological impacts on these individuals and their families represent hidden human costs rarely visible in technical post-mortems but nonetheless real consequences of their unfortunate timing in holding security-critical positions when sophisticated adversaries successfully compromised their institution.

Maia Deguito, the RCBC branch manager whose role in opening and managing accounts that received stolen funds led to criminal charges, has experienced ongoing legal proceedings that have consumed years of her life and depleted her financial resources through legal defense costs. Deguito has maintained that she was an unwitting victim exploited by sophisticated criminals rather than a knowing participant in money laundering, though prosecutors have argued that the suspicious nature and scale of transactions should have been obvious red flags that she ignored or deliberately overlooked. As of recent reports, the legal proceedings continued with uncertain outcomes, leaving Deguito's fate unresolved years after the initial incident. Regardless of eventual legal outcomes, her career in banking has ended permanently, her financial situation has been severely compromised by legal expenses, and her reputation has been destroyed by association with the largest bank heist in Philippine history. The case illustrates how individuals at operational levels in financial institutions can find their lives devastated by sophisticated financial crimes they may not have fully understood, with the complexity of determining culpability creating extended legal uncertainties that compound the harm.

The casino personnel and individuals in the Philippines who facilitated the laundering of stolen funds through chip purchases and cashouts have experienced varying fates ranging from criminal prosecution to disappearance as investigations sought to trace money flows and identify all participants in the laundering operations. Some individuals were arrested and charged with money laundering, facing potential imprisonment and the lifelong stigma of criminal records if convicted. Others have reportedly fled or gone into hiding, seeking to avoid prosecution by removing themselves from jurisdictions where they face legal jeopardy. Still others have claimed innocence or ignorance about the criminal nature of transactions they facilitated, with legal proceedings attempting to sort genuine participants from potentially unwitting tools. The incomplete nature of public information about these individuals reflects both the ongoing nature of some legal proceedings and the reality that many operational-level participants in sophisticated money laundering operations remain difficult to identify or apprehend despite general understanding that the operations required numerous participants to execute successfully.

The actual perpetrators—the sophisticated cyber attackers who compromised Bangladesh Bank's systems and orchestrated the theft—have almost certainly faced no meaningful consequences despite strong evidence pointing to their North Korean affiliation and despite widespread intelligence community consensus about attribution. These individuals, operating from within North Korea or from overseas locations while under North Korean direction, remain beyond the practical reach of arrest or prosecution by any jurisdiction with both the will to pursue them and the legal standing to try them. The frustrating reality that the individuals most directly responsible for planning and executing the heist face no personal consequences while individuals at operational or management levels in victimized institutions experienced career destruction and legal jeopardy illustrates the profound challenges in achieving accountability for sophisticated international cyber crimes. The impunity enjoyed by the actual perpetrators reflects both the protective shield that nation-state affiliation provides and the practical limitations of international law enforcement cooperation when perpetrators operate from hostile or uncooperative countries.

Kim Won Hong and other senior leaders within North Korea's intelligence and cyber operations organizations who would have directed or approved operations like the Bangladesh Bank heist have experienced internal North Korean political dynamics that remain largely opaque to outside observers but that reportedly have included purges and power struggles characteristic of the regime. Kim Won Hong, who headed the Ministry of State Security during the period when North Korean cyber operations intensified, was reportedly removed from his position in 2017, though whether this removal related to cyber operations oversight or reflected broader political maneuvering remains unclear from available information. The internal accountability and power dynamics within North Korea's leadership affect individuals who directed cyber operations but remain fundamentally different from the legal accountability that might apply in other contexts, with leaders facing potential consequences from internal regime politics rather than international legal proceedings. The opacity of North Korean internal affairs means that understanding the ultimate fates of those who directed operations remains largely speculative rather than definitively known.

The security researchers, forensic analysts, and investigators who worked to understand and attribute the Bangladesh Bank heist have experienced professional recognition for their contributions to one of the most significant cybersecurity investigations in history, though most have continued their careers largely outside public attention. Personnel from FireEye's Mandiant division who conducted the initial forensic investigation, intelligence analysts who pieced together attribution evidence, law enforcement officials who coordinated international investigations, and the numerous other professionals who contributed expertise to understanding the incident have generally returned to their ongoing work addressing the continuous stream of cyber threats and incidents. Some have presented their findings at security conferences or published technical analyses that contributed to the security community's collective understanding. Their professional legacies include not just their specific contributions to the Bangladesh Bank investigation but also the methodologies, tools, and collaborative approaches they helped develop or refine that continue benefiting the broader practice of cyber threat investigation and response.

## Status of Recovered Funds

The financial dimension of the Bangladesh Bank heist's aftermath involves complex accounting of the eighty-one million dollars that successfully cleared from Bangladesh Bank's accounts, the substantially larger sums that were blocked before clearing, the portions recovered through various legal and investigative efforts, and the permanent losses that no amount of subsequent recovery efforts could reclaim. Understanding the ultimate disposition of stolen funds requires tracing money through the labyrinthine paths it traveled during laundering operations, examining the legal proceedings that secured return of some assets, and acknowledging the sobering reality that sophisticated money laundering succeeded in converting the majority of stolen electronic funds into forms that remained beyond recovery despite comprehensive understanding of generally where the money went. The accounting provides both encouragement that international cooperation can achieve partial recovery and frustration that most successfully stolen and laundered funds remain permanently lost regardless of subsequent efforts.

The immediate blocking of the majority of the attempted theft represented the first and most significant "recovery" in financial terms, though it might more accurately be characterized as prevention since these funds never actually left Bangladesh Bank's control despite the fraudulent transfer instructions. Of the approximately \$951 million in fraudulent SWIFT messages that attackers generated, roughly \$870 million to \$880 million was blocked through a combination of the fortuitous "fundation" typo that triggered scrutiny at Deutsche Bank, suspicious patterns that the Federal Reserve Bank of New York identified and held pending verification, and possibly other detection mechanisms that prevented transfers from clearing. This prevented loss represents an enormous success in limiting the financial damage, though it also demonstrates how close the attackers came to achieving a catastrophic near-billion-dollar theft had a few more transactions cleared before detection. The blocked funds remained in Bangladesh Bank's accounts at the Federal Reserve, requiring no recovery process beyond simply not executing the fraudulent transfers once they were identified as suspicious.

The eighty-one million dollars that successfully cleared to accounts in the Philippines became the focus of intense recovery efforts through Philippine legal proceedings, diplomatic negotiations, and coordinated law enforcement actions. Of this amount, investigations traced approximately $68 million to $70 million to specific accounts at RCBC and associated entities where the initial transfers landed before beginning their laundering journey. The challenge involved not just identifying where money went but implementing legal freezes rapidly enough to prevent further movement while navigating Philippine legal procedures for asset seizure and repatriation. The delays inherent in international legal cooperation meant that by the time comprehensive freezes were implemented, substantial portions of the money had already been withdrawn and laundered through casinos or converted to other forms beyond the frozen accounts' reach. The frozen amounts represented partial success in preventing complete dispersal of all stolen funds, though disappointingly less than what might have been hoped given that authorities understood generally where the money had gone.

The actual recovery and return of funds to Bangladesh Bank proved a protracted process extending over multiple years as

Philippine legal proceedings worked through competing claims, jurisdictional questions, and procedural requirements before determining how frozen assets would be disposed. The legal proceedings required Bangladesh Bank to prove through Philippine courts that specific frozen assets represented proceeds of crime traceable to the theft—a burden that required comprehensive documentation and legal advocacy extending years beyond the initial freeze. Various parties contested the freezes and sought release of funds, claiming they were innocent parties who had received funds in good faith or arguing that evidence didn't definitively establish criminal proceeds. The proceedings faced delays from normal court congestion, appeals of initial decisions, and the complexity of the legal and evidentiary questions involved. Eventually, settlements and judicial decisions resulted in Bangladesh Bank recovering approximately $15 million to $20 million through Philippine legal channels—a meaningful partial recovery but representing only about 20-25% of the successfully stolen amount.

Additional smaller recoveries came through various other channels including cooperation from financial institutions that had processed suspicious transactions, seizures by law enforcement in jurisdictions beyond the Philippines, and potentially confidential settlements or recovery mechanisms that have not been publicly disclosed. Some financial institutions that handled transfers or processed transactions related to the laundering operations paid compensation to Bangladesh Bank either through legal settlements or as gestures to maintain relationships despite having been exploited in the laundering scheme. These additional recoveries, while adding to the total recovered amount, remained relatively modest additions to the larger Philippine-recovered funds. The cumulative total recovered through all channels likely reached $20 million to $25 million, representing roughly 25-30% of the successfully stolen $81 million but leaving approximately $56 million to $61 million permanently beyond recovery despite comprehensive understanding of the theft and extensive international cooperation on recovery efforts.

The permanently lost funds represent the successful completion of the money laundering operation for the portions that were converted to cash, withdrawn from casinos, transferred through remittance channels, or otherwise moved beyond the frozen accounts before effective interdiction could occur. Once electronic transfers were converted to physical cash carried away from casinos or financial institutions, those funds entered untraceable physical form that could be transported, spent, or converted to other assets without creating the electronic trails that enable investigation and recovery. The individuals who walked out of Philippine casinos with bags containing millions in cash, the funds that were transferred to additional accounts in jurisdictions beyond the investigation's effective reach, and the money that was converted to other forms during the chaotic first days after the theft but before comprehensive freezes were implemented all represent permanent losses. The reality that sophisticated money laundering succeeds in making substantial portions of stolen funds irrecoverable even when authorities understand what happened and pursue recovery aggressively provides sobering context for evaluating the effectiveness of current approaches to financial crime investigation and asset recovery.

The accounting also must consider the substantial costs incurred by Bangladesh Bank in pursuing recovery efforts, implementing security improvements, and managing the institutional fallout from the breach. Legal fees for Philippine proceedings and other recovery efforts, consulting fees for forensic investigations and security assessments, technology investments in improved security infrastructure, and the broader operational and reputational costs of the breach collectively exceeded tens of millions of dollars. When these costs are subtracted from recovered amounts, the net financial position deteriorates further, with Bangladesh Bank bearing substantial indirect costs beyond the direct loss of funds. The comprehensive financial impact thus exceeded the $81 million directly stolen to encompass years of elevated expenses related to recovery, reform, and reputation restoration efforts that the theft necessitated.

## Ongoing Investigations

The investigative work related to the Bangladesh Bank heist has continued far beyond the initial forensic analysis and attribution efforts, with ongoing investigations pursuing multiple objectives including comprehensive understanding of the full scope of the operation, identification of all participants and facilitators, pursuit of additional asset recovery opportunities, and development of intelligence about North Korean cyber capabilities and operations that can inform defensive strategies against future attacks. Understanding these continuing investigations requires recognizing that sophisticated international cyber operations create investigative demands extending years beyond initial incidents, that new information and leads continue emerging as related investigations in other contexts reveal connections to Bangladesh Bank, and that the broader strategic objective of understanding and countering North Korean cyber operations maintains investigative relevance long after specific incident response has concluded. The ongoing nature of investigations also reflects the reality that some aspects of complex international crimes remain incompletely understood years after the fact, with continued analysis occasionally yielding new insights.

The law enforcement investigations in multiple jurisdictions have remained open as authorities continue pursuing leads about individuals who may have facilitated the money laundering operations, seeking to identify participants who have not yet been charged or located, and attempting to understand the full network of facilitators that enabled the rapid laundering of stolen funds through Philippine and potentially other financial systems. These investigations face challenges from the passage of time since the original incident, the difficulty of locating and apprehending individuals who have gone into hiding or who reside in jurisdictions where extradition proves complicated, and the practical resource constraints that limit how much ongoing effort can be devoted to historical cases when new incidents constantly emerge demanding attention. However, major financial crimes typically maintain at least nominal investigative status for years, with authorities occasionally following new leads as additional information becomes available or as participants in other financial crimes provide information that connects to Bangladesh Bank.

The intelligence community assessments about North Korean cyber capabilities continue evolving as additional operations are identified and attributed, as occasional defectors or intelligence sources provide insights into North Korean operations, and as technical analysis of new North Korean malware reveals evolution in capabilities and tactics. The Bangladesh Bank case provides one data point within broader intelligence efforts to understand North Korean cyber operations comprehensively, including the organizational structures that conduct operations, the personnel involved, the strategic objectives guiding operations, and the technical capabilities available. This intelligence work serves both immediate defensive purposes—helping predict and prevent future attacks—and longer-term strategic objectives around understanding North Korean capabilities broadly and potentially developing approaches to constraining or countering operations through diplomatic, technical, or other means. The intelligence value of understanding operations like Bangladesh Bank extends beyond the specific incident to inform comprehension of North Korean strategic thinking and operational patterns.

The regulatory and policy investigations into whether financial institutions and regulators adequately performed their responsibilities before and during the incident have largely concluded their immediate work but maintain relevance as regulatory frameworks continue evolving in response to lessons learned. RCBC faced regulatory sanctions and enforcement actions from Philippine banking regulators for its failures in preventing money laundering through accounts it maintained. Other institutions involved in processing suspicious transactions or failing to report potential money laundering have faced varying levels of regulatory scrutiny and consequence. The regulatory dimension continues affecting institutions years after the incident as examinations assess whether corrective actions have been implemented and sustained, and as regulatory frameworks incorporate lessons from Bangladesh Bank into ongoing supervision and enforcement priorities. The shift from reactive investigation of what went wrong to proactive prevention of similar future failures represents the evolution from incident-specific investigation to broader regulatory and policy implementation.

The technical investigations into the malware and infrastructure used in the attack continue as security researchers identify new samples or infrastructure that can be linked to the same operation or threat actor, providing additional insights into tactics, tools, and procedures. The collaborative nature of security research means that researchers discovering new information about North Korean cyber operations regularly check whether their findings connect to previous incidents like Bangladesh Bank, occasionally revealing new links or insights that weren't apparent in earlier analysis. The accumulation of knowledge about specific threat actors over time through analysis of multiple incidents provides increasingly detailed understanding that helps both attribute new operations and anticipate future tactics. The technical investigation thus never fully concludes but rather transitions into ongoing threat intelligence development that uses historical cases like Bangladesh Bank as reference points for understanding contemporary threats.

The internal investigations and assessments at financial institutions and security organizations evaluating their own procedures, capabilities, and responses to the Bangladesh Bank case have largely concluded their formal work but maintain ongoing relevance as institutions periodically review whether lessons learned remain implemented and whether their security postures adequately address the threats that Bangladesh Bank illuminated. Many institutions conducted internal reviews assessing their vulnerability to similar attacks, evaluating whether their security controls would have detected and prevented the specific techniques used, and identifying gaps requiring remediation. These internal investigations contributed to the broader security improvements implemented across the financial sector, though the proprietary nature of internal assessments means that most findings remained confidential rather than being publicly shared. The ongoing nature of these internal evaluations involves periodic reassessment as threats evolve and as institutions implement new technologies or procedures that might affect their security postures.

## Conclusion

The timeline of the Bangladesh Bank heist reveals an incident far more complex and extended than the dramatic weekend when fraudulent transactions flooded through compromised systems might suggest. The story stretched from months of patient reconnaissance in 2015 through the explosive operational phase in February 2016 to years of investigation, recovery, and reform continuing to the present. The chronological framework demonstrates patterns characteristic of sophisticated cyber operations—extended preparation periods where attackers methodically position themselves for success, compressed execution phases where operations unfold in hours but were enabled by months of groundwork, and protracted aftermath periods where consequences continue emerging long after immediate crises have passed. Understanding events in temporal sequence reveals the calculated patience of sophisticated attackers, the fog and chaos of early response when understanding remained incomplete, and the extended nature of institutional and societal recovery from catastrophic security failures.

The fates of key players whose lives intersected with this historic crime demonstrate the uneven distribution of consequences, with institutional leaders and operational-level facilitators experiencing destroyed careers and legal jeopardy while the actual perpetrators remain beyond accountability's practical reach. The contrast between the visible punishment of those closest to the incident and the impunity of those most responsible reflects fundamental challenges in achieving justice for sophisticated international cyber crimes where technical attribution may be clear but legal jurisdiction and practical enforcement capabilities prove inadequate for imposing meaningful consequences on state-sponsored actors operating from hostile nations. The human cost extends beyond those formally held accountable to affect numerous individuals whose association with the incident damaged careers, reputations, and life prospects regardless of actual culpability for security failures.

The status of recovered funds provides sobering accounting demonstrating both the possibilities and limitations of international asset recovery efforts. The partial recovery of approximately 25-30% of successfully stolen funds represents meaningful success achieved through sustained legal efforts and international cooperation, validating that determined pursuit can reclaim some stolen assets even when sophisticated money laundering operations initially succeed in dispersing funds across international jurisdictions.

However, the permanent loss of approximately 70-75% of successfully stolen and laundered funds demonstrates that current approaches to asset recovery remain inadequate against sophisticated operations that rapidly convert electronic transfers into physical cash or other difficult-to-trace forms. The accounting also reveals that when indirect costs of investigation, recovery, security improvements, and broader institutional impacts are considered, the true financial toll far exceeds the direct loss of stolen funds.

The ongoing investigations in multiple domains demonstrate that sophisticated cyber incidents generate investigative demands extending years beyond immediate response, with law enforcement pursuing remaining participants and facilitators, intelligence agencies continuing to develop understanding of adversary capabilities and operations, regulators ensuring corrective actions remain implemented, and security researchers accumulating technical knowledge about threats. The continuation of investigations long after initial incident response concludes reflects both the complexity of international cyber crimes that span multiple jurisdictions and organizations, and the strategic value of developing comprehensive understanding of threat actors beyond just responding to individual incidents. The investigative work transitions from reactive incident response to proactive threat intelligence development that uses historical cases as foundations for understanding and defending against contemporary and future threats.

The epilogue's comprehensive accounting of timeline, key players, recovered funds, and ongoing investigations provides essential factual grounding for the broader narrative while demonstrating that even years after the dramatic weekend when the world learned of the heist, aspects of the incident remain incompletely resolved. The combination of what is definitively known, what remains uncertain, and what continues unfolding illustrates both how much has been learned about this historic incident and how much remains perpetually beyond complete knowledge when investigating sophisticated international cyber operations conducted by adversaries skilled in operational security and protected by uncooperative nation-states. The Bangladesh Bank heist thus remains a living case study rather than purely historical incident, with its lessons continuing to inform contemporary cybersecurity practice and its unresolved elements reminding us of the persistent challenges in achieving complete understanding and comprehensive accountability for the most sophisticated cyber threats facing the global financial system.

# Appendices

## Glossary of Technical Terms

Understanding the Bangladesh Bank heist and the broader landscape of cybersecurity and financial technology requires familiarity with specialized terminology that appears throughout technical discussions but may not be immediately accessible to all readers. This glossary provides clear, comprehensive definitions of key terms, avoiding circular definitions while explaining concepts in ways that illuminate their relevance to the incidents and issues discussed in this book.

**Advanced Persistent Threat** (**APT**) - A sophisticated, sustained cyber attack campaign typically conducted by well-resourced adversaries such as nation-states or organized criminal groups. APTs are characterized by extended reconnaissance periods, patient operation over months or years, sophisticated techniques designed to evade detection, and specific targeting of high-value objectives rather than opportunistic attacks against any available victim. The Bangladesh Bank heist exemplified APT characteristics through its months-long reconnaissance, sophisticated custom malware, and strategic targeting of central bank foreign exchange reserves.

**Authentication** - The process of verifying that a person, device, or system is genuinely who or what it claims to be before granting access to resources or processing requests. Authentication typically involves credentials such as passwords, security tokens, biometric identifiers, or cryptographic keys that must be presented and verified. Multi-factor authentication requires multiple different types of credentials, providing stronger security than single-factor approaches that rely solely on passwords or other single authentication methods.

**Backdoor** - A method of accessing a computer system or encrypted data that bypasses normal authentication and authorization procedures. Attackers often install backdoors in compromised systems to maintain persistent access even if their initial entry method is discovered and blocked. Backdoors may be created through malware installation, exploitation of undocumented system features, or compromise of legitimate remote access tools that administrators use for system management.

**Blockchain** - A distributed digital ledger technology where transactions are recorded in chronological blocks that are cryptographically linked to form an immutable chain. Each participant in a blockchain network maintains a copy of the ledger, and new transactions require consensus among participants before being added. The technology underpins cryptocurrencies but has potential applications in various contexts requiring transparent, tamper-evident record-keeping without centralized authority.

**Botnet** - A network of compromised computers or devices controlled by attackers without the owners' knowledge or consent. Botnets are typically used to conduct distributed attacks, send spam, steal data, or perform other malicious activities at scale. The term combines "robot" and "network," reflecting how compromised devices act as automated agents following attacker commands.

**Command and Control (C2)** - The infrastructure and communication channels that attackers use to remotely control malware or compromised systems. C2 servers receive data from infected systems and send instructions directing malicious activities. Sophisticated attackers employ techniques to obscure C2 communications, making them appear as legitimate network traffic or routing them through compromised legitimate servers to hide their true origin.

**Cryptocurrency** - Digital or virtual currency that uses cryptography for security and operates without central authority such as a government or bank. Cryptocurrencies like Bitcoin and Ethereum enable peer-to-peer transactions recorded on blockchain ledgers. The pseudo-anonymous nature of many cryptocurrencies has made them attractive for money laundering and ransom payments, though blockchain analysis can sometimes trace transactions despite the absence of traditional banking intermediaries.

**Distributed Denial of Service (DDoS)** - An attack that attempts to overwhelm target systems, networks, or services with massive volumes of traffic from multiple sources, rendering them inaccessible to legitimate users. DDoS attacks exploit the limited capacity of network connections and server resources, flooding them with more requests than they can handle. Mitigation typically involves filtering malicious traffic, distributing load across multiple servers, or absorbing attack traffic through specialized DDoS protection services.

**Encryption** - The process of encoding information so that only authorized parties possessing the correct decryption key can access it. Encryption protects data confidentiality during storage and transmission, preventing unauthorized parties who might intercept or access encrypted data from reading its contents. Modern encryption employs mathematical algorithms that make breaking the encryption without the proper key computationally infeasible even with substantial computing resources.

**Endpoint Detection and Response (EDR)** - Security technology that continuously monitors end-user devices such as computers and mobile devices to detect and respond to cyber threats. EDR solutions collect detailed information about device activities, analyze it for signs of suspicious or malicious behavior, and enable security teams to investigate and remediate threats. This approach provides visibility and control beyond what traditional antivirus software offers.

**Firewall** - A network security system that monitors and controls incoming and outgoing network traffic based on predetermined security rules. Firewalls create barriers between trusted internal networks and untrusted external networks such as the internet, examining traffic to determine whether to allow or block it. Modern firewalls may also inspect traffic contents, not just network addresses and ports, providing deeper security analysis.

**Intrusion Detection System (IDS)** - Technology that monitors networks or systems for malicious activities or policy violations. IDS identifies potential security incidents based on known attack signatures or behavioral anomalies, generating alerts for security personnel to investigate. Unlike intrusion prevention systems, IDS primarily focus on detection and alerting rather than automatically blocking suspected threats.

**Key-logger** - Malicious software that records keystrokes on infected computers, typically to steal passwords, credit card numbers, or other sensitive information entered through keyboards. Key-loggers may transmit captured data to attackers through network connections or store it locally for later retrieval. Protection involves keeping security software updated and being cautious about installing untrusted programs.

**Lateral Movement** - The technique attackers use to progressively move through a network after initial compromise, accessing additional systems and accounts to reach their ultimate objectives. Lateral movement exploits trust relationships between systems, stolen credentials, and security weaknesses in internal networks that may be less hardened than internet-facing perimeter defenses. Effective defense requires internal network segmentation and monitoring that can detect unusual internal traffic patterns.

**Malware** - Software specifically designed to disrupt, damage, or gain unauthorized access to computer systems. Malware encompasses various types including viruses, worms, trojans, ransomware, spyware, and custom tools developed for specific attacks. Modern malware often employs sophisticated techniques to evade detection and may be modular, allowing attackers to deploy different capabilities as needed rather than installing everything at once.

**Man-in-the-Middle Attack** - A type of attack where adversaries secretly intercept and potentially alter communications between two parties who believe they are directly communicating with each other. These attacks can enable eavesdropping, data theft, or injection of malicious content into what appear to be legitimate communications. Protection involves using encrypted communications and verifying the identity of communication partners through cryptographic authentication.

**Network Segmentation** - The practice of dividing computer networks into smaller isolated segments to contain potential security breaches and limit lateral movement by attackers. Properly implemented segmentation means that compromise of one network segment doesn't automatically grant access to others, requiring attackers to overcome additional security boundaries. The Bangladesh Bank case demonstrated the importance of segmenting critical systems like SWIFT infrastructure from general corporate networks.

**Patch** - A software update that fixes security vulnerabilities, bugs, or adds features to existing programs. Security patches address discovered vulnerabilities that attackers could exploit, making timely patching critical for maintaining security. The challenge involves balancing the urgency of deploying security patches against risks that updates might cause operational disruptions if not properly tested.

**Penetration Testing** - Authorized simulated cyber attacks conducted to evaluate the security of systems, identifying vulnerabilities before malicious actors can exploit them. Penetration testers employ similar techniques to real attackers, documenting discovered weaknesses and recommending remediation. Organizations use penetration testing to validate security controls and improve defensive postures through controlled adversarial assessment.

**Phishing** - Social engineering attacks that use fraudulent communications, typically emails, to trick recipients into revealing sensitive information, clicking malicious links, or downloading malware. Phishing messages impersonate legitimate entities such as banks, employers, or service providers, exploiting trust and urgency to manipulate targets. Spear phishing targets specific individuals with customized messages based on reconnaissance about their roles and relationships.

**Ransomware** - Malware that encrypts victims' data and demands ransom payment for decryption keys. Ransomware attacks have evolved from targeting individuals with small ransom demands to sophisticated operations against corporations and institutions that can pay millions for data recovery and operational restoration. The economics of ransomware, particularly when combined with data exfiltration for additional extortion leverage, has made it one of the most financially successful forms of cybercrime.

**Social Engineering** - Manipulation techniques that exploit human psychology to trick people into compromising security. Social engineering attacks leverage authority, urgency, fear, helpfulness, or other psychological principles to convince targets to provide information, grant access, or take actions that benefit attackers. These attacks succeed not through technical exploitation but through manipulating human behavior and decision-making.

**SWIFT (Society for Worldwide Interbank Financial Telecommunication)** - The secure messaging network that banks worldwide use to send payment instructions and other financial messages. SWIFT messages enable international money transfers by providing standardized, authenticated communication between financial institutions. The Bangladesh Bank heist specifically targeted SWIFT systems, demonstrating vulnerabilities in how some institutions implemented and secured their connections to this critical financial infrastructure.

**Two-Factor Authentication (2FA)** - Security process requiring two different authentication factors—typically something you know (password) and something you have (security token or mobile device)—before granting access. 2FA significantly strengthens security compared to password-only authentication because compromising credentials alone proves insufficient for unauthorized access. Modern 2FA implementations may use authentication apps, SMS codes, hardware tokens, or biometric factors as the second authentication element.

**Virtual Private Network (VPN)** - Technology that creates encrypted connections over the internet, enabling secure remote access to networks and protecting communications from eavesdropping. VPNs are essential for remote workers accessing corporate networks and for individuals seeking privacy when using untrusted networks like public Wi-Fi. However, VPN security depends on proper implementation and trustworthy VPN providers.

**Zero-Day Vulnerability** - A security flaw unknown to software vendors and for which no patch exists. Attackers exploiting zero-day vulnerabilities have temporary advantages because no specific defenses exist against threats using these previously unknown weaknesses. Zero-day exploits are particularly valuable and are commonly associated with sophisticated threat actors who discover vulnerabilities through their own research or acquire them from exploit markets.

Understanding these terms provides the foundation for comprehending both the specific technical details of incidents like the Bangladesh Bank heist and the broader landscape of cybersecurity challenges, defensive strategies, and the evolution of threats in our increasingly digital world.

## How SWIFT Works

The Society for Worldwide Interbank Financial Telecommunication operates the secure messaging network that has formed the backbone of international financial communications for decades, facilitating trillions of dollars in daily transactions among more than eleven thousand member financial institutions across two hundred countries. Understanding how SWIFT operates, why it was specifically targeted in the Bangladesh Bank heist, and what security mechanisms protect it illuminates both the sophistication of the attack and the challenges facing financial infrastructure security. SWIFT represents a unique position in global finance—neither a bank nor a payment system itself, but rather the trusted communication layer enabling banks to send authenticated payment instructions to one another with confidence that messages genuinely originate from claimed senders.

SWIFT's core function involves providing standardized message formats and secure transmission infrastructure for financial communications between member institutions. When a bank needs to instruct another bank to transfer funds, pay for securities, confirm transactions, or communicate other financial information, it composes a SWIFT message following standardized formats that specify exactly how different types of information should be structured. These standardized formats ensure that receiving banks can automatically process messages regardless of which institution sent them or what language the sender's country uses, creating the interoperability essential for smooth international financial operations. The messages themselves don't move money directly—they are instructions that direct banks to debit or credit accounts based on bilateral relationships and correspondent banking arrangements, with actual fund settlement occurring through other mechanisms.

The security architecture that protects SWIFT communications relies on multiple layers including physical security of messaging infrastructure, network security protecting message transmission, strong authentication verifying message origin, and message integrity verification ensuring communications haven't been altered in transit. Each member institution connects to SWIFT through dedicated secure network links rather than the general internet, with stringent requirements for how institutions implement and protect these connections. Messages are authenticated using cryptographic techniques that verify sender identity and ensure message integrity, preventing unauthorized parties from injecting fraudulent messages or altering legitimate communications. The Bangladesh Bank heist succeeded not by breaking SWIFT's network security or cryptographic authentication, but rather by compromising Bangladesh Bank's internal systems that had legitimate authority to generate authenticated messages—a crucial distinction that underscores how insider access or compromised legitimate systems can bypass security measures designed to protect against external attacks.

The SWIFT Alliance Access software that member institutions use to connect to the SWIFT network and compose messages became a specific target in the Bangladesh Bank attack. This software provides the interface between a bank's internal systems and the SWIFT network, enabling authorized bank personnel to create payment instructions and other messages that are authenticated and transmitted to recipient banks. The attackers' custom malware specifically targeted Alliance Access, modifying its behavior to inject fraudulent messages while simultaneously hiding those messages from the database queries that bank staff used to monitor SWIFT activity. This sophisticated manipulation demonstrated deep understanding of how Alliance Access operated and represented a concerning evolution in threats against financial infrastructure where attackers targeted not the network itself but the endpoints connecting to it.

The correspondent banking relationships that SWIFT facilitates involve bilateral arrangements where banks maintain accounts with one another or with specialized correspondent banks that provide services to numerous institutions. When Bank A wants to send money to Bank B in another country, the actual movement of funds typically involves Bank A's correspondent in Bank B's country crediting Bank B's account based on SWIFT instructions from Bank A. These correspondent relationships create the actual financial connections that SWIFT messages activate, with the messages serving as secure authenticated instructions about how correspondent banks should adjust account balances. The Bangladesh Bank heist exploited these correspondent relationships by generating fraudulent SWIFT messages that appeared to come from Bangladesh Bank instructing the Federal Reserve Bank of New York to transfer funds from Bangladesh Bank's account to recipient accounts that the attackers controlled.

The SWIFT network's operational characteristics include extraordinarily high reliability, with redundant infrastructure ensuring that message transmission continues even if individual components fail, and comprehensive message tracking that creates audit trails of all communications. However, the network's security depends critically on member institutions properly implementing and protecting their connections—a distributed trust model where SWIFT provides the secure network infrastructure but relies on members to secure their endpoints and properly control access to message generation capabilities. The Bangladesh Bank case demonstrated that this distributed responsibility creates potential weak links where institutions with inadequate endpoint security can be compromised, with attackers then exploiting legitimate authenticated access to inject fraudulent messages.

The post-Bangladesh Bank security enhancements that SWIFT implemented through the Customer Security Program aimed to address the endpoint security weaknesses that enabled the attack. The mandatory security controls require member institutions to implement network segmentation isolating SWIFT infrastructure, comprehensive logging and monitoring of SWIFT activity, regular security assessments, and timely patching of software vulnerabilities. These requirements represent SWIFT's evolution from purely providing secure network infrastructure to also prescribing minimum security standards for how member institutions protect their connections and internal systems. The attestation framework where institutions must annually certify their compliance creates accountability mechanisms that didn't previously exist, though questions remain about verification rigor and consequences for non-compliance.

Understanding SWIFT's operation illuminates why it became an attractive target for sophisticated attackers seeking to steal large sums through electronic means—the system facilitates enormous value transfers with automated processing based on authenticated messages, creating scenarios where successful compromise of authentication could enable massive theft before detection and response could intervene. The combination of high transaction values, automated processing, distributed endpoint security, and the time delays inherent in international coordination created an attractive risk-reward profile for sophisticated actors willing to invest in the technical capabilities and patience required to successfully compromise SWIFT-connected institutions. The Bangladesh Bank case served as wake-up call about these vulnerabilities, catalyzing security improvements but also demonstrating to potential attackers what could be accomplished by those with sufficient sophistication and determination.

## Resources for Further Reading

The Bangladesh Bank heist and the broader landscape of cybersecurity, financial crime, and international relations it illuminates represent rich topics deserving continued study beyond this book. The following resources provide avenues for deeper exploration of specific aspects, offering technical detail, policy analysis, investigative journalism, and scholarly research that complement the overview provided here. The selection emphasizes accessible yet authoritative sources that balance readability with rigor, enabling readers to pursue particular interests while maintaining connection to real-world implications and practical applications.

**Cybersecurity and Financial Sector Security**

The cybersecurity landscape continues evolving rapidly, with new threats, defensive technologies, and best practices emerging continuously. Organizations like the Financial Services Information Sharing and Analysis Center provide threat intelligence and facilitate collaboration among financial institutions on security matters. The National Institute of Standards and Technology publishes frameworks and guidelines for cybersecurity that have become de facto standards across industries, with their Cybersecurity Framework providing comprehensive structure for organizing security programs. The SANS Institute offers extensive training, certification, and regularly updated resources on technical security topics ranging from network defense to incident response. These organizational resources provide current information complementing the historical analysis this book provides.

**SWIFT and International Banking**

SWIFT's own documentation and publications provide authoritative information about the organization's operations, security initiatives, and industry guidance. The Customer Security Program materials explain mandatory security controls and implementation guidance, while SWIFT's intelligence reports share threat information with member institutions. Academic research on international finance and correspondent banking provides theoretical frameworks for understanding how global financial infrastructure operates and what vulnerabilities its structure creates. Books examining the history and evolution of international banking illuminate how institutions like SWIFT emerged and why they became central to global commerce.

**North Korean Cyber Operations and Attribution**

Understanding state-sponsored cyber operations requires synthesizing multiple information sources given the sensitivity and classification level of much intelligence. Cybersecurity firms like Mandiant, CrowdStrike, and Kaspersky publish regular threat intelligence reports that include technical analysis of state-sponsored threat actors including those attributed to North Korea. Academic research on North Korean politics, economics, and strategy provides context for understanding why the regime invests in cyber capabilities and how cyber operations fit within broader strategic approaches. Investigative journalism from outlets specializing in cybersecurity and international affairs has produced comprehensive reporting on North Korean cyber activities beyond what government sources disclose publicly.

**Money Laundering and Financial Crime**

The Financial Action Task Force, an intergovernmental organization focusing on combating money laundering and terrorist financing, publishes standards, guidance, and country assessments that illuminate global anti-money laundering frameworks and their limitations. Academic journals focusing on financial crime publish research on money laundering techniques, effectiveness of countermeasures, and policy debates about appropriate regulatory approaches. Books examining specific major financial crimes provide case studies complementing the Bangladesh Bank narrative, demonstrating both common patterns and unique aspects of different incidents.

**Incident Response and Digital Forensics**

Professional resources on incident response and digital forensics provide practical guidance applicable to responding to cyber attacks similar to the Bangladesh Bank compromise. The SANS Institute's incident response materials offer frameworks and procedures that have become industry standards. Books on digital forensics explain the technical methods investigators use to analyze compromised systems, recover evidence, and reconstruct attacker activities. These resources prove valuable for security professionals but also accessible to general readers interested in understanding how investigations actually unfold.

**Policy and International Cooperation**

Think tanks focusing on cybersecurity policy and international relations publish research and policy recommendations addressing challenges like those the Bangladesh Bank case revealed regarding attribution, deterrence, and international cooperation. Organizations like the Council on Foreign Relations, the Center for Strategic and International Studies, and the Brookings Institution regularly examine cyber policy questions. Academic journals in international relations increasingly address cyber issues, providing scholarly analysis of how digital threats affect traditional concepts of sovereignty, warfare, and diplomacy.

This curated selection provides starting points for continued exploration, with each resource offering connections to additional materials for those seeking ever-deeper understanding of specific aspects. The rapidly evolving nature of cybersecurity means that ongoing engagement with current sources remains essential for maintaining understanding as threats, defenses, and policy responses continue developing beyond what any single snapshot can capture.

# About the Author

Passionate about educating others, David G. Stone has now turned their expertise into an easy-to-follow guide designed to help remote workers, freelancers, and businesses safeguard their online accounts. Through The Remote Worker's Guide to Password Management, they provide practical, real-world strategies to enhance digital security and prevent cyber risks.

www.ingramcontent.com/pod-product-compliance
Lightning Source LLC
LaVergne TN
LVHW052218200926
848481LV00001B/149